DÜRER

Fedja Anzelewsky

DÜRER

His Art and Life

Translated by Heide Grieve

KONECKY&KONECKY

Frontispiece

1 *Self-Portrait*. 1500. Oil. 67×49. Bayerische Staatsgemäldesammlungen, Munich.

The *Self-Portrait* of 1500 is the most famous of Dürer's three painted self-
portraits (cf. Pls. 24, 76). The head, seen full-face, is built up according to
a system used by mediæval painters to represent Christ's face. This
similarity between the self-portrait and the face of the Redeemer is based
on the biblical idea that God created man in His image; and as God can
only be known through His personification in Christ, man has to be like
the Son of God. However, according to Dürer's intention, man has to be
in His image in a symbolic as well as a literal sense, which means that he
has to bear his "cross" just as Christ did. The Christ-like self-portrait also
implies that the artist, whose talent is God-given, is like the creator of all
things by virtue of his creative ability. This is not a presumptuous, but a
religious painting. At the same time, the artist, who during these years
was preoccupied with the problem of human proportions, experimented
in this self-portrait with a long-established system of proportions.

Konecky & Konecky
156 Fifth Avenue
New York, NY 10010

© 1980 by Office du Livre, Fribourg, Switzerland

ISBN: 0-914427-50-4

Printed and bound in Hong Kong

Table of Contents

I. Nuremberg

Patricians · Merchants · Humanists · Artisans · Artists

During the late Middle Ages Nuremberg, Albrecht Dürer's birthplace, was the "unrecognized capital" of the Holy Roman Empire of the German Nation. It was here that the imperial charter of the Golden Bull had been promulgated in 1356, and in Dürer's time the city was called "Augusta praetoria imperii" (principal city of the Empire) by the Humanists. From the eleventh century, when it consisted of a humble settlement under the imperial castle, the town had developed into one of the most important urban centres on German soil. According to the most recent estimates approximately 45,000 to 50,000 people lived within the city fortifications, the third and outer wall of which was completed around the middle of the fourteenth century. Bearing in mind that at that time only Cologne and Augsburg had a comparable number of inhabitants, it is obvious that in Dürer's day Nuremberg must have been one of the foremost German cities.[1]

Towards the end of the Middle Ages the trade connections enjoyed by Nuremberg merchants, who usually operated in companies made up of several members of one family, extended from Cracow to Lyons, Barcelona and Lisbon, and from Antwerp and Lübeck to Budapest, and further into Transylvania and the principalities of Moldavia and Walachia. In Venice merchants from Nuremberg and Augsburg were the joint leaders of the *Fondaco dei Tedeschi*, and up to 1492 the merchant house of Pirckheimer supplied silver to the Venetian mint. From Venice and Genoa trading extended to Rome and from there to southern Italy.

The Nuremberg merchants and their financial power constituted one of the most important sources of money for the kings of the house of Luxembourg; the Pirckheimer family, for instance, who at that time had only recently settled in Nuremberg, played a crucial role in supplying the money for the many wars waged by the members of the house of Luxembourg.[2] Any ruler therefore made sure that he maintained particularly good relations with this rich city. The many tokens of royal favour culminated in 1424 in the transfer of the imperial insignia to Nuremberg, to be kept in the city "in perpetuity".

Nuremberg's foreign trade, which extended throughout Europe, was handled principally by those families who as members of the council were also responsible for governing the city itself. Their names are found as early as the thirteenth century among the families of serfs who were raised by royal pardon to non-aristocratic ministerial rank. Among them were the Behaim, Haller, Stromer, Muffel and Holzschuher families, to name but a few. Members of these families were city administrators from that time onwards. After a short interlude in the fourteenth century, when the guilds succeeded in taking over the municipal administration, the Nuremberg patricians continued to govern the city until 1806, when the constitution of the free imperial city was revoked. As a result of the fourteenth-century revolt of the guilds, artisans were refused the right to organize themselves in guilds, as was the custom in other towns, and this was not repealed until the second half of the sixteenth century. All the different trades were subject to the supervision of the council, which regulated production in a form of economy planned according to the commercial needs of the moment.

From 1392 onwards, the governing body of the city administration was the "Small Council" which was elected annually and consisted of forty-two members of the patriciate. Of these, thirteen were nominated as "younger mayors" *(jüngere Bürgermeister),* and thirteen as "older mayors" *(ältere Bürgermeister).* Seven members of this last group were chosen to be supreme regents *(Septemviri),* and three of these became "first captains" *(oberste Hauptmänner);* two of them acted as treasurers *(Losunger).*[3] The tasks of the municipal administration were so manifold that most of the members of the council were held responsible in an honorary capacity for one particular department – for example that of a city architect, a tax officer or a superintendent of churches.

The council also appointed the government officials, of whom the most important was the town clerk (Stadtschreiber), who was usually a trained lawyer, like the Humanist Nikolaus von Wyle. There were also five municipal physicians, a municipal apothecary and several high-ranking teachers who earned fifty to sixty florins a year, as well as many officials of lower rank who were usually paid in kind, receiving free accommodation, firewood, etc., as well as a small wage. The council also controlled all aspects of civil and criminal jurisdiction.

Apart from the governing patrician families there were 300 to 400 Ehrbare (honorables); among them were merchants like the Landauer, Schreyer and Scheurl families, but there were also lawyers, artists and wealthy artisans. These could be appointed as Genannte (nominated candidates) to the Greater Council, of which Dürer too became a member in 1509.

The most influential of the city's inhabitants were middle-ranking merchant families and master-craftsmen, usually working in a specialized field. However, about a third of the inhabitants belonged to the lower social classes which had to be supported by the city administration in times of need. These were the small artisans, masters as well as journeymen, labourers and the 500 poor and sick who were in the constant care of the city. Lowest in social rank were—here as everywhere else—the "dishonest people": prostitutes, slaughterers, hangmen and privy cleaners.

One trade engaged in by the Nuremberg citizens deserves special mention, not only because all social classes, patricians as well as labourers, were employed in it, but also because the fame of many Nuremberg products was based on it: this was the metal-working trade. Nuremberg merchants had a share in the mining of minerals and ore in the Upper Palatinate as well as in Thuringia and the Ore Mountains. The ore was smelted in numerous furnaces managed by Nuremberg entrepreneurs. Crude metal for processing was also imported from Bohemia, Hungary and Poland. A typical example of a family whose fortune was made in mining were the Landauers, who in the course of three generations rose from a modest economic rank as painters to large-scale entrepreneurs in the metal-smelting industry. The Augsburg merchant family, Fugger, who for a time were represented in Nuremberg by Georg Fugger and Georg Thurzo, made this city their main centre for the transshipment of silver and copper mined in the Tyrol and Hungary.[4]

Enterprising merchants and inventive craftsmen alike were engaged in the Nuremberg metal-working trade. The so-called "Nuremberg Egg", made in 1510 by the locksmith Peter Henlein, was no less important in this context than the mechanical process of wire-drawing by means of water power, which had been invented as early as the mid-fifteenth century. The products of Nuremberg brass and copper foundries, like the Vischer foundry for example, were sold as far away as Magdeburg and Cracow. The most famous of all Nuremberg products were instruments and tools; these "Nuremberg trinkets" were sought after throughout Europe. They, together with Nuremberg's favourable geographical situation, were the main reason why the astronomer Johannes Regiomontanus settled in the city; only here could the measuring instruments that he invented or improved be produced. Regiomontanus was assisted by Bernhard Walther, factor of the Vöhlin-Welser Company, whose house at the Tiergärtner gate was later bought by Dürer. Regiomontanus's work in Nuremberg was probably important for Martin Behaim as well. Behaim had acquired a first-hand knowledge of geography while serving as a sailor for the Portuguese, and because of this had been commissioned by the council to construct a globe. This globe, built in 1491–3 according to Behaim's instructions, was the first ever made. At a later date Erhard Etzlaub from Erfurt became famous as a cartographer and globe-maker.[5]

The council had decided that it was inadmissible for a doctor, even if he belonged to an eligible family, to serve as a councillor. This rule did not mean that the patricians were hostile to education or science, rather it reflected problems of social standing: the title of doctor elevated its bearer to the social level of a knight, that is a member of the lower gentry. By contrast, those Nuremberg families who were eligible to become members of the council remained burghers despite their wealth and high social rank within the city, and despite their efforts to live in greater luxury than the gentry and to emulate them by holding their own tournaments, the journeymen's joustings. One single doctor among the members of the council who insisted on his due privileges could have created immense social and administrative problems.

Humanism became established slightly later in Nuremberg than in other German cities, but from the second half of the fifteenth century onwards the number of Nuremberg citizens, particularly patricians, who had studied at German or Italian universities was greater than is generally known. Sebald Schreyer had studied at Leipzig, Hieronymus Holzschuher at Ingolstadt and Padua, and Dürer's friend, Willibald Pirckheimer, and his sister, Caritas, already belonged to the third generation of Humanists in a family whose

2 *Nuremberg from the West. C.* 1497. Watercolour and gouache. 13.6 × 34.4. Formerly Kunsthalle, Kupferstichkabinett, Bremen.

This watercolour, lost during World War II, shows the west side of the city, looking northwards. The exact spot Dürer painted this picture from is not yet known; it appears to be on the north bank of the Pegnitz, close to where the river leaves the city. Of the buildings, the middle one of the three towers can be identified as the tower of the Neutor. The tall, narrow tower in the middle ground still dominates the Tiergärtner Tor, near where Dürer lived from 1509. In the far distance the great hall, chapel and Heidenturm of the imperial castle can be discerned. Outside the town on the left are groups of buildings and individual houses. On the hills to the left, the tiny church in the cemetery of St. John, where Dürer was later buried (cf. Pl. 240), and the church of the Holy Cross can be seen.

members had originally been merchants. The Nuremberg town physician and chronicler, Dr. Hartmann Schedel, was also a second-generation Humanist. Over a period of time, both the Pirckheimer and the Schedel families had built up large libraries. Hartmann Schedel's library, for instance, comprised 670 printed works and 400 manuscripts. Unfortunately there are no comparable records of the books owned by the Pirckheimer family. However, documentary evidence shows that the library of Dr. Hieronymus Münzer, Hieronymus Holzschuher's father-in-law, consisted of 185 volumes. In 1523, Dürer bought ten works from Regiomontanus's collection of 193 books on mathematics and astronomy which had been enlarged by Bernhard Walther.

Among the group of Humanists which Dürer joined around 1496–7 were Willibald Pirckheimer, the town physician Dietrich Ulsen who came from Kampen in Overijssel, the physician Hieronymus Münzer, the lawyers Peter Dannhauser and Christoph Scheurl, the theologian and mathematician Johannes Werner, the merchant and astronomer Bernhard Walther, and the astronomer Konrad Heinfogel. Sebald Schreyer, who had received a Humanist education but was not engaged in any scholarly work, occupied a special position as a patron and instigator of many literary projects. Schreyer and the other Nuremberg Humanists maintained close ties with Konrad Celtis, who on 18 April 1487 was the first German to be crowned "poeta laureatus" by the Emperor Frederick III. The ceremony was performed in Nuremberg castle. It is interesting, moreover, that Dürer's teachers, Michael Wolgemut and Wilhelm Pleydenwurff, were also praised for their knowledge of mathematics in the final section of Schedel's *Chronicle of the World (Weltchronik)*, the printing of which had been financed by Sebald Schreyer and his brother-in-law Sebastian Kammermeister.

Nuremberg's intellectual climate of that time is also reflected in the number of printers and publishers who, from 1469 onwards, following the example of Johann Sensenschmidt from Eger, had installed their presses in the city and had made it the centre of incunabula printing. Dürer's godfather, Anton Koberger, was the most important of these printers, and his trade connections extended almost as far as Nuremberg's foreign trade in general. In 1489 he moved

from a house near the Dürer family to larger premises at the Ägidienhof. According to a report by Johann Neudörffer, more than one hundred people were employed in Koberger's "large-scale enterprise". Koberger printed or published many theological works, including a treatise by Nikolaus von Kues and Boethius's *De consolatione philosophiae,* and in particular, writings by Italian Humanists such as Poggio, Enea Silvio Piccolomini and Marsilio Ficino. The printer Friedrich Creussner published Tacitus's *Germania* and also works by Lucian and Virgil. Dürer himself had a link with the printing trade in that Wilhelm and Heinrich Rummel, the grandfather and great-uncle of his wife Agnes Frey,[6] had business connections with Johann Sensenschmidt, Nuremberg's first printer.[7]

In Nuremberg as elsewhere artists were classed as artisans, but painting was regarded as a "liberal art". Since the guilds of the imperial city of Nuremberg, in contrast to those of other German towns, were not self-governing, the term "liberal art" really meant that painters were not subject to the direction and control of the council. Thus they were not bound by the rule that everybody who had learnt his craft in Nuremberg had to practise it there as well.[8] It was not until 1534, later than in other professions, that the painters asked for guild regulations. This was after the governing families had passed the so-called "Dance Statute" of 1521 which made them a patrician upper class set apart

3 Michael Wolgemut: Frontispiece for Schedel's *Chronicle of the World.* 1493. Woodcut. 34.3 × 26.5. Kupferstichkabinett SMPK, Berlin.

The *Chronicle of the World,* written by the Nuremberg physician and Humanist Dr. Hartmann Schedel, was published in 1493 by Albrecht Dürer's godfather Anton Koberger, first in Latin, then in German. It is the most richly illustrated printed publication of the fifteenth century. Dürer's teacher, Michael Wolgemut, together with his stepson Wilhelm Pleydenwurff, designed 652 wood blocks — many of which were printed several times, so that the overall number of illustrations amounts to more than 1800 — during the years the young Dürer worked as an apprentice painter in their workshop. Sebald Schreyer and his brother-in-law Sebastian Kammermeister, who financed the printing as well as the illustrations, had discussed the execution of the woodcuts with Wolgemut and Pleydenwurff as early as 1487–8. But the epoch-making importance of the *Chronicle of the World* does not really lie in the great number of illustrations, but rather in the inclusion of many views of towns, mostly based on a very sound knowledge of the localities. This feature may well have been inspired by a travel book entitled *Peregrinationes in terram sanctam* written by the dean of Mainz Cathedral, Bernhard von Breidenbach. It was illustrated and published in 1486 in Mainz by the Utrecht painter Erhard Reuwich, and included large-scale woodcut vedutas. The influence can be proved in the case of Wolgemut's frontispiece to the *Chronicle of the World,* because its preliminary drawing (in London) is a transposition of Reuwich's frontispiece woodcut.

from the rest of the inhabitants, and after their hitherto flexible administration had become increasingly rigid. However, the painters' request was not granted until 1596, and then only after repeated reminders.[9]

Settling in Nuremberg does not appear to have been all that easy, even though painters from other towns frequently came to live there. Michael Wolgemut, for example, son of the Nuremberg painter Valentin, found that the only employment open to him on his return from his travels as a journeyman was in his late father's workshop, then run by his mother. He did not become a workshop owner in his own right until he married the widow of Hans Pleydenwurff, whose husband had moved to Nuremberg from Bamberg and died in 1472; even then Wolgemut owned the workshop jointly with his stepson, Wilhelm Pleydenwurff. The citizens of Nuremberg seem to have thought it important that even the "free" painters conformed to the general rules governing artisan life in the city. It was considered essential, for example, for a man to be married and to possess his "own smoke", or house, since apprentices and journeymen who were single lived with the master's family.

Nuremberg must have appeared particularly attractive to painters because it seemed to offer so many opportunities for work. The two parish churches and various monasteries needed altarpieces and memorials, and the churches in the numerous villages on Nuremberg lands, where many patrician families owned castles or manor-houses, also offered possibilities for painting. Altarpieces made in Nuremberg workshops were exported to Zwickau, Breslau and even Cracow. Just how prolific Nuremberg artistic production could be is demonstrated by the six new altarpieces which in 1486 were consecrated in the Augustinian church alone. A contemporary note mentions that twenty-three altar panels were made in the city between 1488 and 1491.

The term "altar panel" usually denoted a whole retable, that is, a centre panel bearing carved and gilded figures and wings painted on both sides. In general, commissions were given to the painter who made the design and then distributed the work for the centre panel and the sculptures to carpenters and wood-carvers. The treasurer Nikolaus Muffel — who was executed for embezzlement in 1469 — mentioned several times in his *Gedenkbuch* (commemorative diary) that he had spent 200 florins for altar panels which he then donated. In 1479 Michael Wolgemut received 1,400 florins for an extensive altarpiece which had been sent to Zwickau; the sum included the cost of the long-distance transport which Wolgemut had paid in advance. These are

4 Wilhelm Pleydenwurff: *Jephta Receives her Father.* 1491. Woodcut for the *Schatzbehalter*. C. 25 × 17. Kupferstichkabinett SMPK, Berlin.

The second great illustrative work of the Wolgemut-Pleydenwurff workshop consisted of the woodcuts for the *Schatzbehalter* by Father Stephan Fridolin. It was published in 1491 by Anton Koberger. This illustration shows Pleydenwurff's rather more clumsy drawing style. The *Schatzbehalter* and the *Chronicle of the World* may be regarded as prototypes, both in technique and style, for Dürer's work as a designer and woodcutter.

houses have survived. The decorations in the front room of Sebald Schreyer's house, which consisted of paintings of classical gods and philosophers and was unique in the city, is one such sad loss. A number of woodcuts by Michael Wolgemut showing the nine Muses and other classical subjects, which were probably designed for the *Archetypus triumphantis Romae* (a book financed by Sebald Schreyer but never printed) convey an impression of how classical Antiquity was viewed before Dürer.

Michael Wolgemut was one of the "large-scale entrepreneurs" typical of the latter part of the fifteenth century; certain aspects of his artistic practice were comparable to the enterprises of contemporary prosperous merchants. He had a well-organized workshop where large altarpieces and portrait panels as well as designs for tapestries and glass paintings, woodcuts and sculptures were produced.[10] Insofar as Wolgemut's own work can be isolated from that of the rest of the workshop, he showed a predilection for linear draughtsmanship. One noticeable and consistent feature of his innumerable illustrations for books printed in Nuremberg, such as the *Schatzbehalter* and Schedel's *Chronicle of the World*, is the ornamental sweep of his draperies, which contrasts with his often somewhat wooden figures. Wolgemut's design for the frontispiece of the *Chronicle of the World* was based on a woodcut made by Erhard Reuwich to illustrate an account of Dean Breidenbach's travels, which had been published in Mainz in 1486. Wolgemut's frontispiece is characterized by a rather surprising ornamental complexity and a certain overall monumentality. Wolgemut's stepson, Wilhelm Pleydenwurff, born around 1460, appears to have been influenced in his painting by Schongauer and Rogier van der Weyden. However, the warm, balanced colours of his pictures make them superior to most other contemporary Nuremberg paintings.

Recent research suggests that the St. Vitus altarpiece, erected in the Augustinian church in 1487, was produced in the Wolgemut workshop during the time when Dürer was

Pl.20

Pl.3

Pl.4

Pl.5

large sums of money, considering that Dürer later estimated 50 florins annually to be sufficient to maintain adequately a two-person household.

While the wall paintings in churches and monasteries had religious themes, although most now are sadly lost, secular subjects were usually confined to portraits. None of the painted façades of public and private buildings in Nuremberg or the paintings decorating the interiors of patrician

5 Master of the Augustinian Altarpiece: *St. Bernhard's Vision.* 1487. Oil. 273 × 92. Germanisches Nationalmuseum, Nuremberg.   ▷

Around 1487 a polyptych in honour of St. Vitus was erected in the church of the Augustinian order at Nuremberg. The unknown principal master involved in this work executed four scenes taken from the legends of various saints on the inside of the inner wings, among them *St. Bernhard's Vision*. These four panels represent the supreme achievement of Nuremberg painting around the time Dürer entered the Wolgemut workshop. They are also a source for one of the characteristic features of Dürer's art, namely the fusion of figures and landscape.

13

an apprentice there; Wolgemut himself does not, however, seem to have had a hand in its execution. The artist who did paint the four large figures of saints in front of a richly varied landscape background — who for want of a more accurate name is known as the "Master of the Augustinian Altarpiece" — must be regarded as one of the most important German painters of his time. These four panels, his only surviving works, are direct prototypes of Dürer's later altarpieces.

At the end of the fifteenth and the beginning of the sixteenth century, Nuremberg was not a burgher town with a narrow outlook, as the Romantics liked to picture it. Rather, it was more cosmopolitan than most cities of the time, governed prudently by a patrician council, and a centre for German Humanism and printing as well as for foreign trade and the metal industry. For the young Dürer it provided a fertile intellectual background such as could be found at that time in few other cities of the Empire.

II. Early Life until 1489

Family · Youth · Training

According to Albrecht Dürer's family chronicle,[11] which he wrote on 25 December 1523 (Gregorian Calendar) using his father's notes, the Dürer family had originally come from Hungary. Dürer's ancestors had been horse and cattle breeders in the village of Atjósfalva which then lay outside the gates of Gyula, a small town south of Grosswardein, but which no longer exists. His grandfather, Anton, was the first of the family to live in the town itself and train as a goldsmith there. Of his four children – three sons and a daughter – the eldest, Albrecht, the painter's father, also trained as a goldsmith; the second son, Lasslo, became a saddler; and the youngest, Johann, a priest.

Albrecht Dürer the Elder, born 1427, left Hungary when he was very young. As surnames were generally used only by the aristocracy, common people living away from their home usually supplemented their Christian names with the name of their profession or place of origin. This is what the young goldsmith Albrecht did: he called himself "Thürer", translating the Hungarian word Atjós = door, unintelligible to German ears, into its German equivalent (Thür). This new name is first recorded in Nuremberg on 8 March 1444,[12] which implies that Albrecht Dürer the Elder left Gyula at the age of sixteen and started on his journeying after having finished his apprenticeship as a goldsmith in his father's workshop. It can hardly have been by chance that Albrecht Dürer the Elder went to Nuremberg, for trading in ores from the mining country around Hermannstadt was a privilege enjoyed by the Nuremberg merchants. The trading companies of the Landauer and Pirckheimer families, for instance, had a vital share in the metal trade of south-east Europe. It is quite possible that the young goldsmith followed a group of Nuremberg merchants along the trade route – extending from Hermannstadt via Grosswardein, Ofen, Vienna and Ratisbon to Nuremberg – and thus arrived in the latter city on the River Pegnitz.

Hungarian and German scholars have long debated whether or not the Dürer family was of Magyar or German origin. Hungarian scholars have pointed out that Gyula was situated in the heart of Magyar country and that horse- and cattle-breeding was a typically Hungarian occupation. Few convincing arguments have as yet been advanced to support the German theory. The only indication of German, or at least partly German, origins is the fact that Albrecht Dürer the Elder had apparently learnt to write German, as is shown by a letter to his wife written in Linz in 1493.[13] It cannot be stated with any certainty whether the whole family or just the mother was of German origin. The painter Albrecht Dürer later signed himself "Albertus Dürer Germanus" when he wanted to emphasize his nationality.

Albrecht Dürer the Elder's first stay in Nuremberg does not appear to have lasted long, because the family chronicle does not mention it. It says: "Then Albrecht Dürer, my dear father, came to Germany, stayed for a long time with the great artists in the Netherlands and finally came to Nuremberg in the year 1455 after the birth of Christ, on St. Loyen's day (25 June). And on the same day Philipp Birkamer celebrated his wedding." The journeyman, who had been away for more than ten years, entered the service of the goldsmith Hieronymus Holper. In 1467, when forty years old, he married Barbara Holper, the fifteen-year-old daughter of his master. On 4 July of the following year he himself passed the examination necessary to become a master goldsmith. Even before this date he had assisted his father-in-law in his official duty of testing the purity of gold and silver.

The newly-weds lived in a house at the back of Dr. Johannes Pirckheimer's town residence; it was on Winklerstrasse which ran parallel to the west side of the main market place. Such houses at the rear were often only one storey high and separated from the main part of the house by a yard; they fronted a road which ran parallel to that on which the main building was situated. We know from descriptions by Sebald Schreyer that these single-storey buildings usually consisted of just a living room, small bedroom and kitchen.[15] Here, in the house on Winkler-strasse, Albrecht Dürer the Younger was born on 21 May 1471, the third of eighteen children, and was christened in the church of St. Sebald. His godfather, Anton Koberger, had recently started to print books, but seems to have also begun his career as a goldsmith.[16]

As early as 1475 the master goldsmith Dürer was in a position to buy his own house on a street called Unter der Vesten (now Burgstrasse, Castle Street) on the corner of Untere Schmiedegasse.[17] This street, which led from the main market place past the goldsmiths' "display" area (where their wares were publicly inspected) and the choir of St. Sebald up to the castle, was in the oldest and most distinguished quarter of the town. Anton Koberger[18] and Sebald Schreyer — who as the honorary churchwarden of St. Sebald responsible for finance frequently commissioned works by the goldsmith Dürer[19] — lived in houses on the upper part of the west side (as seen from the market place) of this street; the patrician family Kress lived in the house now called the *Fembohaus,* and further along were the homes of Dr. Hart-mann Schedel, Michael Wolgemut, the patrician family Behaim and Albrecht Dürer the Elder and his family. On the lower part of the east side was the Dominican monastery, next the houses of the Harsdörfer and Scheurl families where the young King Maximilian stayed during the second half of August 1489, then the house of the Haller family and finally the residence of the imperial *Schultheiss* (mayor), Nuremberg's highest imperial official.[20] This neighbour-hood, where several members of Nuremberg's intellectual and artistic élite as well as a number of patrician families lived, may well have exerted a considerable influence on the development of the young Dürer.[21]

Dürer appears to have started going to school a few years after the move to the new house. He later wrote: "And my father was particularly pleased with me when he saw that I was a diligent pupil. This is why my father let me go to school, and when I had learnt to read and write he took me away from school again..."[22] Not much can be learnt from this laconic report. But the phrase "to school" implies that Dürer went to a public institution to learn to read and write and not to one of a number of private tutors in Nuremberg who taught writing and arithmetic.[23] Foremost among Nuremberg's schools were those attached to the parish churches of St. Sebald and St. Lorenz. There were also a number of schools run by local religious orders.[24] In the schools attached to the two parish churches, where a basic "trivium" (of grammar, dialectic and rhetoric) was taught, the pupils were divided into three groups according to age.

The youngest pupils learnt to read and write by studying religious texts in Latin, such as the paternoster or the credo, etc. The fact that Dürer was taken away from school once he had learnt to read and write might imply that he attended one of these basic courses at St. Sebald's.

Scholars have long debated about the extent of Dürer's knowledge of Latin, and no satisfactory conclusion has yet been reached. In his drafts of a manual on painting, Dürer stipulated that a painter should be able to read Latin;[26] it is hardly likely that he would have written this if he himself had been incapable of reading a Latin text.[27] In later years he owned a Latin edition of Euclid which he had bought in Venice in 1507.[28] He sent a letter to Pirckheimer from Italy which starts with a mixture of Latin and Italian.[29] It is noticeable that the Italian words in this letter are spelt more or less phonetically whereas the Latin phrases are ortho-graphically correct. If a note by Joseph Heller[30] is to be believed, there still existed in London around 1800 a letter written in Latin sent by Pirckheimer to Dürer when the latter was in Venice. The dedication to Dürer in Pirckhei-mer's Latin translation of Theophrastus' Greek *Characters* is also in Latin. On the other hand, Dürer is known to have asked for a German translation of Euclid[31] and the German writings of Luther.[32] This implies that Dürer gained an elementary knowledge of Latin at school which enabled him to understand reasonably simple texts without the help of his Humanist friends.[33]

To understand Dürer's personality and work, it is most important to know something of the spiritual influences which parents and school exerted on him during his childhood and youth. Foremost among these influences were the religious ideas dominating education at that time. It seems very difficult to learn anything new about the impact

6   Page from Albrecht Dürer's *Gedenkbuch.* 1502–14. Ink and water-colour. 31×21.6. Kupferstichkabinett SMPK, Berlin.

There is one other manuscript apart from Dürer's family chronicle in which he recorded important events such as the death of his father and his mother. Of this so-called *Gedenkbuch* (commemorative book) only a double page remains in the Berlin Kupferstichkabinett. On the *verso* of the first page Dürer describes a rain of crosses, a strange natural phenomenon which occurred at Nuremberg in 1503. He sketched one of these crosses with a few strokes of the brush on the page. This phenomenon, which was recorded elsewhere in Germany around the same time, has been variously interpreted as a rain of ashes or even of a special kind of algae, driven far inland by strong air currents. In any case, Dürer's description testifies to a belief in miracles. As if to emphasize the significance of the apparition even further, he follows his account with a description of a comet he had seen. In Dürer's lifetime comets have been documented for 1490, 1500 and 1506.

16

sy hat mir ach vor den segen geben und den gottlichen frid gewünst mit vill schoner ler auch das ich mich vor sünden solt hüten
sy begert auch vor zu trinken sant Johans segen als sy dan tett und sy forcht den tot sere aber sy sagt für gott zu kumen förcht
sy sich nit sy ist auch hert gestorben und ich merckt das sy etwas grausams sach dan sy fordert das weichwasser und het doch vor
lang nit geret also parchen ir dy augen ich sach auch wy ir der tot zwen gros stos ans hertz gab und wy sy mund und augen zu tet
und verschid mit schmerzen ich pettet ir vor do von hab ich solchen schmerzen gehabt das ichs nit aussprechen kan got sy ir genedig

Das grost wunderwerck das ich all mein dag gesehen hab ist
geschehen im 1503 Jor als auff vill leut krewz gefallen sind sunderlich
mer auff dy kind den ander leut under den allen hab ich eins
gesehen in der gestalt wy ichs hernoch ~~gemach~~ gemacht hab und es
was gefallen auffs Eyrers magt der im pirkamers hinderhaws
sass ins hemt in leinen duch und sy was so betrübt dar um das sy
wainet und ser klagte dan sy forcht sy müst dorum sterben

Sy je menigk freundlich gewest von gott zu leib und sach gern das er gottes hrer was im 63 Jor do sy starb und ich hab sy erlich noch meinem vermügen begraben lassen gott der her verleich mir das ich auch ein seligs end nem und das got mit seinem himlischen her mein vater muter und freund zu meinem end wollen kumen und das uns der allmechtig got das ewig leben geb amen und in irem tot sach sy vill lieblicher dan do sy noch das leben hett

auch hab ich ein komett am hymell gesehen

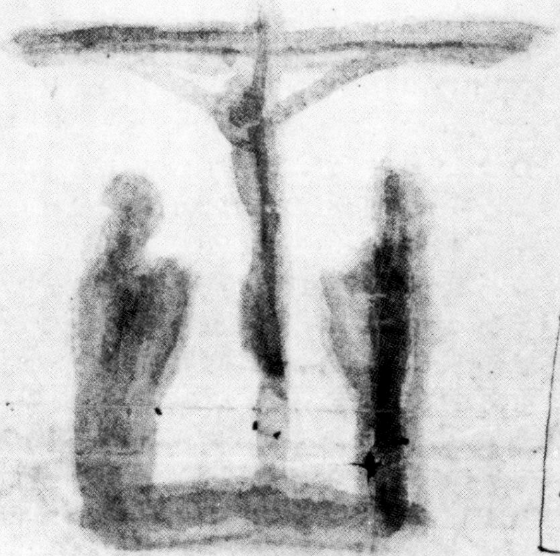

Ich das nochgeschrieben ist mein hab dy ich erarbeit hab redlich
mit meiner hant dan ich hab fast gehabt zu grosser
gewonung hab auch grossen schaden erliten das ich verporgt hab
der mir nit ist worden des gleichen mit knechten dy mir nit
rechnung thetten auch mir einer zu rom gestorben mit verlirung
meins guts des halben do ich im 13 Jor in meiner e pin gewest
hab ich ~~dy auch begaltung~~ grosse schuld bezalt das ich zu fertigen
gewunnen hab ist ein zimlich gutes hawss gutt kleider
von zinnen geschirr guten werckzeug
bettgewant
truhen und behelter
mer dan 100 fl reinisch guts farb

Dz hab Ich aws eim spigell nach
mir selbs kunterfet jm 1484 jar
do Ich noch ein kint was
Albrecht Dürer

18

these ideas had on Dürer, particularly if one remembers the numerous complaints about how ill-educated clerics of all ranks were, and how often they lacked even the basic skills necessary to look after the spiritual welfare of their charges.

The Nuremberg monasteries and churches, which were under the ecclesiastical jurisdiction of the diocese of Bamberg, seem to have cared for the spiritual welfare of their parishioners far better than churches elsewhere; this was largely due to careful guidance by the Nuremberg council. A number of Nuremberg clerics had even received a Humanist upbringing; these included Johannes Werner, the vicar of St. Johann, and provost Sixtus Tucher. The noticeable devoutness of the Nuremberg laity[34] did not find its expression merely in the donation of altarpieces, masses and benefices. Institutions for impoverished elderly artisans, such as Mendel's "Twelve-Brothers'-House" or Landauer's foundation, must be regarded above all as examples of active Christian charity. It is interesting in this context that an inventory of the estate of a rich widow, drawn up in Nuremberg in 1486, lists one Bible and three prayer-books.[35] It seems that all families who could read and write had at least prayer-books. Some Nuremberg citizens may well have possessed Bibles too; this seems to be indicated by the fact that a large number of Bibles were being printed on Nuremberg presses. It is well known, for instance, that Dürer's woodcuts of the *Apocalypse* were influenced by the illustrations of the Nuremberg Bible of 1485 (cf. p.80).

Dürer's parents, according to his own written comments on their religious attitudes, appear to have been firmly pious people, believing that each human action had its reward or punishment. It also seems certain that they were somewhat superstitious as well. Dürer himself believed, even in later years, that dreams and extraordinary events, such as the rain of crosses or the appearance of the comet (18 May–24 June 1500), were omens; he was also convinced that the stars influenced human fate, a conviction he shared with most of his educated contemporaries.

Pl.6
Pl.239

7 *Self-Portrait.* 1484. Silver-point. 27.5 × 19.6. Graphische Sammlung Albertina, Vienna.

During the last years of his life, the artist wrote on this famous drawing (in the Albertina in Vienna): "I have painted this self-portrait from a mirror in the year 1484 when I was still a child. Albrecht Dürer." The silver-point strokes are still uncertain, the pointing finger of the left hand is over-emphasized and the hand doing the drawing is clumsily hidden—yet it is difficult to overestimate the importance of this drawing if one remembers that independent self-portraits did not then exist north of the Alps. The drawing is thus proof both of the ability and the astonishing self-confidence of the thirteen-year-old child prodigy.

Among the material Dürer became familiar with in his early education, there must also have been a basic stock of legends, above all those about the lives of the saints. But he may also have known tales about wild men and witches, or at least seen public performances incorporating such figures, such as the carnival plays and the so-called *Schembart-laufen;* but there are few traces of such themes in his works.

Dürer must have been about ten or twelve years old when his father took him into his workshop to train the talented boy to be his successor, as was the custom. Dürer's training lasted until he was sixteen which implies that he was a qualified journeyman goldsmith by the time he changed his profession. The apprenticeship in his father's workshop influenced his later career as a painter. A goldsmith, in contrast to a painter, is primarily concerned with three-dimensional objects; his work compels him to visualize the sculptural qualities of objects and their spatial relationships. The work of a late Gothic goldsmith often had extremely complicated ornamental tracery which placed very high demands on the goldsmith's ability to imagine his shapes in space, while cast or beaten figures taxed his skill as a sculptor. Dürer's efforts, in his prints, drawings, and paintings, to give his figures sculptural clarity, and his ability to impart the illusion of three-dimensionality in two-dimensional representations of bodies in motion, are explained partly by his innate talent and partly by his training as a goldsmith.

Albrecht Dürer's talent as a draughtsman revealed itself very early. The Imhoffs, Willibald Pirckheimer's heirs, apparently owned two small representations of children's heads drawn by Dürer when he was only ten.[36] Moreover, the famous *Self-Portrait* of 1484 shows such a firm and confident grasp of form on paper that a whole series of attempts must have preceded this drawing, the earliest still in existence. An inscription on the drawing of *A Woman with a Falcon* (W.2), done for a companion in the seclusion of his attic, implies that Dürer's father was not very pleased with his son's intense preoccupation with drawing.

Pl.7

Every goldsmith's workshop in the fifteenth century had pattern sheets which had been pulled from engraved metal plates. Around 1430 a resourceful goldsmith on the Upper Rhine had decided not merely to pull such prints from ornamental plates, but to produce engravings specially for printing and thus provide himself with an extra source of income. The new art form, copper engraving, soon had imitators as well as buyers. It spread quickly throughout Europe, though at first the Upper Rhine remained its centre. Engraving first became important as an artistic technique

Pl.8

goldsmiths throughout Europe can be estimated by the abundance of copies and imitations which still exist.

The early silver-point self-portrait, and even more the pen drawing, now in Berlin, of *The Virgin and Child Flanked by* Pl. 9 *Two Angels Playing Musical Instruments,* show that the young Dürer tried to emulate the clean, regular lines of Schongauer's graphic works. Not only the technique but also the formal arrangement of the drawings of this child prodigy from Nuremberg are closer to Schongauer's engravings than to the woodcuts and paintings of the Wolgemut workshop. From the beginning Dürer's human Pls. 3–5 figures are more lissom and sculptural, and also more consciously attractive than those of his immediate associates in the workshop. On the other hand, the self-portrait of the thirteen-year-old and the painted portraits of the 1490s also show how strongly the compositions of the young artist were influenced by Nuremberg tradition.[37]

It is therefore not surprising that, having decided to let his son become a painter, Dürer's father considered sending him to Schongauer to become his apprentice, even though the master lived far away. According to an account by Christoph Scheurl written in 1515 and based on written and verbal information given by Dürer himself, the boy's father had wanted to apprentice his son to Schongauer as early as 1484 when Dürer was thirteen years old. According to Scheurl the plan foundered because Schongauer died.[38] But as Schongauer only died early in 1491 there must have been other, unknown reasons why Dürer did not train with him.

The work of another artist is always mentioned when the origins of Dürer's art are discussed: that of a painter and engraver working in the region of the Middle Rhine known as the Hausbuch Master because of his illustrations for a *Manual of Warfare,* a manuscript owned by the Princes Waldburg-Wolfegg. It is thought that his graphic works, like those of Schongauer, were known in the Nuremberg workshops and may have inspired the young Dürer. But the works of the Hausbuch Master are drypoint engravings Pl. 10

8 Martin Schongauer: *Crucifixion.* C. 1480. Engraving. 29 × 19.6. Kupferstichkabinett SMPK, Berlin.

Martin Schongauer (*c.* 1445–91), of Colmar, was the most important German painter of the last quarter of the fifteenth century. He came from a family of goldsmiths who had originally lived in Augsburg. He was the first painter to take up engraving at the beginning of the 1470s. His engravings could be found throughout Europe and were favourite models and sources of inspiration for workshops of painters and goldsmiths. His prints, signed with the monogram *MS* and his workshop stamp, were also known in the goldsmith's workshop of Albrecht Dürer the Elder. This engraving, representing the crucified Christ between Mary and John, was probably done around 1480. Engravings of this kind served as examples for the young Dürer.

9 *Enthroned Virgin and Child Flanked by Two Angels Playing Musical Instruments.* 1485. Pen and wash. 21 × 14.7. Kupferstichkabinett SMPK, Berlin. ▷

Dürer showed that he was fully aware of his achievement by not only dating this composition 1485, but also signing it with the initials *A* and *d,* an early version of his later monogram. The composition of this drawing is influenced by Netherlandish art, but there are also formal similarities between it and the engravings of the Master E.S. (who died in 1467) and of Schongauer. Dürer clearly tries to imitate the regular lines of the Colmar master, so that the sculptural forms of the complicated folds of the draperies stand out clearly.

when the Colmar painter Martin Schongauer, who like Albrecht Dürer was the son of a goldsmith, took up the new technique around 1470. The composition as well as the technical execution of his engravings made them works of European importance. Even today the impact of his prints on the workshops of contemporary painters, sculptors and

Pl. 10

10 Hausbuch Master: *Group of People Playing Cards*. C. 1480. Engraving. 13×12. Rijksprentencabinet, Amsterdam.

The artist (Erhard Reuwich?) who is called Hausbuch Master after an illustrated manuscript owned by the Princes Waldburg-Wolfegg was, together with Schongauer, one of the first painters who took up engraving. But he preferred to use a needle rather than a burin for his graphic works, engraving plates of soft metal with his imaginative, lively and often humorous compositions. Although this technique only allowed a small number of impressions to be made, Dürer appears to have seen some of the Hausbuch Master's compositions, such as this *Group of People Playing Cards*, during his years as a journeyman.

pulled from plates of very soft metal, so that only a very few prints could be made of each plate. Similar subject matter alone is not sufficient proof that the young Dürer was influenced at the very beginning of his career by the graphic works of the Hausbuch Master. Dürer's art reflects a knowledge of the Hausbuch Master's works only during and immediately after the years of his journeying.

Albrecht Dürer became an apprentice in the painting workshop of his neighbour Wolgemut when he was sixteen, at an age when his father had already finished his apprenticeship. It can easily be imagined how the talented newcomer had to suffer the mocking and teasing of the other members of the workshop; Dürer still remembered the abuse he had been subjected to as late as 1523 when he wrote his family chronicle.[39]

Little is known about the teaching methods in a painter's workshop in the late Middle Ages. The training was mainly technical. If Dürer's theoretical writings are reliable, his own artistic training consisted mainly in copying other artists' works.[40] Neither the existing drawings by Wolgemut and his workshop nor those of the young Dürer indicate the importance attached to drawing from nature. The drawings which the young Dürer produced during his apprenticeship indicate that the arrangement of a composition was clearly thought to be more important than the study of nature. Dürer's drawings of this time and of the subsequent period show a predilection for sweeping draperies which are extremely complicated and presumably modelled on Wolgemut's. The role Wilhelm Pleydenwurff, the joint owner of the workshop, played in Dürer's training can only be guessed at, because little is known as yet about his artistic output. It is possible that he awakened Dürer's interest in the representation of landscapes and their atmosphere.

Topographically identifiable landscapes and architectural views used as backgrounds in altar panels had become

◁13 *Christ on the Cross, with Mary and John*. 1489. Pen. 31×22.7. Cabinet des Dessins, Musée du Louvre, Paris.

The Crucifixion has always been a central subject of Christian art. As far as can be ascertained Dürer first drew a Crucifixion *circa* 1489, towards the end of his apprenticeship with Michael Wolgemut. The overall composition may have been inspired by Schongauer's great engraving of the Crucifixion (Pl. 8), but the rendering of space in this drawing is already superior to that in the Colmar engraver's work. Schongauer's print gives the impression of stillness, and the individual figures are isolated and passive; in Dürer's drawing Mary and John turn towards the crucified Christ and thus actively express their grief. Dramatic tension is also conveyed by the dark gathering clouds.

11 *Portrait of Dürer's Mother*. C. 1490. Oil. 47×36. Germanisches Nationalmuseum, Nuremberg. ▷

12 *Portrait of Dürer's Father*. 1490. Oil. 47×39. Gallerie degli Uffizi, Florence. ▷▷

Dürer painted his father's portrait during the months after he finished his apprenticeship and before he left on his journeying at Easter 1490. It is known from written documents, and from the two coats of arms of the Dürer and Holper families on the back of this panel, that there was a corresponding portrait of Dürer's mother. From the seventeenth century until recently this was thought to have been lost, but it has been discovered among the paintings of the Germanisches Nationalmuseum in Nuremberg.

increasingly common in Germany after Konrad Witz had depicted Lake Geneva in his *Miraculous Draught of Fishes*. During the last quarter of the fifteenth century most examples of such landscape art were to be found in Franconia. The earliest landscape watercolour, a view of the imperial palace at Bamberg, was painted before 1487 by Wolfgang Katzheimer the Elder. Compared with it, the numerous views of towns in Schedel's *Chronicle of the World*, which were produced in the Wolgemut workshop, appear rather old-fashioned, but do show that there were examples of this kind of art in Nuremberg which could have inspired the young Dürer.

Pl. 4
Pl. 3
Work on the woodcuts for the *Schatzbehalter* (1491) and for Schedel's *Chronicle of the World* (1493), which were executed in Wolgemut's workshop while Dürer was an apprentice there, provided him with a thorough grounding in the art of drawing for woodcuts. There have been many attempts to identify the young Dürer's drawings among the many hundreds of illustrations, but so far they have not been successful.[41] The contemporary rules of the trade can hardly have allowed an apprentice to do independent designs; on the other hand, the process of transferring the design onto the wood block was better paid than the designing itself, so it is unlikely that Dürer collaborated in either process. It may be, however, that Dürer helped execute the drawings from which the blocks were made.[42]

Many woodcut illustrations in books printed in Nuremberg have been thought to show the untrained hand of the young Dürer. However, the only woodcut that can reasonably be attributed to the developing painter is the frontispiece of a pamphlet published by Peter Wagner, probably at the end of 1489, called *Oratio Cassandrae virginis Venetae pro Berthucio Lamberto...* (M.S. 271), to which Celtis contributed an ode to Apollo. The woodcut already exhibits some characteristic Dürer features, especially and somewhat surprisingly the view through the door behind the standing figure of the scholar. It is reminiscent of the
Pl. 15 woodcut of *St. Jerome* produced in 1492.

Six drawings executed during the years of apprenticeship with Wolgemut have survived. Three of them are signed with a monogram and the date 1489 — both added by a later hand. This date must be approximately correct. The "Bremen" drawing (W. 16), which was unfortunately lost during the war, included horsemen and horses shown in varied poses, using difficult foreshortenings, in a landscape of astonishing depth. Schongauer's engraving of *Christ Carrying the Cross* may have been the inspiration for it. The drawing of *Fencing Horsemen*, in London (W. 17), tackles the same problem and depicts such difficult subjects as a horse collapsing underneath its rider. Certain weaknesses in the execution imply that the London drawing was done earlier than the Bremen one. The drawing of *Three Warriors*, in Berlin (W. 18), appears to illustrate a similar subject, but it may well be a study for the soldiers under the Cross. All three drawings show that the young draughtsman tried hard to convey the sculptural quality of his figures and to clarify their positions in space.

The only early drawing with a religious theme is the *Crucifixion* in the Louvre. In this work Dürer far surpasses Pl. 13 not only his teacher, but even his chosen model Schongauer. While the draped figures of the Virgin and St. John under the Cross reflect his sound training as a draughtsman and are Schongauer types, the exaggeratedly slender figure of Christ on the Cross gives the impression that it was Dürer's first attempt to draw a nude figure. The most striking feature of the composition is the perfect integration of figures and space. Although the group around the Cross is in the very foreground of the picture, the figures do not stand in front of the landscape but are part of it. This is one step Pl. 5 beyond the achievement of even the Master of the Augustinian Altarpiece. His painting and other works originating from the Wolgemut workshop taught Dürer to emphasize the expressive power of a landscape, and particularly of the sky. At the end of his apprenticeship the young Dürer was already demonstrating his ability, later praised by Erasmus, to convey more than was visible in nature, purely by means of black lines.[43]

"At that time God gave me diligence, so that I learnt well,"[44] Dürer said later, reflecting on his apprenticeship. But he had not merely learnt how to draw an object in black lines on paper. This was only the most basic skill of a painter (if one ignores the graphic artist for a moment). To prove his real technical and artistic skill he had to be able to painstakingly transfer, with paints, the preliminary design of a composition onto wood or canvas.

As early as 1484 Dürer may well have wanted to prove his ability as a painter with a self-portrait; evidence of this is provided by a copy of a small painting. But the first painting which can be definitely attributed to Dürer is the 1490 portrait of his father; a corresponding portrait of his mother Pl. 11 has recently been rediscovered.[45] The portrait of the Pl. 12 goldsmith Dürer is not only superior to Wolgemut's portraits, its quality surpasses all other portraits done in Germany during this period. One would have to go back to the portraits of the great Flemish painters of the fifteenth century to find a comparable achievement.

III. Journeying Years: 1490–5

The Lower Rhine · The Upper Rhine · Italy

The period from Easter 1490 to spring 1495 must be regarded as one unit in Dürer's life. The impressions he gained during these five years had a decisive influence on the whole of his later development. In order fully to understand the importance of this period in the young artist's life, one has to try to visualize what art was like in Europe at the end of the fifteenth century.

The human figure had been at the centre of high mediæval art. Earthly reality surrounding man had only been included to demonstrate the working of God's plan for salvation in human history. Pictorial representation, be it in wall paintings, panels, book illustrations or stained glass windows, was not a copy of reality but its symbolic representation. The portrayal of realistic spatial relationships was therefore unimportant. But cross-currents between Italian art on the one hand and the art of France, the Netherlands and Germany on the other, started a development in the last quarter of the fourteenth century which in the course of fifty years almost entirely replaced the idealistic mediæval conception of the world. Christ's Passion, the life of the Virgin and the figures of the confessors and martyrs of the faith were now depicted with a degree of realism which must have seemed almost miraculous to the people of Europe at that time. Boccaccio's praise, in the *Decamerone,* of Giotto as the painter who rediscovered nature clearly reflects the fascination he and his contemporaries felt for the *buona maniera moderna* or *ars nova*.[46]

The various stories taken from the Bible and the legends of saints were now no longer shown against a background of transcendental gold or a neutral ground of delicately ornamental tapestry-like patterns, but in a setting composed of fragments of the real world which suited the subject depicted. For artists including Masaccio, the brothers van Eyck and Konrad Witz, the main representational problem was to show human figures in space, i.e. in a landscape or an interior. The Italian artists had developed a theoretical system for the correct rendering of the visual impression made by objects seen at varying depths, which they called *prospectiva* (view through). North of the Alps, where the painters in the Netherlandish provinces were the leading artists, the problem of the human figure and space was first tackled by concentrating on the actual visual impression they made, in which light and colour were predominant elements. The painters' rendering of space was based on such close observation that the lack of correct perspective was usually not even noticeable.

The Netherlandish painters strove for realism in the depiction not only of figures and space but of the entire material world. One of the most important aims of the great masters was to reproduce the various textures of the world using paint. For this purpose they had developed a new technique which enabled them to reproduce the most delicate shades of colour. This technique, which has been attributed to the brothers van Eyck, is called oil-painting—not entirely correctly, as it really involved mixed media (oil and tempera). The great Netherlandish painters, above all Rogier van der Weyden, also proved to be masters of composition, inventing new, impressive formal arrangements which were to influence the whole of later European painting.

In the course of the fifteenth century painters and sculptors from all over Germany had moved to the Netherlands to gain first-hand knowledge of the artistic and technical achievements of the great artists. Hans Memling left eastern Franconia and settled in Bruges; today he is regarded as an important exponent of early Netherlandish painting. On the other hand, Netherlandish artists like the sculptor Nikolaus Gerhaert von Leyden or the painter Erhard Reuwich had begun to work in the towns along the Rhine. In this context it should be remembered that most of those parts of the Netherlands in the possession of the princes of France and Burgundy were situated on the territory of what then constituted the German Empire. Ghent and Bruges, and increasingly Antwerp as well, must have been as important for contemporary artists as Paris was to be for the German Impressionist painters. Examples such as Friedrich Herlin, who visited the Netherlands in 1467 after he had finished his works for Rothenburg ob der Tauber, or Hans Holbein the Elder, who went to the Netherlands in 1490 when he too had already finished his training and was a master painter, clearly show that ambitious painters thought it very important to meet the leading artists of the north, while art produced south of the Alps continued to be ignored.

In accordance with tradition the young Dürer set out after Easter, on 11 April 1490, to start his travels as a journeyman. All he himself said in his family chronicle about this time was that he went away after Easter, 1490 and was called back by his father early in 1494.[47] But the previously mentioned report by Christoph Scheurl gives a rather more detailed account: "Then, when he (Dürer) had travelled the length and breadth of Germany he came to Colmar in the year 92, and there the goldsmiths Casper and Paulus and the painter Ludwig, and similarly in Basle, Georg, all four of whom were brothers of Schon Merten (Martin Schongauer), kept him good company."[48]

There is no agreement among scholars as to where Dürer could have spent the two years between his departure from Nuremberg and his arrival in Colmar in the summer of 1492. Some believe that Dürer spent the first years of his journeying in southern German art centres, such as Augsburg and Ulm; others think that the young artist finished his training in the Netherlands. Neither assumption can be proved. Nothing in Dürer's art indicates, for instance, that he was particularly familiar with the art of Swabia and the area around Lake Constance.

Christoph Scheurl's statement that Dürer travelled the length and breadth of Germany[49] gives the impression that he went from one town to the next. But the phrase used in the printed Latin version, *tandem peragrata Germania*, implies a journey over large distances. All the same, it cannot be deduced from these three words alone that the young Dürer went as far as the Netherlands.

The same applies to a description in the *Schilder-Boek* by Karel van Mander, the painter and artists' biographer, which appeared in 1604. In his biography of the Haarlem painter Geertgen tot Sint Jans (who died in 1495), he says that Dürer, on seeing an altarpiece by Geertgen in Haarlem, exclaimed: "Truly this man was already a painter in his mother's womb!"[50] As Dürer did not go to Haarlem during his stay in the Netherlands in 1520–1 it must be assumed that he said this during his earlier journeying. But it is doubtful whether Dürer, a talented but still very young artist, could already have made such an impression on the Netherlandish town that his words were still remembered many years later. This artist's anecdote thus does not prove much, even though Joachim von Sandrart also mentions that Dürer stayed in the Netherlands during his journeying years.[51]

Which were the most likely centres for the young Dürer to have perfected his training? There were three which might have determined his route: the first was the south-west where Schongauer lived. Then there was a route from Franconia through the south-east, to Austria. Throughout the fifteenth century there were lively commercial and artistic links between Franconia and Austria. The most prominent artist to take this route was the young Cranach. The third and probably most important link was with the north-west, with the Netherlands. As the goldsmith Albrecht Dürer was one of the people who had stayed "in the Netherlands for a long time and visited the great artists",[52] he may well have advised his son, whose training he guided with obvious care throughout, to perfect his abilities in the Netherlands before going to work with Martin Schongauer.[53]

If the young Dürer really went to the north-west first, there should be traces of his acquaintance with Netherlandish art in his work. This raises an additional problem, however, in that one would have to be able to distinguish those traces which show a direct influence from those which merely reflect the general influence of the Netherlands on German art. But some features which show a personal debt have indeed been found by scholars in early Dürer drawings.[54] The woodcut of the *Martyrdom of the Ten Thousand* Pl. 45 is yet another work which reveals the influence of the Netherlands, both in composition[55] and iconography.[56] Many scholars have moreover pointed out that the composition of Dürer's *Feast of the Rose Garlands* is closely related Pl. 114

14 *Holy Family*. C. 1492. Pen. 29×21.4. Kupferstichkabinett SMPK, Berlin.

Dürer's rapid development is clearly illustrated by a comparison of the *Crucifixion* of 1489 (Pl. 13) with this *Holy Family*, executed *circa* 1491–2. The group of figures is integrated into the landscape even more strongly than in the earlier drawing. The depth of the picture can be clearly measured by following the row of trees. Dürer's first direct contact with the art of the Netherlands, and particularly that of the Haarlem painter Geertgen tot Sint Jans, was presumably responsible for the clear conception of space in this drawing. This drawing, together with several other, mostly sketchy studies, constitutes a preliminary design for the engraving of the *Holy Family with a Grasshopper* (Pl. 29).

15 *St. Jerome Pulling the Thorn from the Lion's Paw.* 1492. Woodcut. 19 × 13.3. Kupferstichkabinett SMPK, Berlin.

This woodcut was used as the frontispiece for the first volume of the second edition of St. Jerome's letters, published by Nikolaus Kessler in Basle in 1492. The Basle Kupferstichkabinett has the wood block which was signed on the back by the young artist in calligraphic script: *Albrecht Dürer von nörmergk.* The most surprising feature of this illustration is the wealth of detail in the interior (which anticipates the engraving of *St. Jerome* of 1514, Pl. 169). No artist before Dürer had attempted to represent an interior with a comparable wealth of realistic detail. It is true that Dürer had not yet mastered the laws of perspective, but many of the spatial ambiguities may be the result of clumsiness on the part of the cutter, who had not yet undergone the intensive training typical of Nuremberg craftsmen.

to the centre panel of Stephan Lochner's famous altarpiece of the *Three Magi* in Cologne. There has even been a recent attempt to establish that the young Dürer stayed in the Bruges workshop of Hans Memling.[57]

It may be assumed that Dürer's early journey took him to Pl. 14 Cologne, perhaps even to Haarlem.[58] It is unlikely that he

went as far as Flanders and Brabant, the heart of early Netherlandish art, since the southern provinces and towns, which had been rebelling against King Maximilian for more than a decade, were at that precise time being subjugated by Duke Albert of Saxony in a harsh campaign.[59] When Haarlem also rebelled against Hapsburg rule at the beginning of 1492, Dürer may well have left the Netherlands and gone to Colmar to work and study with Martin Schongauer.

On his way to the Upper Rhine he may have stopped at Mainz where the painter Erhard Reuwich, the so-called Pl. 10 Hausbuch Master, and possibly also Wolfgang Peurer (Master WB)[59a] worked. It is more likely that Dürer met these two painters, who were also competent graphic artists, at this time rather than at the beginning of his journeying,[60] because those of his drawings showing traces of their influence indicate that he was also familiar with Netherlandish art.

Martin Schongauer was already dead when Dürer arrived in Colmar. He had died on 2 February 1491 in Breisach, where he had been working on a wall painting at the minster since 1488. Martin's brothers, the goldsmiths Casper and Paul and the painter Ludwig who had taken over the Colmar workshop, gave a warm welcome to the journeyman. But it must have been a great disappointment to the young, self-confident artist to find not Martin Schongauer but his brother Ludwig, who was a much less important painter. This may be why Dürer seems to have left quite early, travelling along the Upper Rhine and arriving in Basle in the early summer of 1492.

The imperial city of Basle, which was also a diocese, had had a university since 1460; it was donated by the citizens and granted many special privileges by the Humanist Pope Pius II. Chairs in both the faculty of arts and the faculty of law had early been occupied by Humanists. The growing university had attracted several well-known early printers who had received a Humanist education such as Johann Amerbach from Amorbach in the Odenwald; this meant that the city had rapidly developed into one of the most important centres for book printing.

In Basle, as in Nuremberg, it was the general practice that a journeyman wanting to work was only allowed to do so in the workshop of a local master. Two Basle painters who had originally come from Nuremberg, Hans Schaltensdorfer and Konrad Kögel, have been mentioned in connection with Dürer.[61] But as no definite works are known by these two painters—nor by other painters mentioned in Basle documents—it is impossible to say any more about the workshop in which Dürer may have worked. However, a predella in

16 *The Martyrdom of St. Sebastian.* 1494. Woodcut for a broadsheet. C. 11.5 × 15.3. Öffentliche Kunstsammlung, Kupferstichkabinett, Basle.

In 1974, sixteen fragments of an unknown print of the late fifteenth century were discovered during restoration work on the receipt book for 1525–1659 of the Basle Guild of Wine Growers. They had been used as maculature when the volume was bound in 1525. They belong to eight broadsheets of a Latin poem on St. Sebastian by Sebastian Brant. The woodcut is two and a half columns wide and appears on the upper left-hand side of the sheet. It shows the saint on the right-hand fragment, archers with long-bows and crossbows together with a group of onlookers on the left hand. This woodcut was correctly identified as a work by the young Dürer very shortly after it was discovered.

the Basle museum (A. 6) which is today generally accepted as a work by Dürer proves that he must indeed have worked with a Basle master. A votive panel representing the *Rescue of a Drowned Boy* (A. 5), presumably produced for a particular commission, may also have been executed in Basle, or possibly during a short stay somewhere on the way from Colmar to Basle. The style of the figures and the energetic treatment in general relate this painting very closely to Dürer's Basle illustrations.

The first of many illustrations done in Basle was a woodcut for the frontispiece of an edition of St. Jerome's letters published in the autumn of 1492. The Father of the Church and translator of the Bible is shown in his study as he pauses in his translating to pull the thorn out of the lion's paw.[62] No German book illustration or individual woodcut had ever represented a comparable interior in which furniture and household equipment as well as the view through to the street are depicted in such loving detail. The illustration made a great impression on Basle painters, as a woodcut of *St. Ambrose*[63] inspired by Dürer's frontispiece clearly shows. And Dürer himself seems to have been fully conscious of his achievement, because he signed the back of the wood block "Albrecht Dürer from nörmergk". A

recently discovered woodcut of the *Martyrdom of St. Sebastian* for a broadsheet by Sebastian Brant must also have been made at the beginning of Dürer's Basle period.[64]

After the success of the *St. Jerome* woodcut the foreign journeyman-painter received virtually all the important commissions for illustrations issued by Basle printers in those years. First of all, he produced fifty-five designs for a book by the Knight de la Tour Landry called *Examples of the Fear of God and of Worthiness*, which the Württemberg Knight Marquart von Stein had translated from French into German. Dürer demonstrated his narrative talent in partly humorous, partly serious woodcuts for this collection of *novellae* with a moral purpose. His pictures are among the best German incunabula illustrations.

While the stories of the French knight provided many scenes and situations which could easily be turned into illustrations, the next work to be illustrated by Dürer presented him with entirely new problems. The *Ship of Fools* by Sebastian Brant (1457–1521) is an intricately structured didactic poem in German which the Humanist lawyer wrote while working in Basle. In the course of 112 chapters and more than 7,000 couplets, he characterizes human excesses, weaknesses and transgressions, as well as

Pl. 15

Pl. 18

31

17. *The Woman and the Hermit.* 1493. Woodcut. C. 10 × 12.5. Kupferstichkabinett SMPK, Berlin.

This woodcut for the *Knight of the Tower,* a typical devotional book of the time, shows Dürer as a humorous illustrator. "The good hermit who was bereft of his reason" is brought back to his senses by the woman, by means of a cold bath. The original French text of 1371, written by the knight Geoffrey de la Tour Landry, had been translated into German by the Württemberg *Landvogt* of Mömpelgard (Montbéliard), Marquart von Stein, between 1478 and 1490 and was printed by Michael Furter in Basle in 1493.

18 *The Fanatical Falcon- and Dog-Lover.* 1494. Woodcut. 17 × 14.3. Kupferstichkabinett SMPK, Berlin.

By far the most famous work which Dürer illustrated at Basle was *The Ship of Fools,* a moralizing epic poem by the Strasbourg Humanist Dr. jur. Sebastian Brant. It was published by Johann Bergmann von Olpe in Basle in 1494. The various kinds of folly are interpreted in a late mediæval Humanist sense as moral failings, rather than as acts of stupidity, let alone carnival pranks. The book became a world-wide success when it was published in a Latin version in 1497.

such simple pleasures as folly. The poet believes that these are signs of a topsy-turvy world heading for catastrophe on an apocalyptic scale.[65] Brant's main conclusion is that a wise man should stay at home and weigh all his actions carefully lest he become one of the company of fools on the ship.[66] At the same time it is his duty to teach his fellow men that God has given them the choice between eternal damnation and the opportunity of making mankind in the image of the divine cosmos.[67] This idea comes close to Count Pico della Mirandola's conception of man.

The young Dürer designed seventy-six illustrations, including the frontispiece, for this difficult poem with its wealth of examples taken — or simply translated — from the Bible, Virgil and Ovid. Each new theme is summarized in three lines at the head of each chapter and usually provides the subject of Dürer's illustration, which he supplemented with details from the text. Some illustrations, on the other hand, are almost entirely independent of the text, which raises the question as to whether Dürer invented them himself or designed them according to the wishes and suggestions of the author. Brant says in the preface: "If there were someone who … could not read about the portraits which I have created here, he would understand their meaning by looking at the pictures" (fol. a ij *verso*); this implies that he had a say in the illustrations even if he did not literally "create" them.[68]

19 *The Poet Terence.* 1492–4. Drawing on a wood block. C. 9.25 × 14.55. Öffentliche Kunstsammlung, Kupferstichkabinett, Basle.

This drawing on a wood block, now in the Basle Kupferstichkabinett, was designed as a picture of the author for an edition of Terence's comedies that was never printed. Of the 129 wood blocks for the edition of Terence which remain, only a few were cut at a later date. Iconographically the picture of the poet is closely related to representations of St. John on Patmos receiving his visions of the Apocalypse. However, in contrast to the author of the New Testament, Terence wears the poet's laurel wreath. In 1487 Dürer had witnessed the crowning of the Humanist Konrad Celtis as poet laureate by the Emperor Frederick III at Nuremberg castle; Celtis was the first German to receive this honour. This picture of Terence may well reflect memories of events of this kind.

Dürer's woodcuts are lively and often dramatic. Their liveliness is emphasized by spontaneous, sometimes even nervous strokes of the pen which survive in the print made from the wood block. The book was a universal success; Brant's contemporaries compared him to Aristophanes, Dante and Petrarch and considered his poem superior to Homer's.[69] Dürer's illustrations are sure to have contributed

to this success, as the young painter had succeeded so well in giving a visual expression to Brant's ideas.

Other commissions which Dürer received while in Basle were less fortunate; without doubt the most interesting of them was a commission to illustrate an edition of Terence's Pl. 19 comedies. Dürer had already produced all 147 designs and transferred them to the wood blocks when work was stopped. Draughtsman and editor did not visualize the people and settings of these ancient comedies in a classical context. The classical protagonists are dressed in the latest fashion of 1493 and move through landscapes of the Upper Rhine, even though the illustrations were based on sources going back to a late classical cycle of illustrations. The woodcut of the "theatre" shows that although the editor must have been generally familiar with the design of ancient theatres, he misunderstood the tiered rows of seats. The discrepancy between the classical text and its late mediæval illustrations clearly demonstrates that the understanding of Antiquity which the Humanists of the Upper Rhine had at that time was inadequate. They were only familiar with the

20   Michael Wolgemut: *The Muse Terpsichore.* C. 1493–4. Woodcut. 21.3 × 13.2. Kupferstichkabinett SMPK, Berlin.

This representation of the muse of dance belongs, in all probability, to a group of woodcuts designed as illustrations for an anthology of classical Latin poetry, planned around 1493 by the Nuremberg jurist Peter Dannhauser. The coarse woodcuts, which are still entirely late Gothic in conception, are generally attributed to Michael Wolgemut. When faced with the problem of representing figures from classical mythology, he fell back on a series of north Italian engravings of *circa* 1470 which have mistakenly been identified as tarot cards. Wolgemut's versions based on the Italian models reveal only a rather vague idea about classical art, but by using these engravings—thought to be "in the manner of the ancients" by artists north of the Alps—he was one step ahead of the majority of his contemporaries in his understanding of classical Antiquity.

young Dürer's intensive study of Renaissance art modelled on the ancients, the great variety of names and topics taken from classical mythology which he encountered in the *Ship of Fools* must have made a lasting impression on him, judging by the extent of his knowledge of this subject in later years.

It is likely that Dürer moved on from Basle to Strasbourg in the autumn of 1493, or at least before the beginning of the winter. There are two documents testifying to his stay in the most important city of Alsace: two portraits of the master with whom Dürer worked in Strasbourg and of his wife (A. 7v–8v) are listed in the inventory of Willibald Imhoff, the grandson of Pirckheimer, which unfortunately have been lost. However, a canon illustration of the Crucifixion for the *Opus speciale*, which appeared in Strasbourg on 13 November 1493, still exists and very clearly illustrates Dürer's development since the Paris drawing of 1489. In spite of their late Gothic slenderness, the figures now possess a certain monumentality. The landscape extends without a break into the depth of the picture. It is likely that during this last stage of his journeying Dürer worked with the painter whose workshop is responsible for the panels of the *St. Dominic Altarpiece* in Darmstadt. It seems likely that Dürer at least collaborated on the upper panels. His *Christ* Pl. 21 *as the Man of Sorrrows* in the Karlsruhe Museum is so

21   *Christ as the Man of Sorrows.* C. 1493–4. Oil. 30 × 19. Staatliche Kunsthalle, Karlsruhe.   ▷

It has recently been doubted that this small work, painted towards the end of Dürer's years as a journeyman, probably in Strasbourg, is a work by Dürer's hand, because its technique is closely related to that of a number of panels in Darmstadt, which come from an altarpiece dedicated to St. Dominic in Colmar or Strasbourg. However, the almost terrifying realism of this work, the carefully painted details, the figure's expressive power and stylistic idiosyncrasies, such as the repoussé drawing on the gold ground, solidly connect this panel with Dürer's œuvre.

literary productions of classical times. Neither scholars nor artists in the Upper Rhine region were as yet familiar with the rich visual arts of the ancients. Perhaps Sebastian Brant, who is thought to have been the editor, would have had a greater understanding of these matters if he had known Italy; he was certainly fully aware that this lack of knowledge was a great drawback.

It is against this background that the significance of Michael Wolgemut's work must be seen. At about the same time as Dürer was working on the edition of Terence, Pl. 19 Michael Wolgemut modelled his woodcuts of the Muses on engravings of the Ferrara school, which in their turn were based on classical models. Though it cannot really be maintained—as some scholars have done—that the Humanists of the Upper Rhine were responsible for the

22 *Self-Portrait with the Head Supported on one Hand*. C. 1492–3. Pen. 20.4×20.8. Graphische Sammlung der Universitätsbibliothek, Erlangen.

This study must be seen in the context of the drawing for the *Holy Family* (Pl. 14) and the painting of *Christ as the Man of Sorrows* in Karlsruhe (Pl. 21), regardless of whether it represents youthful melancholy or simply a headache. The gesture of supporting the head on the hand, common to all three pictures, gives clear expression to a variety of feelings: melancholy in the case of the self-portrait, grief in the case of the *Man of Sorrows* and weariness in the case of Joseph, the old man in the picture of the *Holy Family*.

closely related to the *St. Dominic Altarpiece* that this small work by Dürer is sometimes thought to be by the Strasbourg master.[70]

PL. 22 Also closely related to the *Man of Sorrows* is the slightly earlier self-portrait at Erlangen. It could be a preliminary drawing for the painting of Christ, a study in which the young artist realized how the cheek is distorted when the head rests on the hand. But the two works have more than this gesture in common: both faces show an expression of sorrow. It would be unfair to say that the *Man of Sorrows* was deliberately used to express Dürer's youthful problems, but the picture does represent an objective correlative to the artist's own problematic nature.[71]

There is yet another self-portrait of the 22-year-old Dürer which seems to have been completed in Strasbourg; it is inscribed with a couplet which appears to have been inspired by the Strasbourg Friends of God at the Grünen-wörth monastery.[72] The mystic strand in Alsatian theology, exemplified by Johann Geiler von Kaysersberg, the famous preacher at Strasbourg minster, and others, seems to have greatly impressed Dürer, especially as Geiler—like Brant in his *Ship of Fools*—preached the imminent end of the world.[73]

A few drawings, which are generally taken to be studies from nature, show a completely different aspect of the young Dürer's art; they are the *Young Couple* in Hamburg PL. 25 and the *Female Nude* in Bayonne, dated 1493. It is doubtful whether the two elegant young people really are a study from nature, but the *Female Nude* is very obviously a faithful portrayal of a model. It is the first nude study of a living model north of the Alps.

After more than four years of journeying Dürer obeyed his father's summons and returned home from Strasbourg, arriving in Nuremberg after Whitsun (18 May) 1494. On 7 July he married a girl of his father's choice. Agnes PL. 27 Frey—who to judge from Dürer's drawing seems to have been between fifteen and eighteen years old—came from a family of merchants who had formerly been very affluent. Hans Frey, the father of the bride, was a "Mechanicus" and as *Genannter* of the large council belonged to the "honour-ables". His wife Anna came from the patrician family Rummel, and was related to the Haller family. The elevated social position of the Frey family was reflected in a dowry of 200 florins. It was the same as that of Magdalena Haller when she married the town physician, Dr. Hartmann Schedel.[73a]

Even if Dürer followed Nuremberg tradition[74] and lived with his young wife in the house of his parents-in-law or,

more likely still, in that of his parents[75] during these first months, he must have worked hard to be able to establish his own household and his own workshop. The young painter probably found work in Wolgemut's workshop.

Dürer seems to have painted his first watercolours—of views around Nuremberg, the *Cemetery of St. John* (W. 62), the *Wire-Drawing Mill* and studies of trees (W. 63, 64)— PL. 26 during the summer of 1494. Together with the Bamberg vedutas by Wolfgang Katzheimer the Elder, they are among the first landscape paintings in their own right in German art. Dürer's watercolours are still slightly awkward at this time: buildings and clumps of trees seem to be arranged on top of each other rather than receding gradually into the distance; there is still more interest in the precise rendering of detail than in the overall effect; the colours are somewhat heavy due to a lot of bodycolour. However, it is this very naïvety, the loving care with which even the smallest detail is recorded, which make these watercolours so charming. They may not be very naturalistic, but the task which this young artist set himself and fulfilled represents an excep-tional achievement.[75a]

Dürer's first attempts as an engraver were also made at this time. It is very likely that he had already become familiar with the technique of metal engraving in his father's workshop. He could now use his knowledge to realize his designs without having to be dependent on the wishes of patrons or the skill of wood-cutters. And there may well have been other, economic reasons for turning to engraving, because it must often have been more profitable to sell

23 *Young Couple.* C. 1493–4. Pen. 25.8×19.1. Kupferstichkabinett, Kunsthalle, Hamburg. ▷

This drawing in the Hamburg Kunsthalle is a genre scene in the manner of the Hausbuch Master, though there is no evidence of a direct link. Neither is there any evidence for the assumption, often made by early Dürer scholars, that the man is a self-portrait of the young Dürer. There may, however, be a connection with the engraving of *The Walk* (Pl. 53) which was done a few years later.

24 *Self-Portrait.* 1493. Oil. 56.5×44.5. Musée du Louvre, Paris. ▷▷

Dürer added an inscription of two lines at the top of his self-portrait: *My sach die gat/ Als es oben schtat* ("My fate is determined above"). This verse, in language imitating the Alemannic dialect of the Upper Rhine, indicates his religious conviction. The trust in God is further emphasized by the eryngo, a kind of thistle, which Dürer holds in his hand. It is a symbol of Christ's Passion, both in this picture and in the Karlsruhe *Man of Sorrows* where it appears on the gold ground, and not a symbol of love as its popular German name of *Männertreu* (man's devotion) implies. Since Goethe saw a copy of the picture at Göttingen, scholars have often wrongly thought that it was Dürer's gift to his fiancée Agnes Frey (Pl. 27) whom he was to marry in July, 1494.

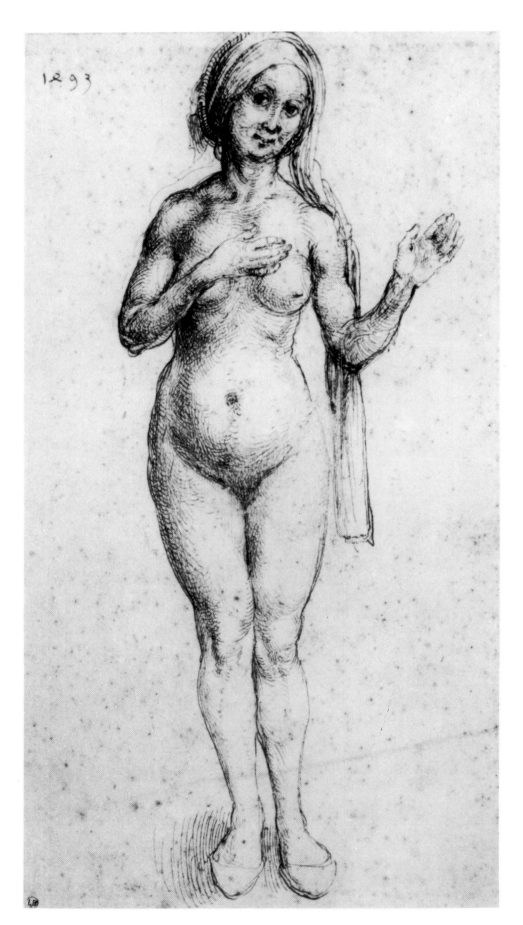

25 *Female Nude*. 1493. Pen. 27.2×14.7. Musée Bonnat, Bayonne.

This is a very important drawing, because – as the date in Dürer's own hand proves – it shows that the artist was interested in depicting the human body very early on in his career. It is the first drawing of a nude from a living model to be executed north of the Alps, and in the context of Dürer's work it must be seen as a preliminary version of his later studies of human proportions.

26 *The Wire-Drawing Mill*. 1494. Watercolour. 28.6 × 42.6. Kupferstichkabinett SMPK, Berlin.

Dürer painted this watercolour (with bodycolour) of a group of buildings
on the River Pegnitz to the west of Nuremberg in the summer of 1494. He
painted it from a hill on the north bank above the Grossweiden Mill
where water power had been used to make wire since the middle of the
fifteenth century. Beyond the river are the buildings of the Kleinweiden
Mill where grain mills, polishing mills and a forge operated. This
"industrial centre" was in the immediate vicinity of the Haller Meadows,
a walled recreation ground which is visible in the foreground on the left.
The Deutschherren bleaching green lies between trees on the opposite
bank; it extends to the hamlet of Gostenhof, where the Nuremberg
bailiff's hospital is recognizable by its roof turret. The hamlet was situated
to the south-west of Nuremberg, outside the Spittler gate, whose tower
can be seen on the extreme left. In the centre of the picture the
Himpfelshof (cf. Pl. 54), a farm, lies hidden behind trees; behind it rises
the tall choir of the small church of St. Leonhard. Immediately beside it
are the high buildings of the two manor houses of Sündersbühl.

several hundred prints which could be pulled from one plate
than individual paintings. Three engravings made in these
years are traditionally attributed to the young Dürer, but of
these only the *Violent Man* is really likely to be Dürer's Pl. 28
work and even here the handling of the burin is still
uncertain. The picture does not yet bear the monogram
consisting of the letters "A" and "d" with which Dürer
signed a number of drawings made in Venice a little later.
During these months Dürer may also have created four
designs for the woodcut cycle of the so-called *Albertina
Passion* (M. 109–112). In his interiors, he used perspective
correctly for the first time.[76]

None of the drawings dated 1494 and signed with the
monogram seem to have been made in Nuremberg during
the summer before Dürer left for the south. But he could

28 Le Violent. 1494. Gravure sur cuivre. 11,4 × 10,2. Berlin, Cabinet des Estampes SMPK.

Dürer a probablement commencé dès son retour du tour de compagnonnage, au printemps 1494, à travailler comme graveur. Il avait déjà assimilé l'art du burin lors de son apprentissage d'orfèvre à l'atelier paternel. L'un des premiers essais dans cette technique est la planche du *Violent*. Elle montre un homme sauvage importunant une femme. Le sens de la représentation n'est pas encore éclairci. Le tracé est inégal, ce qui parle en faveur d'un travail de débutant.

27 *Agnes Frey*. 1494. Pen. 15.6 × 9.8. Graphische Sammlung Albertina, Vienna.

Agnes Frey's hair-style, with a plait down her back, implies that this drawing was done before she married Dürer on 7 July 1494. The sketch was done quickly and unhesitatingly, without any corrections, and there is a strong impression of pensiveness in this portrait of Agnes who was still very young. (The average age when women married was between fourteen and eighteen.) Monogram and inscription were only added later by Dürer. The study reveals little about the character of Agnes who was about nineteen years old. The fact that she travelled to the Frankfurt fair in 1506 (cf. p. 135) is rather more revealing, and the portrait drawing of her, which Dürer made in 1521 (Pl. 209), is also quite expressive: Agnes Dürer appears to have been a resolute woman who displayed a degree of initiative unusual for her time.

29 *The Holy Family with a Grasshopper*. 1494. Engraving. 24 × 18.6. Kupferstichkabinett SMPK, Berlin. ▷

This is the first of Dürer's prints which is signed. The signature is made up of the same letters as in the Berlin drawing of 1485 (Pl. 9), but the 'd' is already put between the oblique bars of the 'A', as in Dürer's well-known later monogram. The theme of the picture is closely related to that of the Berlin drawing of the *Holy Family* (Pl. 14), done during Dürer's years as a journeyman, although the figure of the Virgin is based on another early drawing. Such formal references to earlier works, which can be found throughout Dürer's career, go back to mediæval practices when features based on prototypes collected in pattern books were used in all kinds of new combinations. The only indication that this is an engraving of the Holy Family, rather than a human idyll, is the apparition of God the Father and the dove in a bank of clouds in the sky.

31 *Southern Mountains.* 1494. Watercolour. 21×31.2. Ashmolean Museum, Oxford.

Dürer's own inscription, calling this view *welsch pirg,* southern mountains, means that the locality lies beyond the German-speaking area in the region where Romance is spoken. In all probability, it is the Val di Cembra which branches off to the north-east from the valley of the River Adige, north of Trent. Stylistically, the Oxford picture belongs to a group of landscape watercolours painted in the spring of 1495 during Dürer's return home from Italy.

◁ 30 *Virgin and Child in Front of an Archway.* 1494. Oil. 47.8×36. Magnani Collection, Parma.

This is another of Dürer's paintings which has only recently been discovered; it came from a convent near Ravenna. The Virgin is still painted in the German late Gothic tradition while the child is already based on Italian models, as two drawings in the Louvre and the Uffizi show. Clearly the picture never left Italy.

32 *Penitent St. Jerome.* 1494. Oil. 23.1×17.4. On loan to the Fitzwilliam Museum, Cambridge, from Sir Edmund Bacon, Bart., O.B.E., T.D., J.P.   ▷
33 *Celestial Phenomenon (verso* of 32).   ▷▷

Dürer, a journeyman without means, went to Italy to complete his training, but had to earn a living by his own work. A number of small paintings stylistically related to this period appear to have been painted in Venice. This small panel, a penitent St. Jerome, was only discovered about twenty years ago in an English private collection. It is still late Gothic in style, yet its landscape is so closely related to the watercolours of the Italian journey that it may be assumed that the panel was painted in the south. The back of the painting shows a very surprising picture, clearly a representation of an unusual celestial phenomenon. This may be a reminiscence of the "thunderstone of Ensisheim" whose fall Dürer may have witnessed in Basle in 1492.

45

have drawn several of his twenty copies of the so-called "tarot cards" (W. 122–41) during this time. This seems likely because Michael Wolgemut was engaged in transferring the same series of engravings to woodcuts during the same period. These woodcuts had been commissioned by Sebald Schreyer and were to be illustrations for an edition of selected works by Roman writers and poets planned by Peter Dannhauser and Konrad Celtis. Dürer, who had first come into close contact with classical subjects in Basle, must have been greatly impressed by these works which a Ferrara engraver made around 1460–70 and modelled on classical prototypes. During the summer of 1494, first preparations seem to have been made for alterations to the front room of Schreyer's house further up the road which were completed in 1495. In this Humanist neighbourhood, Dürer may well have received the decisive impetus to acquaint himself with the art of Italy, where attempts to revive classical culture had been going on for almost a hundred years.

Dürer's opportunity came in August, 1494 when there was an outbreak of the plague in Nuremberg; the newly-married painter left and travelled across the Alps to Venice. Such behaviour is not so surprising if one remembers that as early as 1483 a report by the Nuremberg town physicians commissioned by the council had advised that the safest way to avoid the plague was to leave the affected area; in this they followed a recommendation of the Florentine physician and philosopher, Marsilio Ficino.[77] One of the authors of the report, Dr. Hieronymus Münzer, followed his own advice quite faithfully by fleeing to Naples in 1483 and going on as far as Spain in 1494.[78] In the same year Dr. Hartmann Schedel and his family retired to his country house some twenty miles outside Nuremberg.[79] And Dürer's godfather, Anton Koberger, is known to have moved to Amberg because of the plague[80]. Dürer therefore merely did what most of the educated and affluent citizens did—which throws some light on his social status or, at any rate, his social aspirations.

Dürer seems to have travelled first to Innsbruck (via Augsburg) where Peter Rummel, a relation of his wife, lived. He painted two watercolours of the courtyard of Innsbruck castle (W. 67, 68). Continuing south he went across the Brenner and through the Eisack valley. But he then appears to have turned east before reaching Trent. Joseph Meder has pointed out that the Glockendon map of around 1485 showed a route to Venice through Brunico, Belluno and Treviso.[81] Rusconi,[82] on the other hand, maintains that several of Dürer's watercolour landscapes appear to show PL. 31 the palace of Segonzano and views of the Val di Cembra.

The Venetian republic, whose sovereignty on the Italian mainland extended almost to the gates of Milan and reached far south along the Dalmatian coast, was at that time the richest and most important mercantile and maritime power in Europe—regardless of the Ottoman advance on the Balkans and the discovery of America. It was the ships of Venetian merchants that carried the bulk of the trade with the Near East. Furthermore, this city built on lagoons had more than 100,000 inhabitants and was among the most densely populated in Europe.

There were many Germans in Venice, and the members of the House of the German Merchants, the only foreign trading establishment of its kind in the city, must have represented a particularly important contact for Dürer. Augsburg and Nuremberg merchants jointly headed the governing body of the *Fondaco dei Tedeschi*. In 1494 and 1495 two Imhoffs were the Nuremberg consuls. Contacts with Venetian painters, which were of vital importance to Dürer, may well have been established informally through the help of the Nuremberg merchants. One of these Nuremberg merchants was the affluent Anton Kolb, who financed the publication of the great woodcut plan of Venice by Jacopo de' Barbari which appeared five years later; he also acted as Koberger's commission agent and as the distributor of Hartmann Schedel's *Chronicle of the World*.[83] On the other hand, the two half-brothers Gentile and Giovanni Bellini each owned one of the prosperous broker's patents for the *Fondaco dei Tedeschi* and thus had to be present at the German trading centre on the Canale Grande from time to time, if only "on business".

The leading artists in Venice at that time were the painters Gentile and Giovanni Bellini, Vittore Carpaccio and Cima

34 *Large Crucifixion*. 1494–5. Woodcut. 57×38.9. Kupferstichkabinett SMPK, Berlin.

It seems very likely that Dürer tried to design woodcuts in Venice just as he had done whilst on the Upper Rhine. However, only the large Crucifixion, printed from two blocks, can be attributed to this period with any certainty. The lower part with the group of figures around the Virgin is very Italianate in style while the upper half is typical of Dürer. This difference in style between the two parts may mean that an Italian artist drew the group around the Virgin, or that Dürer drew it but a Venetian wood-cutter cut the block. The second alternative is more likely because there are many Italian motifs in the upper part as well. The figures of Christ and the unrepentant malefactor, for example, are based on an unfinished painting by Lorenzo di Credi (now at Göttingen), the figure of the repentant malefactor is based on drawings by Leonardo da Vinci. This woodcut, more than any other work by Dürer done during his first stay in Venice, demonstrates how strongly the young artist was influenced by Italian art.

35 Andrea Mantegna: *Bacchanalia with Silenus*. C. 1485. Engraving. 32.7 × 45. Kupferstichkabinett SMPK, Berlin.

da Conegliano. Their works were distinguished by a highly developed sense of colour. Local colour was still predominant in Venetian painting, as in the painting of other Italian schools, but large areas of unbroken, brilliant colour were balanced by a whole range of mixed hues and neutral background. While Giovanni Bellini's and Cima's pictures are usually quietly solemn compositions, Gentile's and Carpaccio's works reflect a naïve pleasure in narrating a story. The Florentine artists' preoccupation with theory was generally alien to the Venetians, and interest in ancient themes, which inspired Mantegna's art, scarcely influenced their paintings.[84]

There can be no doubt that Dürer gained admission to several workshops of painters and sculptors during the months of his first stay in Venice.[85] The pen and wash drawing of two Turks and a negro (W. 78), for instance, must have been made in the workshop of Gentile Bellini, who was then working on his painting *The Relic of the Cross Being*

Carried in Procession through St. Mark's Square, in which the same group appears. The impressive composition and brilliant colour of the pictures by Giovanni Bellini (who was a much better artist than his brother) influenced Dürer's paintings deeply. This influence is seen in the paintings of a *Madonna in Front of a Landscape*, presumably done in Pl. 65 Venice, and the *Haller Madonna* of around 1497, although Pl. 70 the small panel of a *Penitent St. Jerome* and the *Madonna* of Pl. 32 Bagnacavallo are still largely late Gothic.

Dürer may well have learnt about the art of Andrea Mantegna through the Bellinis whose sister was married to Mantegna. The severe and monumental style of the Mantua master, which is particularly apparent in his engravings, must have deeply impressed the young Nuremberg painter.

36 Dürer: Copy of Mantegna's Engraving. 1494. Pen. 29.8×43.5. Graphische Sammlung Albertina, Vienna.

Dürer's drawing is not really a copy of Mantegna's engraving but a tracing. In fact, Dürer only traced the outlines and substituted complex hatchings for the simple parallel hatchings of the Italian master, emphasizing the sculptural quality of the bodies. This drawing, and a corresponding copy of Mantegna's engraving of the *Battle of the Sea-Gods*, show the same aims as *The Death of Orpheus* (Pl. 37), also completed during Dürer's first stay in Venice.

Dürer familiarized himself with Mantegna's art by making Pls. 35, 36 copies, even tracings, as *Bacchanalia with Silenus* and *Battle of the Sea-Gods* (W. 60) prove. Yet he added his personal touch to the engravings by substituting complex hatchings, which emphasize the internal modelling of the figures, for the simple parallel hatchings of Mantegna's works. The young Dürer was probably more impressed by the strongly sculptural, spatial quality of the nude bodies, depicted in forceful movement, rather than by the "classical" subject matter, although this is found in his drawing the *Death of* Pl. 37 *Orpheus,* based on a lost work by Mantegna.[86]

Dürer made similar copies of works by Antonio Pollaiuolo and Lorenzo di Credi (W. 84) and other masters, mostly of nude figures. In the workshop of Lorenzo di Credi, who was in Venice for several years to supervise the completion of the equestrian statue of Colleoni by Verrocchio, Dürer may have seen studies by Leonardo da Vinci for a St. Sebastian. He made use of these studies soon afterwards in a large woodcut of the *Crucifixion* which must Pl. 34 have been started while he was still in Venice.[87] Other extant drawings show that he was fascinated above all by strange and exotic subjects, such as the magnificent robes of Venetian ladies and the unfamiliar costume of Turks Pl. 38 (W. 78–81), as well as creatures of the sea which he had Pl. 41 never seen before (W. 91).

It is not yet known how important the painter and graphic artist, Jacopo de' Barbari, the only theorist among the

51

37 *The Death of Orpheus.* 1494. Pen. 28.9×22.5. Kupferstichkabinett, Kunsthalle, Hamburg.

This drawing, treated entirely like a painting, is signed and dated 1494 by Dürer on the lower margin. It is generally assumed that it was made in Nuremberg in the summer of 1494, though there is no evidence that it was Dürer's "masterpiece" qualifying him for the rank of master in the Nuremberg Guild of Painters, as Joachim von Sandrart, the first German art historian, believed it to be (in 1675). However, it seems more likely that this drawing was actually made during Dürer's first stay in Venice. It reflects both his interest in classical myths and the correct representation of moving human figures in space. In both these aspects, Italian art was almost a century ahead of northern art. It hardly seems likely that Dürer used a rather primitive Italian engraving (which is also kept in the Hamburg Kunsthalle) as his model; his drawing is much more closely related to a painting by Mantegna.

38 *Venetian Lady.* 1495. Pen and brush. 29×17.3. Graphische Sammlung Albertina, Vienna.

Venice was like a new world for the young Nuremberg painter, and he tried to capture its exotic features with his pen. He was not interested solely in the works of the Venetian artists, but also in the people and objects he saw on the streets and canals of the city, all of which were new and unfamiliar to him. Several of his drawings show that he was fascinated by the elegant, exotically dressed Venetian ladies who could be seen in the streets, squares and churches, walking around in their high, cothurnus-like shoes. The costume study in the Albertina, which records every detail of the woman's dress and jewellery and has a view of her from the back as well, is the most important of these studies. A drawing in Frankfurt (W. 75), in which a Nuremberg and a Venetian woman are depicted side by side, shows how impressed the young Nuremberg artist must have been by the unfamiliar fashions of the Venetian ladies.

39 *View of Arco*. 1495. Watercolour. 22.1×22.1. Cabinet des Dessins, Musée du Louvre, Paris.

This view of Arco, a small town situated a few kilometres north of Lake Garda, which Dürer painted in the spring of 1495 when he was on his way back from Venice to Nuremberg, is rightly held to be the most famous watercolour of this journey. Dürer did not take the usual route from Verona up the valley of the River Adige, but went further west and presumably north across Lake Garda by boat. In contrast to the watercolours painted on the way to Italy, this one no longer attempts simply to be a topographically faithful view, but is a consciously arranged composition. The sheer rock face on the left, for instance, could not be seen from the point of view from which the watercolour was painted, and involved a change of position on Dürer's part.

40 *Innsbruck from the North.* 1495. Watercolour. 12.7 × 18.7 (enlarged). Graphische Sammlung Albertina, Vienna.

Scholars disagree whether this view of Innsbruck, the favourite residence of Emperor Maximilian I, was painted in the autumn of 1494 or in the spring of 1495. The low horizon, unusual for Dürer at this time, the inclusion of a cloudy sky, the mountains largely covered with snow, and the light green trees and bushes, make it more likely that this watercolour was executed on Dürer's return journey in the spring of 1495, rather than in October of the previous year. Local scholars have identified individual buildings. The high tower on the extreme left belonged to the castle of the reigning prince; Dürer had painted two watercolours of its courtyards on his outward journey. The tower on the river bank, the Kräuterturm, strengthens the corner of the fortification. The small tower in the city wall to the right of it is the Tranktörl, so called because this was the watering-place for cattle. The tower on the extreme right marks the Inntor where a bridge crossed the River Inn. Next to it the Ottoburg is recognizable by its turreted oriels; immediately next to that is the Tänzelsche Haus. Of the two towers rising behind the wall in the centre the left-hand one is the Stadtturm, the right-hand one the Wappenturm which was unfinished.

Venetian painters, was for Dürer while he was in Venice. Dürer himself said that as a young man he had been shown figures by Jacopo which were constructed according to a proportional system.[88] This must have been in approximately 1494–5, since Dürer certainly made his own first attempts at such figures before 1500, although Jacopo had not explained to him how the original figures were constructed. The 1495 *Female Nude seen from the Back* (W. 85) may be taken as evidence of Dürer's knowledge of Barbari's work. There are surprisingly many formal points of correspondence between the figure in Dürer's drawing and the figure seen from the rear in Barbari's *Victoria and Fama*, though the quality of the work is quite different.

In the spring of 1495 Dürer started on his journey back to Nuremberg. This time he went via Arco, situated a few miles

north of Lake Garda. Here he painted the watercolour (now in Paris) which shows the small town nestling among olive groves at the foot of the massive *Burgberg*. Its delicate colours make it one of Dürer's most successful watercolours. From there he travelled north via Trent where he painted watercolours of the town and the bishop's castle.

He stopped at Klausen on the River Eisack to draw a view of the town from a hill on the left river bank, a view which included Branzoll Castle and the Säben Monastery. The landscape in this drawing, now lost, became the model for Pl. 86 that of the *Large Nemesis*. It may be that Dürer's idea of a view from this angle was inspired by Jacopo de' Barbari, who must have made preparatory studies for his bird's-eye plan of Venice while Dürer was still living there.

Passing through Innsbruck, Dürer painted what was probably the last watercolour of this journey, the *View of*

41 *Crab*. 1494–5. Watercolour. 26.3×35.5. Museum Boymans-van Beuningen, Rotterdam.

The crab *(eriphia spinifrons)*, and a watercolour of a lobster done in 1495 (W. 91, now in Berlin), are among the first drawings of animals done from nature that can be attributed with certainty to Dürer. This crab, drawn from a living animal, is very common in the Adriatic.

Innsbruck from the North. This cannot have been painted Pl. 40 earlier, as some have argued, as the light green of the trees as well as the snow-covered mountain tops imply that the picture was painted in the spring of 1495.

Dürer returned to Nuremberg in the spring of 1495, full of impressions of the various currents in Italian Renaissance art he had gained during this first stay in Venice. They were to inspire him and to give a new direction to the whole of his art.

56

IV. The Founding of Dürer's own Workshop: 1495–9

Graphic Works · Commissions for Paintings · Apocalypse

When Albrecht Dürer returned from Italy in the spring of 1495 he had been journeying for almost five years (except during the summer months of 1494). Like any journeyman of his time, Dürer did not choose his own work during this period, but worked on tasks set for him by a master painter who in turn had been commissioned by a patron. It can no longer be established whether or not recommendations by Dürer's godfather, Anton Koberger, who was a close friend and business associate of Johann Amerbach in Basle, were partially responsible for Dürer obtaining so much work as an illustrator.[89]

Dürer must have taken it for granted that in his home town, too, he would use his ability as a woodcut designer to earn some money, this time to establish his own household and open his own workshop. His graphic work would enable him to survive until the first commissions came in. It had the added advantage of being a regular source of income, once the initial period was over when copper plates had to be engraved or wood blocks cut, as prints could be pulled from plates over several years. The young Dürer may well have had this in mind when in July, 1497 he concluded a contract with a man called Konrad Schweitzer, whereby Dürer paid him a weekly wage of half a florin and an additional three pounds as expenses for selling his engravings and woodcuts outside Nuremberg.[90] In 1500 Dürer engaged Jakob Arnold for the same service.[91]

Dürer had been unlucky in that the relatively small sheets of the *Albertina Passion* had been badly cut, while the two large single sheets of the *Lamentation* (M. 186) and the *Martyrdom of St. Sebastian* (M. 196) — which presumably were cut while Dürer was still in Italy — had been much more successful; this seems to have made the artist decide, once back in Nuremberg, to use the larger format. It is the format — corresponding to half a sheet of paper (32 × 22.5 cm) — of his large-scale publications, the *Large Passion* and the *Apocalypse* as well as the individual prints of the

Men's Bath, Hercules and the *Martyrdom of the Ten Thousand*, all of which were done before 1500. Pls. 43–5

In 1496, after his return to Nuremberg, Dürer seems to have resumed his intention of publishing a Passion cycle. It seems likely that the first design of the sequence was the *Flagellation* (B. 8), because of its somewhat archaic composition. It is influenced by the corresponding scene in the 1491 *Schatzbehalter* by Wilhelm Pleydenwurff, and in it figures crowd together in the middle ground in regular rows. The subsequent designs of the *Entombment* (B. 13), *Christ on the Cross* (B. 11) and the *Lamentation* (B. 12) show how the compositional arrangement of the often numerous figures becomes more and more accomplished. Important individual figures are now set apart, by their size and by light effects, from the accompanying crowd of figures who remain in shadow. Sculptural and spatial effects, which Dürer aimed at from the very beginning, are achieved in these works by subtly differentiated lines, first drawn and then cut into the wood block. Rows of parallel lines, drawn closely together or in wide sweeps as necessary, follow the internal modelling of figures and shapes. Dürer's use of a richly varied scale of light and shade meant that woodcuts no longer needed colouring, as had formerly been the prac- Pl. 46 tice.

The last compositions for the woodcut sequence of the *Large Passion* were designed shortly before 1500; the sequence then remained unfinished for more than a decade. Dürer's imagination and energy may well have been taken up by other works, such as the designs for the fifteen woodcuts of the *Apocalypse*. Pls. 78–9

Immediately after his return, Dürer also seems to have resumed his experiments with engravings. But engravings take longer than woodcuts, because the artist has to do both the design and the actual engraving, while in the case of woodcuts the blocks are cut for him by a wood-cutter. None the less, Dürer produced about twenty-seven engravings in the period up to 1500, ten of which were of quarter-sheet size, the others smaller.

The format of the paper was quite important for Dürer's engravings and woodcuts. It may be assumed that standard sheets supplied by contemporary paper mills measured about 32×45 cm varying by a few centimetres according to the different manufacturers.[92] The printing presses must have been designed to take sheets of paper with these basic measurements. Judging by the few surviving illustrations of presses, they seem to have been used for the printing of books and graphic work alike. As is shown by surviving trial prints of small-format woodcuts by Dürer, prints from plates and wood blocks of this size were not pulled on individual sheets of paper, but several to a sheet. Dürer sold the cut prints either separately or as half- and quarter-sheets, as an entry in his own hand in his diary of the journey to the Netherlands shows.[93] He charged one florin for twenty half-sheets (one florin equals 252 pfennigs); thus half a sheet — such as one illustration of the Large Passion — cost twelve pfennigs and one heller. Around 1500, this was roughly the equivalent of half a day's wages for a Nuremberg stone-mason.[94]

42 *The Women's Bath*. 1496. Pen. 23.1×22.6. Formerly Kupferstich-kabinett, Kunsthalle, Bremen.

Dürer's small-format prints, like those of earlier fifteenth-century engravers, show single figures or groups of two or three figures against a white background. They are mostly figures of saints or of common people, such as the *Three Peasants Talking,* but there is also the *Turkish Family* (B. 85) and, as an exception, an allegorical subject, the *Small Nemesis* (B. 78). The engravings, with an almost square transverse format, have the same subject matter of general interest, but are aesthetically more complex since the figures are seen in front of various landscapes. About half of the ambitious large engravings have religious themes, the remainder are mythological and allegorical. The landscapes, which usually consist of both real and imaginary scenes, play an important role. The *Prodigal Son,* for instance, faithfully reproduces the *Himpfelshof* near Nuremberg, and on the shore of the *Sea Monster* is a view of Nuremberg castle from the north. Pl. 47 / Pl. 48 / Pl. 54 / Pls. 51–2

Only one of the landscape studies which Dürer must have made for these engravings has survived; it is a watercolour of the *Little Pond House* (in London) which reappears in the middle ground of *The Virgin with the Long-tailed Monkey.* The other studies were also presumably watercolours like the *Little Pond House.* Even when transformed into the linear motifs of the engravings they retain a certain "emotive realism"[95] which characterizes Dürer's existing landscape watercolours of this period. This later group of landscape watercolours is differentiated from those painted before and during the Italian journey by a faithful rendering of detail combined with an emphasis on atmosphere. Pictures like the *Pond in the Woods* and *Weiden Mill* are among the best of early European landscape paintings, even though Dürer thought of them only as studies and occasionally left them unfinished. A group of drawings of a quarry near Nurem-berg were even more obviously intended as sketches. Dürer used all manner of techniques from pure pen drawings to sketches done with the brush and carefully executed water-colours. Such studies often formed the basis for landscapes in Dürer's engravings and paintings. Pl. 57 / Pl. 56 / Pls. 55, 58 / Pl. 59

43 *The Men's Bath*. 1496–7. Woodcut. 39.1×28. Kupferstichkabinett SMPK, Berlin. ▷

Dürer had been preoccupied with the problem of the human body since executing his first study of a nude (Pl. 25). In Venice he had made a fine drawing (now in Paris) of a female model. Further efforts resulted in this picture of the *Men's Bath,* done about a year later. Dürer may have planned a corresponding picture of a Women's Bath, as the lost drawing formerly in Bremen indicates. It seems doubtful that the picture is a mere genre scene, and the suggestion that the *Men's Bath* should be interpreted as an allegory of the five senses or the four temperaments seems quite reasonable.

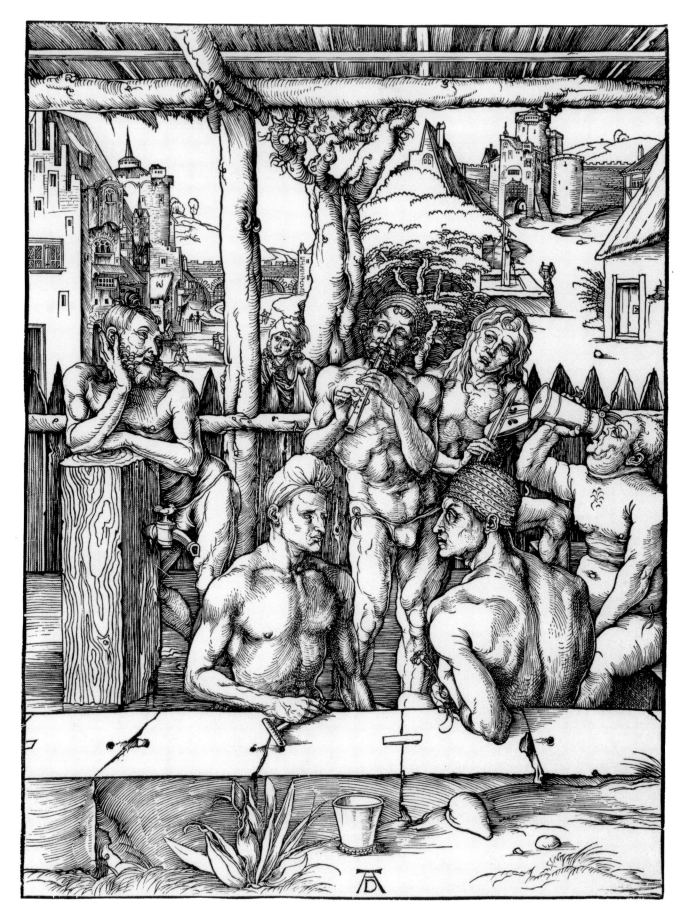

The four large engravings of *Four Witches* (B. 75), *The Dream, The Sea Monster* and *Hercules* have themes which are even now not fully understood by scholars. Even in Dürer's time their rather obscure subject matter must have meant that there was only a restricted market for these engravings, since they presupposed an understanding of allegorical ideas in the buyer as well as the artist. The way in which Dürer used these themes in his work must mean that he had a more thorough knowledge of them than can be explained merely by his short contact with Italian art or advice given him by his Humanist friends. Presumably they did suggest themes of this kind and may have supplied characteristic details based on their knowledge of literature, but Dürer must already have been more familiar with classical mythology and Humanist allegory than existing documents suggest.[96]

Dürer may first have come across similar subjects at home, and it is certainly documented that he came into contact with Humanist ideas in Basle. Almost every chapter of the *Ship of Fools* has admonitory examples taken from classical mythology; Pythagoras, Plato and Socrates are shown to be paragons of classical wisdom. Work on the Terence illustrations may well have strengthened Dürer's interest in this new world of ideas and pictures, and the Ferrara tarot cards must have given him an added insight into Humanist thinking. The contemporary conception of the world is represented in this series of engravings, and Dürer came to understand it by copying them. His copies may be of little artistic value, but they were extremely important for his intellectual development.

When in June, 1495 Sebald Schreyer invited his Humanist friends to a festive opening of a newly decorated palatial room on the first floor of his house, the interested young painter may have been invited as a neighbour to join the circle which included the lawyers Johann Löffelholz and Peter Dannhauser, and the physicians Hartmann Schedel, Hieronymus Münzer and Dietrich Ulsen (Theodoricus Ulse-

nius). Willibald Pirckheimer, who had just returned home after more than seven years in Italy, was presumably also a guest at the Schreyer celebrations.[97] However, the most important person in this society must have been the "arch-Humanist" Konrad Celtis who had come to Nuremberg in June of the same year to present the council with his paper entitled *Norimberga*.[98] It was he who had thought up the scheme for the decorations which consisted of pictures of Apollo and the Muses as well as of classical philosophers, and had also written explanatory verses in Latin which were put underneath the pictures.

The members of this circle had studied in Italy, in many cases for several years, and been influenced by philosophical ideas current there. As is demonstrated by the library of Dr. Münzer[99] and the lists of books to be bought in Italy which Dr. Johannes Pirckheimer sent to his son Willibald,[100] Nuremberg scholars avidly studied the Neoplatonic philosophy of late classical times which had been resurrected by Marsilio Ficino in Florence. According to Ficino, the artist plays an essential role because through his creative power he makes visible the beauty of God's world, just as the scholar

45 *The Martyrdom of the Ten Thousand Christians.* 1497–8. Woodcut. 38.7 × 28.4. Kupferstichkabinett SMPK, Berlin. ▷

According to legend, the Emperor Hadrian recruited 9,000 mercenaries under Acatius (or Achatius) for his campaigns in Asia Minor. Under the guidance of two angels these 9,000 men defeated enemy troops which far outnumbered them. They were then sent by the angels to Mount Ararat where they were converted to Christianity. Hadrian, supported by King Sapor of Persia, had the apostates tortured to death. Moved by the steadfastness of Acatius' men, a thousand of Hadrian's soldiers also became Christians and suffered martyrdom in their turn. Apart from the saintly warrior Acatius there were a number of canonized priests of the same name, which seems to have led to a confusion between the warrior Acatius and one of the bishops. In the Rhine/Maas area this confusion can be traced back to the fourteenth century. Dürer shows a bishop being tortured in his woodcut, though this version of the subject was not common in Nuremberg, nor indeed anywhere in South Germany.

44 *Hercules Kills the Molionides.* C. 1496. Woodcut. 39 × 28.3. Kupferstichkabinett SMPK, Berlin.

Scholars have long argued about the subject of this woodcut which Dürer inscribed "Ercules" on the upper margin. In 1971, the "Dürer year", a Soviet and a German scholar found the solution independently of each other. The subject is taken from a legend handed down by Apollodorus and Pausanias: at Kleonai near Corinth, Hercules kills Eurytus and Kteatus, the sons of Molione, whose bodies were joined together and who were stronger than any other human being. Only Pausanias also mentions the desperate mother of the twins, who, in Dürer's woodcut, is driven on by an avenging Fury.

46 *Christ Carrying the Cross (Large Passion).* 1497–8. Woodcut. C. 39 × 28. Kupferstichkabinett SMPK, Berlin. ▷▷

Nothing reflects Dürer's great creativity more clearly than the fact that the young artist worked on two woodcut sequences of monumental format at the same time: the *Apocalypse* (Pls. 78, 79) and *Christ's Passion.* Apart from the dramatic events which dominate every scene of this latter cycle Dürer's main emphasis is on the plasticity of his figures and on spatial effects. These could be developed more strongly in the *Passion* than in the *Apocalypse,* because the former was based on real events. The group depicting Christ and the mercenary shows particularly well the powerful sculptural quality of Dürer's figures. A multitude of figures and incidents in one picture was, moreover, a feature much admired by Dürer's contemporaries.

62

47 *Three Peasants Talking.* 1496–7. Engraving. 10.9×7.7. Kupfer-stichkabinett SMPK, Berlin.

This is one of Dürer's well-known early engravings. In contrast to the preliminary drawing in Berlin, where the three men are represented as country yokels rather like the peasants in Hans Sachs's Shrovetide plays, this engraving has no trace of caricature. Rather it shows three distinct "characters" who are clearly differentiated by their pose and physiognomy. They carry weapons, which means they are freemen. The man wearing leggings and spurs and carrying a basket even poses almost as if he were a knight.

does by examining the laws of nature.[101] These ideas of the Italian philosopher explain why the young, gifted Dürer was accepted so readily by the Nuremberg Humanists. The Florentine version of Neoplatonic thought, which attempted to combine classical Greek philosophy with the teachings of the Christian faith, became moreover the basis for the whole of Dürer's art.[102]

The acquaintance with Celtis, one of the spokesmen of Neoplatonic philosophy in Germany, must have given added impetus to the artist to continue the study of the proportions of the human body which he had begun under Barbari's influence. Celtis had studied under Rudolf Agricola in Heidelberg in 1484 and must have known his works on the theory of art.[103] This is shown for example by his use of the Greek word "symmetria" instead of the Latin "proportio" in an epigram written before 1500 and addressed to Dürer.[104] Dürer must have made his first studies of the proportions of the human body around 1496. This is confirmed by many works between 1496 and 1498 which depict nude figures — for example, the *Men's Bath*, the *Four Witches* and Pl. 43 the *Martyrdom of the Ten Thousand* — that could not have Pl. 45 been done without preliminary studies of the body's proportions. He may well have based his own attempts on reproductions of classical statues, such as the Farnese Hercules, the Apollo Belvedere and presumably a *Venus pudica,* since one of the four witches in the engraving (B. 75) is derived from such a figure. In the earliest existing study of proportions, a female figure in the *Dresden Sketchbook*

48 *Six Warriors.* 1495. Engraving. 13.2×14.6. Kupferstichkabinett SMPK, Berlin.

Only four of the six figures in this engraving are truly warriors; three of them are mercenaries *(Landsknechte),* the fourth represents a Turkish horseman. The two other figures are elegantly dressed men. This combination is reminiscent of groups often shown under the Cross in pictures of the Crucifixion. But it cannot be determined whether a part of the crowd of a typical Crucifixion scene has been made the subject of an independent picture here, or whether the *Six Warriors* is merely a fragment of an unfinished plate.

49 *Pupila Augusta*. C. 1496–7. Pen. 25.4×19.5. By gracious permission of Her Majesty Queen Elizabeth II; Windsor Castle.

49 *Pupila Augusta*. C. 1496–7. Pen. 25.4×19.5. By gracious permission of Her Majesty Queen Elizabeth II; Windsor Castle.

(St. 1500/13), there seems to be as yet no systematic process of construction, but in subsequent studies Dürer was already trying to construct contours and internal modelling of female figures purely from circles drawn with the compass.[105] With male figures the first stages of this development are less clear. The first study of this type appears to be the *Male Nude with a Mirror* (W. 419) based on the Farnese Hercules. This was followed by manuscript pages, now in London[106] and Dresden,[107] where the figures are drawn

50 *View of a Town*. Detail of Pl. 49.

The drawing, which bears the inscription PUPILA AUGUSTA in mirror-writing, was presumably a preliminary design for an engraving. It shows the birth of Venus Urania (celestial love) who even in classical texts was sometimes given the appellation of Pupila Augusta (august ward). Venus and the two female figures accompanying her appear in the middle ground, standing on a dolphin. This group of figures is based on an Italian niello engraving. The recumbent woman with the winged cap who reads the goddess's fate from a flat bowl or mirror, and the woman sitting beside her, also go back to Italian prototypes. The background view, of a town dominated by a castle, combines motifs from Nuremberg and Innsbruck. It is possible that the engraving was not executed because all the figures would have appeared left-handed in it; but the view of the town was used twenty years later (cf. Pl. 192).

53 *The Walk*. 1496–8. Engraving. 19.5 × 12. Kupferstichkabinett SMPK, Berlin.

The traditional title of this engraving does not do justice to its meaning. The elegant couple is reminiscent of couples who could often be seen walking outside the walls of Nuremberg in places such as the Haller Meadows. They are spied upon by a skeleton carrying an hour-glass, the symbol of time passing, hiding behind the tree. If one remembers that in the years between 1496 and 1498 Dürer not only did the engravings illustrated here, but also the woodcuts for the *Apocalypse* (Pls. 78, 79) and the Madrid *Self-Portrait* (Pl. 76), it becomes clear that at this time he must have been torn between a love of the world and the belief that its end was imminent.

◁51–2 *The Sea Monster*. C. 1498. Engraving. 24.6 × 18.7. Kupferstichkabinett SMPK, Berlin. (Detail on p. 66)

Dürer himself gave this engraving its title, which implies that the subject was familiar at least to his Nuremberg buyers, and is not taken from an obscure classical legend as is often supposed. There was indeed a legend called "the Sea Monster" known in Nuremberg; it was a ballad based on earlier texts, written in 1472 by the Franconian nobleman Kaspar von der Rhön. There are a number of discrepancies between the poem and the engraving, yet there can be no doubt that Dürer was inspired by this legend, which he used together with the classical figures of a sea god and a Nereid to construct an impressive composition.

according to the same principles of construction as the female nudes.

As far as is known today, Dürer received his first commissions for paintings from Frederick the Wise of Saxony. It is possible that Celtis, who owed his acclaim as a poet to Frederick's recommendation, drew the Elector's attention to the young Nuremberg painter. It is apparent that the prince, the Humanist and the painter were associated until Celtis's death in the spring of 1508. This is reflected in the painting of the *Martyrdom of the Ten Thousand*, commissioned by Pl. 125 the Elector, where there is a double portrait of the painter and the "arch-Humanist" who had only recently died.

When the Elector Frederick and his brother, Duke Johann, visited Nuremberg from 16 to 18 April 1496, it is

A preliminary study for the figure of the Prodigal Son, and a sketch of the overall composition in which many of the main elements are traced in detail, show how carefully Dürer prepared his graphic works. He must also have made — or reused — a drawing of the group of buildings. It has recently been established that these are modelled on the Himpfelshof west of Nuremberg (Pl. 26). In the parable in the Bible (Luke XV, 11–32) the Prodigal Son fed swine in a field, while Dürer shows the scene taking place in the courtyard of a farm; his source for this version may have been the commentary to Luke by St. Ambrose.

This is one of Dürer's most famous watercolours. In 1970 a second, very sketchy watercolour study was discovered on the back of this sheet. It is a study of the evening sky, dominated by greys and crimsons with a little yellow and blue. As the sketch on the back was presumably done immediately after the watercolour on the front, the latter was probably also painted shortly before dusk. Dürer's sensitivity to colour and atmosphere is illustrated more clearly in these watercolours drawn from nature than in many of his paintings.

possible that the Elector not only gave Dürer a commission for his own portrait painted on canvas, but also for an altarpiece of the Virgin. The sum of 100 florins, paid by the Saxon fiscal office late in 1496, may well have been remune-

ration for this work which, according to later descriptions, was extensive, but of which only the panels of the inside of the left wing remain. Such a considerable sum could not have been paid for an altar picture painted on canvas.

Pl. 66

Pls. 63, 95 Paintings on canvas, so-called "little cloths", were considered substitutes for the usual panel paintings on wood. Since artists used water-soluble paints for canvas pictures which allowed them to work quickly, and since the price of a picture depended on the materials used and on the time the work took, pictures on canvas were much cheaper than paintings on wooden panels. Panel painting involved the application of several layers of oil paint on a grounding of chalk. The execution of such a picture often took months, because each layer of paint had to be thoroughly dry before work could be continued. This process could only be shortened if the painter used paints with less oil (i.e. tempera) for some parts, particularly for the finishing touches.

Dürer painted the majority of his pictures using this technique with extreme skill, as is shown for instance in his Pl. 67 *Lamentation*. But he himself called this kind of painting "fiddling" *(kläubeln)* and contrasted it to "common painting" *(gemeine gemäl)*.[108] This may refer to a small group of his paintings which were most often executed on the back of Pl. 71 other panels. These pictures, such as *Lot Fleeing Sodom* Pl. 70 *with his Family* painted on the back of the *Haller Madonna*, have the immediacy characteristic of sketches because the paint has been applied so thinly that the preliminary design shows through in places. The front of the panel, on the other hand, is a model of extremely careful "layer painting". The fact that both sides have been painted implies that the picture was originally part of a small folding altarpiece consisting of two panels. The lost panel presumably showed the donor worshipping the Virgin and Child. The composition and colours of the half-length figure of the Madonna and the nude standing child clearly show the lasting influence of Giovanni Bellini's art on Dürer.

The number of religious paintings Dürer was commissioned to produce up to the end of the fifteenth century was surprisingly low. The brothers Stephan and Lukas Paumgartner ordered a large altarpiece, presumably to commemorate the happy conclusion of a pilgrimage to Palestine in 1498; but the work does not seem to have been completed Pl. 69 until about 1503–4. During the same year, Dürer may have been commissioned by Dr. Sebald Bamberger, the newly elected abbot of the Cistercian monastery at Heilbronn,[109] to paint an altarpiece of St. John the Baptist, now lost. Dürer also received commissions for a number of portraits. Unless the patrons themselves decided on the formal layout Pl. 64 of a picture, as did the Tucher family, Dürer generally chose half-length figures, and usually placed them in front of a landscape view. The people in Dürer's portraits have very animated expressions; this is particularly noticeable in the

56 *The Virgin with the Long-tailed Monkey.* 1497–8. Engraving. 19.1 × 12.2. Kupferstichkabinett SMPK, Berlin.

Majestically, yet with her head thoughtfully inclined, the Virgin sits holding the Child on the bank of a stretch of water. The Child plays with a bird, the symbol of the sinful soul which is redeemed by Christ's death on the Cross. The long-tailed monkey tethered at the Virgin's feet symbolizes evil, which has already lost its power over mankind through the birth of the Child. Dürer appears to have based the group of the Virgin and Child on a painting by Lorenzo di Credi in Pistoia Cathedral. The pond house in the background is based — with a few alterations — on the London study (Pl. 57).

portrait of Oswald Krell, a Lindau merchant. Dürer's por- Pl. 77 traits of this period, like his landscapes, are characterized by an "emotive realism".

Dürer's true artistic ability revealed itself most fully when he could work independently of his customers' wishes. Thus

57 *The Little Pond House.* C. 1497. Watercolour. 21.3×22.2 (enlarged). Department of Prints and Drawings, British Museum, London.

In contrast to the dramatic clouds of the sky in the *Pond in the Woods*

(Pl. 55) here Dürer depicts the evening stillness. Small tower-like moated castles like the one shown were very popular in the late Middle Ages. One such building, the small Toppler Castle near Rothenburg ob der Tauber, still survives.

58 *The Weiden Mill.* C. 1498. Watercolour and gouache. 25.1×36.7. Cabinet des Estampes, Bibliothèque Nationale, Paris.

This is Dürer's most accomplished watercolour. It gives the effect of a completed picture, although parts are unfinished. The *Weiden Mill* (i.e. the Grossweiden Mill) shows the same group of buildings as the *Wire-Drawing Mill* (Pl. 26), but Dürer painted it from the Haller Meadows directly next to the River Pegnitz, looking west. The locality also implies that Dürer's aim was to capture the atmosphere of a sunset near the water. This is three centuries in advance of his time, for "atmospheric paintings" of this kind, i.e. pictures conveying the mood of a certain landscape, only began to be painted in the early nineteenth century. On the right of the gently flowing river are the buildings of the wire-drawing mill, to the left the interlocking roofs of the Kleinweiden Mill. A footbridge spans the river. On the right behind the trees is the wall which separated the Haller Meadows from the mill complex.

59 *Quarry.* C. 1497. Watercolour. 23.2×19.7. Biblioteca Ambrosiana, Milan.
▷

This sketch, inscribed "quarry" in Dürer's own hand, is one of a number of studies of rock formations done in various techniques in quarries near Nuremberg. The Milan sketch is a pure brush drawing and the brush-strokes give a strong, direct impression of how Dürer worked. The *Quarry* is very similar to the rocks in *Lot Fleeing Sodom* (Pl. 71).

the supreme achievement among the portraits painted at this time is the self-portrait completed in 1498. The painter in his fashionable, elegant clothes, with his hair worn long and carefully curled and a beard—which at that time was still unusual—looks out at the spectator with serenity and self- Pl. 76

73

confidence; his pose is almost identical to that of the Elector (A. 19). Dürer combined this self-portrait of 1498 with a portrait of his father, painted for his seventieth birthday in 1497 (A. 48), to form a portrait-diptych.

Looking at the self-portrait it is difficult to see the man who at the same time was working on the last designs for the

60 *The Dream.* 1497–8. Engraving. 18.8 × 11.9. Kupferstichkabinett SMPK, Berlin.

The stout but youthful man asleep behind the stove has sinful thoughts blown into his ear by the devil, which results in the appearance of a naked woman in his dream; this man symbolizes indolence. The devil has a dual function in the picture: on the one hand he seduces the sleeping man, on the other he serves to indicate that according to the morals of the time the behaviour of this potentially vigorous man is sinful. Even though the engraving has a moralizing subject, Dürer clearly tried to make the temptress beautiful. This female figure is clearly related to the Paris drawing of a *Nude* of 1495.

61 *Hercules.* 1498–9. Engraving. 31.7 × 22.1. Kupferstichkabinett SMPK, Berlin.

The subject of this engraving is still obscure. Dürer himself called it "Hercules" in an entry in his diary of the journey to the Netherlands of August, 1520. It is closely related to the drawing of the *Death of Orpheus* (Pl. 37): the group of trees, the woman wielding the stick, and the fleeing child have been taken from it. The popular titles, "Jealousy" and "The Cuckold", do not help with the interpretation. It is true to say that the engravings of *Hercules* and the *Sea Monster* as well as the woodcut of *Hercules* show that Dürer was familiar with unusual subjects from classical mythology even before the turn of the century.

62 *The Holy Family.* C. 1495. Gouache. 16 × 11.2 (enlarged). Museum der Schönen Künste, Leipzig. ▷

The forms of this small painting on parchment seem distinctly late Gothic, but its iconography is closely related to several works by Giovanni Bellini and his workshop. The painting is heightened with gold which underlines its precious character; it must have been one of Dürer's first works after he set up on his own account in Nuremberg.

64 *Portrait of Elsbeth Tucher.* 1499. Oil. 29×23.3. Gemäldegalerie, Kassel.

The brothers Hans and Nikolaus Tucher and their wives had their portraits painted by Dürer in 1499. The portrait of Nikolaus (1464–1527) has long been lost; the only remaining portrait is that of his wife, née Pusch, who was the daughter of the man in charge of the Nuremberg artillery arsenal. Each brother had his portrait panel linked to his wife's by hinges, so that the two panels could be folded. Diptychs of this kind were usually kept in closets and chests and only displayed on special occasions.

goldsmith's craft. Dürer's decorative talent is also shown in the book-plates painted for Willibald Pirckheimer. Pl. 75

Throughout the Middle Ages people had believed that the end of the world was near. It was thought certain, for instance, that the year 1000 would mark the end. Five hundred years later, in Dürer's time, the end of the world was expected again. The entire fifteenth century had been characterized by lamentations and doom-ridden prophecies of a major catastrophe. This expectation of impending disaster is very clearly expressed by the authors of the *Hexenhammer*, published in 1487, in an "Apologia" at the beginning of the book: "…quando, mundi vespere ad occasum declinante et malitia hominum excrescente, novit in ira magna, ut Johannes in Apocalypsi testatur, se

Apocalypse and on compositions dealing with the omnipresence of death. For instance, a large composition incorporating many figures, entitled the *Joys of the World,* for which only a preliminary drawing in Oxford (W. 163) still exists, must have progressed far beyond the design stage, as a number of direct and indirect copies testify. But the whole range of Dürer's talent can only be appreciated when one considers his drawings for various decorative schemes together with his paintings and graphic works. His designs for elaborate tableware reveal the early years spent as an
Pl. 74 apprentice goldsmith; among them the *Large Table-Fountain* is outstanding for the extreme demands it makes on the

65 *The Virgin and Child in Front of a Landscape.* 1495–6. Oil. 89×74. Dr. G. Schäfer Collection, Schweinfurt. ▷

This picture very strongly reflects the influence of Venetian painting on Dürer. The composition of the figures is closely related to a painting by Giovanni Bellini done only slightly earlier. It must have been painted either in Venice or just after Dürer returned to Nuremberg when the impression Bellini's art had made on him was still vivid in his mind. Parts of the panel are in bad condition.

◁ 63 *Portrait of the Fürlegerin with Braided Hair.* 1497. Tempera on canvas. 58.5×42.5. Gemäldegalerie SMPK, Berlin.

There are two versions of this portrait. The canvas version, which has been owned by the Gemäldegalerie in Berlin-Dahlem since 1977, must be considered the original. The coat of arms identifies the attractive girl as a member of the Nuremberg family of Fürleger. Until the nineteenth century this picture, and a corresponding painting (in Frankfurt) of a young girl wearing her hair loose, were kept together; the second sitter was probably a sister of the girl portrayed here.

66 *The Seven Sorrows of the Virgin and the Mater Dolorosa.* 1496. Oil. Centre panel 109.2×43.3, remaining panels 63×45.5 each. Bayerische Staatsgemäldesammlungen Munich, and Gemäldegalerie, Dresden. ▷▷

When Frederick the Wise first visited Dürer's workshop he seems to have commissioned not only his own portrait but also an altarpiece for the palace and university church at Wittenberg, the city where he resided. This is suggested by an entry in the Saxon account books late in 1496 which shows that the considerable sum of 100 florins was paid to a Nuremberg painter for an altarpiece. The original altarpiece was extensive, but only the seven panels, representing the seven sorrows of the Virgin, survive; they were arranged around a centre panel showing the Mater Dolorosa being pierced by a sword, as shown by the reconstruction illustrated here. Only a few copies of the second wing have survived.

67 *Lamentation*. Painted for Albrecht Glimm. 1500–3. Oil. 151×121. Bayerische Staatsgemäldesammlungen, Munich.

deformed pig of Landser may well have been Dürer's source for his engraving of the *Miraculous Pig of Landser*.

Pl. 80

When Dürer did this minor engraving in 1496 he must already have been occupied with the most important work of these years, the woodcuts for the *Apocalypse* (B. 61–75). The wood-cutter's work on the fifteen large, carefully cut wood blocks took a long time, probably much more than a year. The finished work appeared as a book in 1498; there was a Latin as well as a German version, both printed by Anton Koberger.

The sources for Dürer's pictures were the woodcuts of a Bible in Low German, printed in Cologne in 1479, which had already been used by Koberger in his German Bible of 1485. Dürer selected primarily the same topics for illustration as were contained in the Bible of 1479, but added *St. John is Called to the Throne of Heaven* and *The Rejoicing of the Elect*. But where the earlier Bible combined several episodes in one picture, Dürer usually separated these and turned them into individual illustrations; only in the case of *The Seventh Trumpet* did he combine two woodcuts from the earlier cycle in one composition.

The most striking difference between Dürer's works and his model was the changing of the small transverse format of the earlier Bible illustrations into an upright format of half-sheet size. Only with the help of this monumental format could he give a coherent account both of the celestial happenings described in the visions of St. John and their effect on earth. The drama of these bizarre visions is perfectly expressed in the rippling, broken, late Gothic lines of Dürer's woodcuts.

As stylistic differences show, Dürer did not design the prints in the sequence in which they appear in the text. Rather, there is a clear division into an early group with many small figures covering the whole picture plane, and a later group characterized by a few large figures. This change in conception may well reflect a belated response to Dürer's Italian experience which only developed gradually; figures

modicum tempus habere." Johannes Lichtenberger, court astrologer to Emperor Frederick III, wrote in his *Prognosticatio* on 15 November 1484, on the occasion of a conjunction of Jupiter and Saturn in the constellation of Scorpio: "For when the Holy Roman Empire ceases to exist then the whole world must end too."[110] Sebastian Brant also prophesied the collapse of the Empire and the end of time in chapter 103 of his *Ship of Fools*.[111]

Even educated men regarded catastrophes or freaks of nature—such as the yearly invasions by the Turks, the meteorite which came down near Ensisheim in 1492, the flooding of the Tiber on 4 December 1495,[112] the Siamese twins born at Worms in 1495, and a pig with two bodies and eight legs born in Landser, Alsace, in 1496—as sure signs of an impending divine judgement on an apocalyptic scale. Sebastian Brant commented on these events in long, moralizing poems which were published as broadsheets dedicated to King Maximilian. Brant's broadsheet about the

68 *Landscape*. Detail of Pl. 67. ▷

Duke Maximilian of Bavaria had the figures of the donors obliterated by overpainting; the same was done in the *Paumgartner Altarpiece* (Pl. 69). The portrayal of such donor figures obviously did not conform with the seventeenth-century idea of realism. This early *Lamentation* is a type of composition which had been developed in the Netherlands as early as the fifteenth century, but was virtually unknown in Germany before Dürer. Compared to the corresponding woodcut of the *Large Passion* and the so-called *Holzschuher Lamentation* in Nuremberg, the composition of this picture is much clearer, and the arrangement of the figures in tiers is justified by the rising ground of the hill on which the event takes place.

69 *Paumgartner Altarpiece.* 1498–1503. Oil. Centre panel 155×126, wings 157×61 each. Bayerische Staatsgemäldesammlungen, Munich.

The centre panel of this altarpiece, which was donated by the Paumgartner family, represents the birth of Christ and the adoration of the shepherds. The figures on the wings are St. George and St. Eustace, both in the costume of knights. The exterior of the wings showed a picture of the Annunciation of which only the figure of the Virgin on the left-hand panel remains. Restoration work in 1902–3 uncovered the figures of the donors – which had been overpainted in the seventeenth century – on the lower margin of the centre panel. On the left are Martin Paumgartner (who died in 1478) and his sons Lukas and Stephan, and also a man with a white beard who is as yet unidentified. The women are Barbara Volkamer, the widow of Martin Paumgartner, and her daughters Maria and Barbara. According to a seventeenth-century manuscript account Dürer is supposed to have used the portraits of the brothers Lukas and Stephan as sources for the figures of the saints on the wings which were painted in 1498. This dating is borne out by the style of the two wings. The centre panel must have been painted later, though not later than 1502. Panofsky has pointed out that the composition of Dürer's centre panel is related to Hugo van der Goes's *Portinari Altarpiece.* Both pictures show a ruined palatial building with a wooden lean-to roof, and angels gathering around the Child. But Dürer can only have known drawings or copies of the *Portinari Altarpiece,* as the work itself had been erected in Florence as early as 1483.

70 *Virgin and Child at a Window.* C. 1497. Oil. 52×41. Samuel H. Kress Collection, National Gallery of Art, Washington. ▷

This panel, now in Washington, is painted on each side. Along with the *Virgin and Child in Front of a Landscape* (Pl. 65), these show – most clearly among all Dürer's works – the influence which Venetian art had on him after he came into contact with it for the first time. The strictly frontal presentation of the figure of the Virgin, the standing Child, and also the harmony of red, blue and green are reminiscent of similar compositions by Giovanni Bellini. The beautifully painted marble panelling also recalls the art of the south. In contrast to the carefully executed front of this panel, the back, which shows *Lot Fleeing Sodom,* is done in a loose technique reminiscent of watercolour painting. Other panels by Dürer were also painted on both sides (cf. Pl. 120). The coat of arms in the bottom left-hand corner of the picture of the Virgin shows that this panel was painted for a member of the Haller family.

◁ 71   *Lot Fleeing Sodom with his Family*. Oil. (*Verso of Pl. 70*).

72   *Valley near Kalchreuth*. C. 1500. Watercolour. 10.3×31.6. Kupfer-stichkabinett SMPK, Berlin.

Otto Mitius has identified the locality as a valley near the village of Kalchreuth, approximately fourteen kilometres east of Nuremberg. The patrician Haller family, with whom Dürer was on friendly terms, owned a castle in nearby Heroldsberg (cf. Pl. 154). This view and a view of the village of Kalchreuth (W. 118, now lost) must have been among Dürer's latest landscape watercolours judging by their loose, painterly style and lack of detail. They have been dated as late as 1514 to 1520; but in the few landscape views executed during this period Dürer's interest centred so exclusively on the rendering of spatial relationships by purely graphic means (cf. Pl. 154) that these watercolours cannot have been painted at that time. Judging by their colours they belong to the period between 1498 and 1500.

73   *Horseman in Armour*. 1498. Brush. 41×32.4. Graphische Samm-lung Albertina, Vienna.

Dürer later added the following inscription at the top of the drawing: "This is what a suit of armour looked like in Germany at the time. 1498". Traditionally this brush drawing, which was worked over with the pen, is believed to represent the mounted soldier Philipp Link, a member of the Paumgartner family. Mounted soldiers were used by the trading companies, because armed escorts were necessary to guard their large merchant convoys and their wares against attacks by robbers, as the roads were generally unsafe. This costume study by Dürer (cf. Pls. 38, 97, 197) is often thought to have been based on a lost study from nature. However, corrections to the two front hooves and the saddle, and particularly to the horse's head, which originally had been much too small and narrow and had to be altered by Dürer, imply that this is a drawing from a living model. It was worked over with the pen, possibly later, by a member of the workshop. Dürer considered the drawing very important: he used the horse again in his engraving of *St. Eustace* (Pl. 110) and the horseman for his master engraving of *Knight, Death and the Devil* (Pls. 166–8). It is not certain whether the figure of St. George in the engraving of 1505–8 is also based on this study or on another one which has been lost.

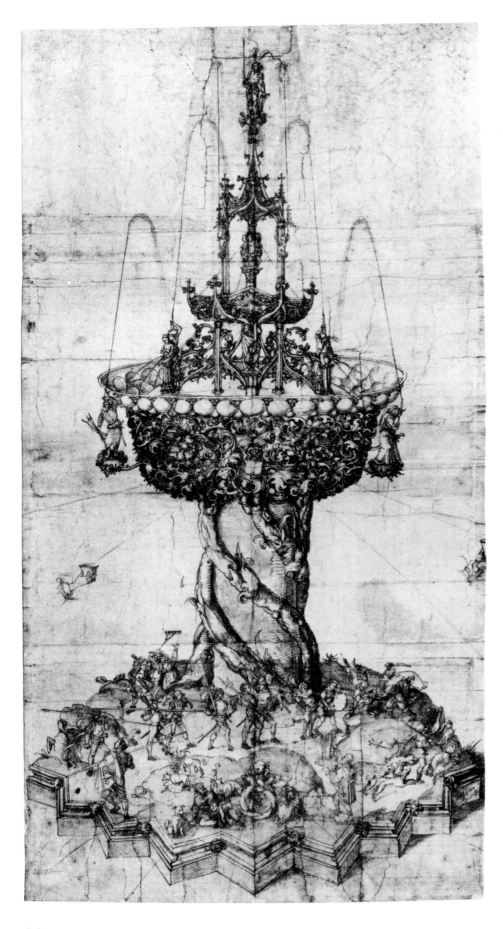

74 *The Large Table-Fountain.* C. 1499. Pen and wash. 56 × 35.8. Department of Prints and Drawings, British Museum, London.

Table-fountains like the one Dürer designed on this sheet (which has detailed measurements on the back) were intended as decorative features on royal tables at festive occasions. This fountain was presumably to be made of metal, either cast in brass or chased in silver, and enamelled in several colours, as the delicate washes of the drawing indicate. The jets of liquid caught in a cup are inked in red which implies that red wine was to flow from this fountain.

75 Miniature for the Title-page of an Edition of the *Idyllia* by Theocritus. C. 1496. Gouache. Private Collection, Franconia.   ▷

Dürer decorated the first page of a Greek edition of the *Idylls* by Theocritus, published by the famous Venetian printer Aldus Manutius in 1495–6, for his friend Willibald Pirckheimer and his wife Crescentia. The illustration decorates the border of the page and is executed in bodycolour heightened with gold. Dürer depicts the idyllic life of the shepherds which is described in the text. The Pirckheimer coat of arms hangs in a tree on the left; that of his wife's family, the Rieters, in a tree on the right.

ΘΕΟΚΡΙΤΟΥ ΘΥΡΣΙΣ Ἢ ὨΔΗ
ΕΙΔΥΛΛΙΟΝ ΠΡΩΤΟΝ.
ΘΥΡΣΙΣ Ἢ ὨΔΗ.

Ἁδύ τι τὸ ψιθύρισμα καὶ ἁ πί-
τυς αἰπόλε τήνα,
Ἁ ποτὶ ταῖς παγαῖσι μελίσ-
δεται· ἁδὺ δὲ καὶ τὺ
Συρίσδες· μετὰ Πᾶνα τὸ δεύ-
τερον ἆθλον ἀποισῇ.
Αἴκα τῆνος ἕλῃ κεραὸν τρά-
γον· αἶγα τὺ λαψῇ.

Αἴκα δ' αἶγα λάβῃ τῆνος γέρας· ἐς τὲ καταρρεῖ
Ἁ χίμαρος, χιμάρω δὲ καλὸν κρέας ἔστε κ' ἀμέλξῃς.
ΑΙ. Ἆρ' ὦ ποιμὰν τὸ τεὸν μέλος ἢ τὸ καταχές
Τῆν' ἀπὸ τᾶς πέτρας καταλείβεται ὑψόθεν ὕδωρ.
Αἴκα ταὶ Μῶσαι τὰν οἴϊδα δῶρον ἄγωνται·
Ἄρνα τὺ σακίταν λαψῇ γέρας· αἰ δὲ κ' ἀρέσκῃ
Τήναις ἄρνα λαβεῖν· τὺ δὲ τὰν ὄϊν ὕστερον ἀξεῖς.
Θ. Λῇς ποτὶ τᾶν νυμφᾶν λῇς αἰπόλε τῆδε καθίξας
Ὡς τὸ κάταντες τοῦτο γεώλοφον ἅ τε μυρῖκαι
Συρίσδεν; τὰς δ' αἶγας ἐγὼν ἐν τῷδε νομευσῶ;
ΑΙ. Οὐ θέμις ὦ ποιμὰν τὸ μεσαμβρινὸν, οὐ θέμις ἄμμι
Συρίσδεν· τὸν Πᾶνα δεδοίκαμες· ἦ γὰρ ἀπ' ἄγρας
Τανίκα κεκμακὼς ἀμπαύεται· ἔστι δὲ πικρός
Καὶ οἱ ἀεὶ δριμεῖα χολὰ ποτὶ ῥινὶ κάθηται.
Ἀλλὰ τὺ γὰρ δὴ Θύρσι τὰ Δάφνιδος ἄλγε' ἀείδες
Καὶ τᾶς βωκολικᾶς ἐπὶ τὸ πλέον ἵκεο μώσας.

Α. Α ii

◁ 76 *Self-Portrait*. 1498. Oil. 52×41. Museo del Prado, Madrid.

The twenty-six-year-old Dürer sits in front of a window; he wears elegant, even dandyish clothes and his hair and beard are well-groomed. Here is the artist whose fifteen woodcuts of the *Secret Revelation* of St. John (Pls. 78, 79), which appeared in the same year, were to hold all of Europe spellbound with their dramatic subject matter. A recent critic maintained that this self-portrait expresses "pharisaical self-adoration", but this seems unjust; the comment in the catalogue of the Nuremberg exhibition of 1971, which interprets Dürer's elegant appearance as an expression of high social rank within a civic hierarchy, is more acceptable. None the less Dürer's beard and hair-style must have appeared extravagant to his Nuremberg contemporaries, because even in later years the "hairy, bearded painter" was the constant target of the—sometimes coarse—mockery of his friends. The formal arrangement of a figure in front of a window with a landscape view in the distance had been commonly used in Germany and Italy before Dürer's time. The severe composition of the picture, which is dominated by horizontals and verticals, reflects a particularly strong influence of Italian (Florentine?) prototypes.

77 *Portrait of Oswald Krell*. 1499. Oil. 49.6×39. Wings 49.3×15.9 each. Bayerische Staatsgemäldesammlungen, Munich.

This picture of the factor (i.e. head of a branch) of the Great Ravensburg Trading Company in Nuremberg is the most impressive of Dürer's portraits of 1499. Krell, who came from Lindau and later became mayor of his home town, worked in Nuremberg from 1495 to 1503. The two side wings show the coats of arms of Krell and of his wife, Agathe von Esendorf.

like the four angels, for instance, clearly derive from Mantegna. These Italian features help make the compositions less complicated without affecting the overall style.

Dürer's personal involvement, creative imagination and artistic talent reveal themselves in every one of these woodcuts, but most strongly in the prints of *The Four Horsemen*, Pl. 78

89

78 *The Four Horsemen of the Apocalypse*. 1498. Woodcut. C. 39.5 × 28.5. Kupferstichkabinett SMPK, Berlin.

The book which immediately made Dürer famous throughout Europe was the *Apocalypse* of St. John, published in 1498. This text had been frequently illustrated during the Middle Ages, even though its apocalyptic visions, which unfold before the reader in quick succession almost like the reel of a film, are difficult to encapsulate in individual pictures. From an early date, printed Bibles — like the Cologne Bible of *circa* 1479 and the Nuremberg Bible of 1483 — illustrated themes from the Apocalypse.

Dürer's cycle of illustrations is based on the woodcuts of these two printed publications. However, in his version, these modest prototypes become pictures of high drama, as the *Four Horsemen* (Apoc. VI, 1–8) or *John Eats the Book* (Apoc. X, 1–11) show. The impression these pictures made on contemporaries, most of whom expected the end of the world in the year 1500, must have been immense. Dürer's woodcuts were something of a definitive version of the subject, influencing all later illustrators. Dürer's godfather, Anton Koberger, printed both the Latin and the German edition of the book. Dürer's well-known monogram appears for the first time; it was added to each woodcut of the sequence.

Pl. 79 *St. John Eats the Book* and *St. Michael's Fight with the Dragon*. These are among the last and most mature compositions of the *Apocalypse*.

Dürer created a new type of book with his woodcuts for the *Secret Revelation* of St. John, in which text and illustrations are of equal importance. When it was published it was an immediate success and Dürer became famous throughout Europe. It is true though that this success was not entirely

79   *St. John Eats the Book*. 1498. Woodcut. C. 39.5 × 28.5. Kupferstich-kabinett SMPK, Berlin.

based on the artistic strength of the woodcuts, but also on the general belief that apocalyptic events were imminent. Some contemporaries feared such events would signify the end of the world; others expected, or perhaps even hoped for, major political and religious changes.[113]

80 *The Miraculous Pig of Landser*. 1496. Engraving. 12.1×12.7. Kupferstichkabinett SMPK, Berlin.

This work commemorates a specific event, namely the birth of a misshapen pig which occurred in the village of Landser, Alsace, on 1 March 1496. Dürer's source was presumably a broadsheet by Sebastian Brant commenting on this event. In Dürer's time — in contrast to our age of television — representations of such monstrosities had a lasting impact, as they were considered to be miracles or signs of God's wrath.

81 *The Syphilitic*. 1496. Coloured woodcut. 24.6×9.3. Kupferstichkabinett SMPK, Berlin.

This woodcut of 1496, representing a man suffering from the "French disease", is a cultural and medical document. Dürer designed it as an illustration to a broadsheet of 110 Latin hexameters written by the Frisian Dietrich Ulsen, who had been the town physician of Nuremberg since 1486. Ulsen, who, in the Humanist manner, called himself Theodoricus Ulsenius, was a friend of Konrad Celtis and Sebald Schreyer. He was the first to comment publicly, via his broadsheet, on the syphilis epidemic which had been raging throughout Europe from 1494 onwards. He thought the cause of these "malignant smallpox", which had been unknown until then, was a conjunction of the planets of Saturn and Jupiter in the house of Scorpio, which had been observed on 25 November 1484. Dürer shows this astrological constellation in a sphere with the signs of the zodiac above the sick man. The third house of the front row shows Scorpio together with several stars; below it appears the date 1484.

V. Rise to Maturity: 1500–5

The Image of God · Theory · Neoplatonism

Dürer's friend Konrad Celtis was one of the people who did not expect apocalyptic doom at the turn of the century. Rather, he hoped that the new era, under King Maximilian's rule, would be the beginning of a Golden Age.[114] And Ficino, whom Celtis had met in Florence in 1488, had already interpreted the revival of interest in grammar, poetry, rhetoric, painting, architecture, music and classical singing as a sign of the approaching Golden Age,[115] as had Enea Silvio Piccolomini. Although Celtis was never in Nuremberg for long, he and Pirckheimer gave the greatest encouragement to Dürer's interest in Ficino's Neoplatonic philosophy and his understanding of it.[116]

PI. 1 How strongly Dürer was influenced by the precepts of Florentine Neoplatonism by the turn of the century is evident in his self-portrait of 1500, which marks the beginning of a new phase in his artistic development. It is completely different from the self-portrait of 1498, which showed an elegant, cosmopolitan young man; the portrait of 1500 is a formal expression of specific ideas.

According to the Nuremberg calendar at that time, the year started on 25 December. The portrait must have been painted between the end of 1499 (Gregorian calendar) and 21 April 1500, the painter's twenty-ninth birthday, as the inscription on the picture says that Dürer was twenty-eight years old when it was executed. The stark frontality, unusual for portraits of that time, and the only slightly softened symmetry of the depiction were suggested to Dürer by the idea that God had created man according to his own image. Dürer took the biblical text literally and created a stylized portrait reminiscent of the Redeemer. He used a geometric system, which was common at that time in idealized pictures of the head of Christ.

The basic concept, that man is the image of God, is strengthened by associated ideas. Ficino had said that man was the crowning glory of God's creation because man's own creative ability, among other things, made him resemble the "divine artist".[117] This belief must have

appealed to Dürer, since it reinforced his conception of his own vocation. The idea of man as a dual image of God suggests that the self-portrait could be interpreted as representative of the creative artist in general. But for Dürer such a conception would have been too one-sided; he thought that being the image of God committed man (as a believing Christian) to the "imitatio Christi" (cf. the self-portrait of 1493)[118] and also (as a painter) to a meaningful use of his artistic talent.[119]

Between 1500 and the start of his second journey to Italy in the autumn of 1505 Dürer, whose work up to now had been entirely bound by established artistic and craft traditions, made a conscious attempt to find a new basis for his art. Panofsky has rightly called this period one of "rational synthesis".[120] Scholars and artists of Dürer's time believed in general that only theoretical principles provided a sound basis for artistic endeavour. In a letter of 1502 addressed to Frederick the Wise, Jacopo de' Barbari, who had been living in Nuremberg since the end of April, 1500, as "contrafeter and illuminist" of King Maximilian, refers to geometry and arithmetic as the foundation of painting. And Jacopo believed, as Ficino had before him, that because the art of painting was based on mathematical principles, it was necessarily a part of philosophy, as it enabled man to recognize the nature of things. Thus Barbari argued that painting should be classified among the "artes liberales" and not among the "artes mechanicae" as hitherto.[121]

According to Italian art theorists the mathematical principles underlying painting applied to two areas in particular: first to the depiction of the ideal proportions of the human body and second to perspective. Up to the turn of the century Dürer's attempts to construct human figures "with compass and ruler" had not led to any useful results, even though Celtis flatteringly praised Dürer's studies of proportions in these years.[122] But around this time Dürer must have read Vitruvius' De architectura where he found in the third book information on classical teaching concerning human

82 *Apollo and Diana.* 1502–3. Engraving. 11.6 × 7.3. Kupferstich-kabinett SMPK, Berlin.

This engraving is closely related to Dürer's studies on proportions carried out in the years after 1500. A seated female figure had already been added to the drawing of the sun god (now in London, Pl. 83) whose figure was traced from one constructed according to a system of proportions. Dürer had first seen the god Apollo and the goddess Diana, who are brother and sister, represented together in an engraving by Jacopo de' Barbari, but his own composition is quite independent.

proportions. Reading Vitruvius and, at about the same time, seeing an illustration of the statue of Apollo which had been excavated in Rome in 1492, seem to have given Dürer the vital incentive to continue with his studies. The drawings of *Aesculapius* (W. 263) and the London *Apollo,* both based on preliminary sketches, are the result of these renewed efforts. Dürer changed the *Apollo,* begun as a study of the body's proportions, into a composition of *Apollo and*

Pl. 82

Diana, under the influence of an engraving of the same theme by Jacopo de' Barbari.[123] His own engraving, small yet powerful compared to Barbari's rather insignificant work, was done around 1502–3. Dürer applied his studies of female proportions—which in the first few years after 1500 were still based on Vitruvius' teachings—to his engraving of *Nemesis,* which had been inspired by a work of the Florentine Neoplatonic poet, Angelo Poliziano.[124] The first work to reflect Dürer's theoretical studies of male proportions is his engraving of *The Standard Bearer* (B. 87). The most mature result of this first phase of Dürer's studies of human proportions was the engraving of *Adam and Eve,* executed in 1504. It is highly accomplished, both technically and artistically.

Pls. 82, 84

Pl. 86

Pl. 87

While Dürer's efforts to understand the laws governing the structure of the human body had proved successful within a few years, his knowledge of the theory of the mathematical principles underlying painting and the use of perspective remained superficial, and he did not progress beyond the simplest constructions.

From about the middle of the fourteenth century, painters on both sides of the Alps had been aware that lines receding

83 *Apollo.* C. 1500. Pen. 28.5 × 20.2. Department of Prints and Drawings, British Museum, London. ▷

This fine work, which appears to be a preliminary drawing for an engraving, shows Apollo standing and Diana seated at his feet. It is one of Dürer's most problematical works. Many possible sources for it have been listed: a drawing of the Apollo Belvedere, a classical statue of Hermes in Augsburg, Jacopo de' Barbari's engraving of *Apollo and Diana* (K. 14) of 1498–1500 which has the same theme as Dürer's drawing, and the man with a cornucopia in Mantegna's engraving of the *Bacchanalia with a Vat* (B. 19). All these works may indeed have been more or less important sources for the final version of Dürer's drawing, except for the Augsburg sculpture, which was not discovered until a later date. It is quite certain that the figure of Apollo was originally a figure constructed according to a system of proportions. Traces of constructional lines are still visible on the figure and the proportions are indicated on the left-hand margin of the sheet. Dürer appears to have owned a drawing based on the Apollo Belvedere, a marble statue which had been excavated in Rome between 1450 and 1490; this is not only implied by the present work, but also by many other drawings of these years which represent figures of Apollo. The statue's right arm was damaged, and Dürer based the arm of his god on that of the man with the cornucopia in Mantegna's engraving. Finally, he completed his constructed drawing by adding the figure of Apollo's sister Diana; this reflects the influence of Barbari's engraving. This last change may well have been made somewhat later, after Barbari had settled in Nuremberg (in April, 1500). It would explain why Dürer did not as usual construct the latter figure on the back of the sheet with the help of lines indicating the proportions and then trace it through to the other side, but added it directly to the final drawing. At any rate this change in the subject matter, which alters the original conception, must have been an afterthought.

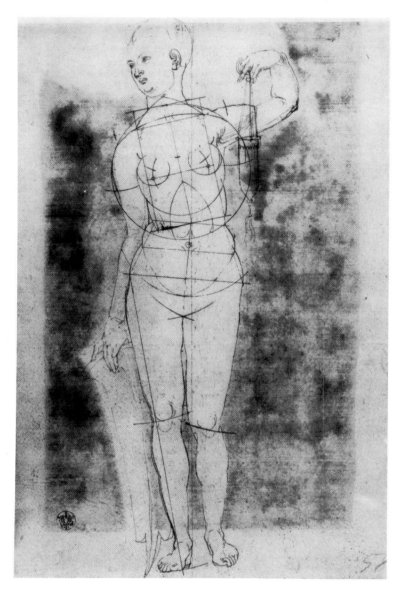

84 *Study of a Female Nude Indicating Proportions*. C. 1500. Pen. 30.3 × 20.5. Kupferstichkabinett SMPK, Berlin.

85 *Female Nude Holding a Shield* (*Verso* of Pl. 84). Pen and wash.

In an epigram written shortly before 1500, Konrad Celtis praises Dürer for his efforts in studying the proportions of the human body. In 1523, Dürer himself wrote that his interest in studies on proportions had been awakened by Jacopo de' Barbari, although he had not learned from the Venetian painter the secret of how to construct human figures accurately. Together these two documents prove that Dürer must have met Jacopo de' Barbari in Venice as early as 1494–5, and that the Venetian painter must have shown him drawings demonstrating human proportions on that occasion. This drawing in Berlin shows how far Dürer's studies had advanced around 1500.

86 *Nemesis*. 1501–3. Engraving. 33.3 × 22.9. Kupferstichkabinett SMPK, Berlin. ▷

This engraving is called "Nemesis" in Dürer's diary of his journey to the Netherlands. The monumental female figure, who hovers in the air above a panorama of the Eisack Valley and the small town of Klausen, is based on Vitruvius' system of proportions. The literary source for Dürer's figure was a Latin poem by the Florentine Humanist Angelo Poliziano, in which the Roman goddess of luck, Fortuna, and the Greek goddess of retribution, Nemesis, are described as one and the same divine figure. The fickleness of luck is symbolized by the sphere on which Fortuna hovers. Nemesis, however, is carried along by her wings and holds out a cup, which is the reward for good deeds, and a harness, which is to be worn by immoderate humans. Dürer conveys the figure's restless hovering, which the text emphasizes, by means of the fluttering draperies behind Nemesis and her (well-observed) uncertain stance on the sphere. The bank of clouds dips in the centre as if giving way under the force of fate.

98

88 *Adam and Eve.* 1504. Pen. 24.2 × 20.1. The Pierpont Morgan Library, New York.

89 *The Birth of Christ.* 1504. Engraving. 18.3 × 12. Kupferstichkabinett, SMPK, Berlin.

The period after 1500 marks an early peak in Dürer's achievement as an engraver as well as a painter. This engraving of the *Birth of Christ* echoes, in mirror image, the composition of the centre panel of the *Paumgartner Altarpiece*. The simple wooden lean-to roof has been replaced by a dilapidated timber-framed building. On the ground floor, in a loggia-like structure, the Virgin kneels before the Child. The figure of Joseph, who was already set apart from the Virgin and Child in the altarpiece, is here separated even more strongly from the main event. He is engrossed in his own activity and hardly seems to notice what has happened. By contrast, one of the shepherds already kneels at the entrance to the loggia, adoring the child. The landscape seen through the large archway is also very reminiscent of the *Paumgartner Altarpiece*. The tiny figures represent the angel bringing the tidings of joy to the shepherds.

into the depth of a picture appear to merge in the distance. Dürer's first use of this basic rule on the rendering of space appears in the woodcut of the *Flagellation* (M. 109) from the *Albertina Passion,* designed around 1495.[125] The woodcut of *Ecce Homo* (B. 9), created several years later, shows how Dürer long remained uncertain in his application of this most primitive of structural laws. It is true that the steps of the stairs recede correctly, but all other architectural elements seem to have been added freehand, without any attempt at correct perspective.

◁ 87 *Adam and Eve.* 1504. Engraving. 24.8 × 19.2. Kupferstichkabinett SMPK, Berlin.

This engraving of *Adam and Eve* of 1504 is the most accomplished of Dürer's early attempts at depicting ideal male and female nudes. The figure of Adam is still very reminiscent of the classical statue of the Apollo Belvedere. A number of allegorical pointers have been added to this representation of the first human couple. Their contrasting nature is reflected three times: by the tree of knowledge (fig) as against the tree of life (mountain ash), parrot as against snake, and mouse as against cat. The Fall of Man not only resulted in human beings losing their paradisiacal innocence, but also their ideal form; from this point onwards humans were no longer alike, but were distinguished by their many different temperaments; these are represented by the animals.

92 *The Annunciation.* 1503–4. Woodcut for the *Life of the Virgin.* 29.5×21. Kupferstichkabinett SMPK, Berlin. ▷

Compared with the preliminary drawing for the *Birth of the Virgin* (W. 292), the one for the *Annunciation* is a carefully executed design in which all major elements of the composition have already been established. However, Dürer did make some alterations when he transferred the design on to the wood block: in the final version the figures are larger in relation to the surrounding space; the hall-like room in which they stand is made more intimate by the introduction of additional horizontal elements. The medallion with the half-length figure of Judith, the candle on the wall-mounted cupboard, the water urn in the niche and the lily in the vase in the foreground are all symbols of the Virgin. Just as Judith saved her people from the threat of the enemy, so the Virgin Mary will save mankind by giving birth to the Redeemer. The evil one, in the shape of an animal, is already chained in a dungeon below the stairs.

91 *The Annunciation.* C. 1503. Pen and wash. 31.2×20.4. Kupferstich-kabinett SMPK, Berlin.

90 *Joachim Receives the Glad Tidings.* C. 1504. Woodcut for *The Life of the Virgin.* 29.5×21. Kupferstichkabinett SMPK, Berlin.

Apart from the woodcuts for the *Apocalypse* (Pls. 78, 79), and early designs for a Passion cycle, Dürer designed seventeen woodcuts for the *Life of the Virgin* cycle in quick succession after the turn of the century. The most impressive of these compositions are those which include complex landscapes, like *Joachim receives the Glad Tidings*, and *The Visitation* (B. 84). Joachim and Anna had been married for a long time without having had any children. Then one day, when Joachim was tending his flock, an angel appeared and told him that he would have a daughter, Mary. Dürer represents the scene as a real event rather than as a vision of Joachim, because the shepherds see the angel too.

The Coburg drawing of the *Flagellation* (W. 185),[126] dated 1502, is the first work to show a definite attempt by Dürer to construct correct perspective in views of interiors and exteriors of buildings. The use of framing arches in the Coburg drawing as well as in the woodcuts of the *Meeting at the Golden Gate* (B. 79), the *Annunciation* and *Christ*

101

93 *Philosophy.* 1502. Woodcut for Konrad Celtis's *Quatuor libri amorum.* 21.7 × 14.7. Kupferstichkabinett SMPK, Berlin.

Like the woodcuts for the writings of Hrosvitha, Dürer's two illustrations for Celtis's book are somewhat sketchily drawn. Yet both woodcuts show a wealth of imagination, even though the artist had to comply with detailed instructions from the author. The enthroned figure of Philosophy is surrounded by a garland which symbolizes the four seasons. The four winds — which also represent the four elements and the four temperaments — occupy the four corners. The four medallions in the garland represent the four most important philosophers of the various nationalities.

among the Doctors (B. 91) from the *Life of the Virgin* cycle shows that at that time, Dürer must have already known about Italian theories of perspective. This kind of framing device is not, as might be thought, an archaic element. The motif is always linked to systematically constructed architectural views and must therefore be considered a conscious application by Dürer. The idea, as first expressed by Leon

Battista Alberti, is that a picture which uses perspective is like a view through a window, i.e. literally a "perspective".[127] Although Dürer seems to have known about only one of the devices used by the Italians for constructing perspective views, namely the vanishing point, his highly developed sense of space enabled him to use it to represent surprisingly complicated spatial arrangements convincingly, as the drawings of the *Green Passion* show. Such complicated foreshortened architectural elements as those in the *Ecce Homo* from the *Green Passion* (W. 308) might suggest that Dürer knew not only Alberti's *Della pittura,* a copy of which was owned by Bernhard Walther in Nuremberg, but also consulted Filarete's *Treatise on Architecture,* because similarly complex constructions are found there.[128] However, Dürer does not seem to have known or understood the more advanced methods of construction described in both theoretical treatises. This would explain why he planned to travel on horseback from Venice to Bologna late in 1506 in order to receive instruction in perspective drawing.

During this same period Dürer also tried to work out the proportions of the horse by means of geometric construction. It is not certain whether he did this of his own accord or because he had heard about similar attempts by Italian masters. In any case, the proportions of the horse in the engraving of *St. Eustace* show a systematic construction. Pl. 110 Similar studies by Leonardo may have inspired Dürer in 1502. For several months preceding the so-called "Battle by the Wood", fought on 19 June 1502 and lost by Nuremberg, Galeazzo da Sanseverino, an old Italian friend of

94 *Christ Being Crowned with Thorns (Green Passion).* 1504. Pen and brush on green primed paper, heightened with white. 28.3 × 18. Graphische Sammlung Albertina, Vienna. ▷

The development leading up to the execution of twelve sheets comprising the *Green Passion* can be followed in greater detail than that of any other Passion cycle by Dürer. Tracings were made of the preliminary drawings and were then used (with minor alterations) as the basis for the final versions. It is not known for what purpose this Passion cycle was intended. A comparison with a sequence of stained-glass panels in a church near Nuremberg suggests that the sheets could have been designs for a glass painter. However, the designs Dürer executed for the Fugger tombs (Pls. 155, 156) employed the same technique. This suggests that the drawings of the *Green Passion* might well have been intended as preliminary designs for reliefs in the manner of Adam Kraft. Kraft had created the first "Stations of the Cross" in European art in 1507 to 1508. These reliefs were placed along the road leading from the city to the cemetery of St. John. The perspective construction underlying Dürer's interior is very simple. The vanishing point, slightly to the side of the central axis of the composition, lies in Christ's left eye. The gradual diminution of equidistant transversals is not yet constructed systematically, but based on free judgement.

Pirckheimer's, had been staying in Pirckheimer's house.[129] Galeazzo, the Duke of Caiazzo, son-in-law and cousin of Ludovico il Moro, the Duke of Milan, imprisoned in France, kept the most beautiful horses in Italy in his Milan stables.[130] Notes by Leonardo prove that he based his studies for the Sforza monument on Sanseverino's fine animals.[131] Since the horses Dürer drew between 1502 and 1505 (W. 247, 360, 361) are clearly influenced by these and earlier studies of Leonardo's,[132] it seems reasonable to suppose that Sanseverino was the link between the two artists; there is, however, no documented contact between Dürer and Sanseverino before 1511.[133] In the autumn of 1503, a canon, Dr. Lorenz Beheim, who came from a Nuremberg family of bronze-founders and architects, had returned home from Rome. He had served the Borgias as a builder of

96 *Portrait of Willibald Pirckheimer Wearing a Beret*. 1503. Charcoal. 28.1 × 20.8. Kupferstichkabinett SMPK, Berlin.

This is the first of a large group of charcoal portraits. Compared with the silver-point portrait of Pirckheimer (W. 268) the charcoal drawing appears more stylized and deliberately monumental; this impression is strongly emphasized by the profile view.

95 *Head of a Woman*. 1503. Tempera on canvas. 25.5 × 21.5. Cabinet des Estampes, Bibliothèque Nationale, Paris.

This portrait of a woman (now in Paris) was painted on very fine canvas in 1503. The sitter's features resemble those of Agnes Dürer. However, the blue cloak and red gown indicate that this is a picture of the Virgin. Dürer possibly modelled it on his wife. He used Agnes as the model for St. Anne in the painting of *The Virgin and Child with St. Anne* of 1519 (Pl. 184).

97 *Young Nuremberg Lady Dressed for Dancing*. 1500. Pen and wash. 32.4 × 21.1. Kupferstichkabinett, Öffentliche Kunstsammlung, Basle. ▷

The inscription reads: "This is how the young women go dancing in Nuremberg. 15." The Basle drawing is one of a group of four costume studies; the remaining three are in the Albertina. They show the costumes worn by Nuremberg women to suit various occasions. They are carefully executed drawings which were presumably based on preliminary studies from nature. Dürer, who liked splendid dress himself, was always interested in the costumes of his contemporaries, particularly strange and exotic ones (cf. Pls. 38 and 197). The figure of the girl in this drawing was used again in the engraving of *The Coat of Arms of Vanitas* (Pl. 109).

fortifications and as first commander of the artillery for many years. These functions had presumably also brought him into contact with Leonardo, because from June, 1502 to the end of February, 1503, Leonardo had been an engineer in charge of fortifications in the service of Cesare Borgia. The material which Dürer seems to have had access to as early as 1502 — either through Sanseverino or Beheim — presumably consisted at least in part of engravings

98 *Head of a Stag.* C. 1502. Wash. 22.8 × 16.6. Nelson Gallery of Art, Atkins Museum, Kansas City.

This *Head of a Stag,* now in the Kansas City Collection, illustrates the working process which Dürer also applied to the *Hare.* First he made a preliminary line drawing with the brush, which established all the essential elements of the head. Two further stages of work followed, both including corrections: firstly whole areas of the drawing were painted in large sweeps of colour, and secondly, the final details and the highlights were added.

99 *Death as an Archer on Horseback.* 1502. Pen. 38.7 × 31.2. Kestner-Museum, Hanover.

A corresponding picture of the Provost Sixtus Tucher in front of the church of St. Lorenz (W. 214) belongs to this picture of Death on horseback. Both are shaped like a trefoil, and both are dated 1502. The Tucher drawing is in the Städelsches Kunstinstitut in Frankfurt-on-Main. The glass panels made from these designs in the workshop of the glass painter Veit Hirschvogel the Elder are in the Germanisches National-museum in Nuremberg. They appear to have originally been part of an oriel window in the vicarage of St. Lorenz.

100 *Hare.* 1502. Watercolour and gouache. 25.1 × 22.6. Graphische Sammlung Albertina, Vienna. ▷

Dürer's *Hare* has been reproduced countless times and has become one of the most popular works of German art. However, this excessive popularity has led certain critics, equally vehemently, to condemn this kind of realistic picture. It should be pointed out, however, that Dürer succeeds in conveying the characteristic features of the animal, its couchant pose and its soft fur, by comparatively simple means. An undercoat of colour applied with a thick brush established areas of light and dark, then the fur was painted in detail with a fine brush. It is a commonly held opinion that Dürer "painted every single hair", but he worked rather more economically than that. The illusionist effect, on which the fame of this work partly rests, is achieved by groups of lines which are longer or shorter, coarser or finer according to which part of the body they define. The work certainly represents an astonishing artistic achievement, but it should also be remembered that during the Renaissance, and for a long time afterwards, artistic "feats", that is works which displayed virtuosity and unique craft skills, were also much admired.

107

101 *The Ascension of Mary Magdalene.* C. 1503. Woodcut. 21.3 × 14.4. Kupferstichkabinett SMPK, Berlin.

This woodcut represents a subject which had been popular since the fifteenth century. Strictly speaking, it does not show the ascension of the saint, but her daily translation into heaven. This is why Dürer shows her hovering over a landscape, rather like *Nemesis* (Pl. 86). In both works the onlooker is on the same level as the main figure, and looks down upon the earth. In representations of an ascension, on the other hand, the onlooker remains on earth while Christ or the Virgin ascend to heaven.

from drawings by Leonardo,[134] as the 1503 Cologne drawing of a horse (W. 361) suggests.

Dürer's preoccupation with the mathematical and theoretical principles underlying painting ran parallel to his own work and directly influenced it, as the engraving of *Adam* Pl. 87 *and Eve* or the cycles of the *Life of the Virgin* and the *Green* Pls. 92, *Passion* testify. This linking of theory and artistic practice 94 no doubt enabled him to solidify a plan for a manual on

painting as early as 1505, before he went to Italy for the second time.[135] Such a project seems all the more likely since by now Dürer had built up a proper workshop with apprentices and journeymen. Hans Süss of Kulmbach, for instance, is documented as having been a member of the workshop from 1500–1; in 1502, the year Albrecht Dürer the Elder died, Frederick of Saxony sent an apprentice (called Frederick) to Dürer, and from about 1503, Hans Baldung and Hans Schäufelein were members. With the exception of the *Ober-St. Veit Altarpiece* which Schäufelein painted from designs by Dürer (W. 319–23), existing works known to have been produced by Dürer's pupils in the years before the second journey to Italy are confined to a number of prints which appeared as illustrations in Nuremberg publications. Dürer clearly ran his workshop along traditional lines, accepting commissions of all kinds and leaving their execution largely to the members. Thus, when a set of illustrations had been commissioned he himself usually contributed only one or two woodcut designs. This was the case in Konrad Celtis's *Quatuor libri amorum* and in the *Opera Hrosvithae* Pl. 93 (B. 277 a, b); only one manuscript copy of the latter existed, which Celtis discovered in the library of the monastery of St. Emmeran near Regensburg. Hans von Kulmbach produced most of the illustrations for both publications. Kulmbach, Baldung and Schäufelein also did illustrations for Dr. Ulrich Pinder's *Beschlossenen gart*; Dürer contributed only one illustration.

Designs for stained glass played a major role in the works produced by the Dürer workshop during these years. Dürer himself made designs for church windows, pictorial stained- Pl. 99 glass panels or entire cycles, and executed the drawings which were the patterns for the glass-painters, the drawings for the St. Benedict panels (W. 198–209), for example. His sometimes strange drawing style is explained by the fact that

102 *The Large Piece of Turf.* 1503. Watercolour and gouache. 41 × 31.5. Graphische Sammlung Albertina, Vienna. ▷

The *Large Piece of Turf* is Dürer's most famous plant study; it is uncertain whether his pictures of plants were preliminary studies for other works or paintings in their own right. By adding the date in the lower right-hand corner (beneath a leaf coming into the picture from the right) Dürer suggests that he himself regarded this study as something special. He appears to have been conscious of the fact that no painter before him had dared to represent such an insignificant piece of nature not even distinguished by very charming or interesting colours. Dürer's brush captures on paper the apparent arbitrariness and lack of order of natural growth; this reflects a conception of a nature study which is ahead of its time, and also conveys something of the very life of plants. Moreover, this picture expresses the artist's awe at the beauty of even such an insignificant part of God's creation.

he adapted his lines to the requirements and technical possibilities of glass. The drawings for stained glass executed by Dürer and his workshop had a strongly pictorial character which altered the course of Nuremberg stained glass painting.[136]

Dürer's creative energy led him to explore new aspects of his art continually. Although judging by existing works he had started out as a portraitist, in 1503 he produced his first portrait drawings in their own right, those not intended merely as studies for paintings. Dürer may have considered such drawings as substitutes for paintings, for no portrait-

103 *The Saints Nicolas, Ulrich and Erasmus.* 1502–3. Woodcut. 21.3 × 14.3. Kupferstichkabinett SMPK, Berlin.

"Simple woodcuts" like this one appear to have had a wide distribution and to have been highly esteemed by other artists. Copies by Grünewald and Titian after such woodcuts are proof of this.

paintings attributable to Dürer with absolute certainty were produced during the years before he set out on his second journey to the south. But for us his portraits in charcoal, pen and silver-point or, more rarely, painted on canvas, more than compensate for this loss. These works appear more Pl. 95 relaxed than the panel paintings where Dürer had to heed the wishes and social pretensions of his clients as well as pictorial traditions. In the drawn character studies, on the other hand, Dürer could follow his own inclinations, particularly if the sitters were members of his family or friends, as is the case in several of the portrait drawings. Dürer's independence of convention, his understanding of his sitters' characters as well as his own creative power, make each of these studies a work of art in its own right — though in an entirely different way from the portrait drawings of, say, Hans Holbein the Younger. The impression of finality is often explicitly emphasized by Dürer by adding a date, monogram and inscriptions (as on a painting).

Even the quick silver-point sketch of his friend Willibald Pirckheimer (W. 268) is consciously composed. The ugly but vigorous profile with the boxer's nose emphasizes only one side of Pirckheimer's character: the commander-in-chief who had led the Nuremberg contingent in the Swiss War of 1499 and had covered the retreat of the local troops after the attack on Nuremberg in 1502 by Margrave Casimir of Ansbach. However, the drawing also shows the patrician known for his many love affairs, who occasionally seems to have exhibited an interest in "handsome southern mercena-

104 *The Madonna with a Multitude of Animals.* 1503. Pen and wash. 32.1 × 24.3. Graphische Sammlung Albertina, Vienna. ▷

This drawing in the Albertina is difficult to interpret. The traditional iconographic type of the Madonna and Child on a grassy bank is combined with scenes of the angel bringing the glad tidings to the shepherds and the approach of the Magi from different directions, guided by the shining star on the central axis of the picture. The figure of Joseph is separated from the main group of figures, both as far as the composition and the conception of the event depicted are concerned. The picture therefore does not represent a specific moment in the life of Jesus or the Virgin. The strangest features of all, however, are the many animals and plants which can be seen, mostly in the foreground around the Virgin and Child. The chained fox and the two owls hiding in holes provide the key for an interpretation. The chained fox — like the long-tailed monkey (cf. Pl. 56) — is a symbol of evil, and the two nocturnal birds similarly represent the forces of darkness. Christ's appearance in this world has deprived them of their power. The glad tidings of His birth are given to all men, shepherds as well as kings, by the angel and the star; all hurry to adore the new ruler of the world. The various landscape formations represent the world; the animals similarly represent the whole animal kingdom, for there are not only mammals but also many birds and insects, as well as a crab symbolizing marine life, and a toad and a lizard symbolizing amphibians.

106 *Drummer and Piper* from a Wing of the *Jabach Altarpiece.*
1503–4. Oil. 94×51. Wallraf-Richartz-Museum, Cologne. ▷

In or around 1503 Dürer painted a "plague altarpiece" with wings; its
surviving parts are now in collections in Cologne, Frankfurt-on-Main and
Munich. The panels in Cologne and Frankfurt were originally the
outsides of the wings (cf. Pl. 105). Together they represent Job being
mocked by his wife and two musicians. The drummer has Dürer's
features. In the background, Job's flock is being driven away by robbers.

105 *Reconstruction of the Jabach Altarpiece.* Above: with wings closed.
Below: with wings open.

ries"[137] as well, and who added an ambiguous Greek inscription to his own portrait. In Dürer's monumental charcoal portrait based on this sketch, Pirckheimer's massive strength is played down in favour of the "choleric complexion" of the diplomat, the skilful speaker, the translator and Humanist polymath.

Pl. 96

An entirely different side of Dürer's talent is revealed in his drawings from nature, particularly in the studies of animals and plants made during these years. They were meant

Pl. 97
Pl. 98

107 *The Adoration of the Magi.* 1504. Oil. 100×114. Gallerie degli Uffizi, Florence.

In 1504 the Elector Frederick the Wise of Saxony, who had been Dürer's patron for some time, commissioned the artist to paint a small altarpiece showing the adoration of the Magi; it remained in the palace church of Wittenberg until the seventeenth century. The painting is the first classical composition by a German painter. Dürer himself must have sensed that this picture represented a special achievement, since he repeated the composition, with slight alterations, in a later drawing.

108 *The Adoration of the Magi.* Detail of Pl. 107. ▷

grass.[138] The charm of Dürer's compositions from the time before his second journey to Italy is partly based on the element of vitality introduced by such nature studies.

Plants and animals are not optional additions to works; they are always of an allegorical or symbolic significance related to the subject matter. In the engraving of *Adam and Eve,* for instance, the animals symbolize the four temperaments of future mankind. The pen and wash drawing of the *Madonna with a Multitude of Animals* symbolizes Christ's all-embracing rule over creation, comprised of animals and plants as well as human beings. In Dürer's largest engraving, *St. Eustace,* animals and many kinds of plants also play an important role. But here they are an essential component of the legend itself, and their symbolic significance is therefore emphasized. In contrast to these works, which are usually very ambitious in both subject matter and composition, Dürer also designed a group of exclusively religious woodcuts, which he aptly termed "simple wood-work".[139] These consist of eleven sheets showing either single figures or groups of two or three saints.

During the years leading up to his masterpieces of 1504–5, Dürer paid constant attention to intellectual achievements in Italy: the theoretical principles developed there, Jacopo de' Barbari's painting style, reflected in the paintings of *The Virgin and Child* (A. 71) and *Salvator mundi* (A. 83), and the ideas of Florentine Neoplatonic philosophy. The *Jabach Altarpiece,* painted for Frederick the Wise, is a prime example of applied Platonic ideology. On the outside of the wings is a depiction of Job's wife throwing water at her long-suffering husband while a piper and a drummer play a tune. This is a scene which no artist before Dürer had illustrated, and he—or his advisers—clearly adopted a legend about Socrates, known since late classical times, and transferred it to the long-suffering Job of the Old Testament.[140] Only an artist who knew about Ficino's comparison between the pious Hebrew and the

(margin references: Pl. 87, Pl. 104, Pl. 110, Pl. 105)

109 *Coat of Arms of Vanitas.* 1503. Engraving. 22 × 15.9. Kupferstichkabinett SMPK, Berlin.

The subject of this engraving is often linked with an illness which Dürer suffered from in 1503, and called "The Coat of Arms of Death". But it is actually an allegory of the transitoriness of life. The effect of the engraving is essentially based on two things: the balanced, ornamental composition, and the superbly rendered surface textures of the various objects shown. It is Dürer's first dated engraving. The female figure was engraved after the drawing of Pl. 97.

Pl. 100 for future use in other works but are masterly renderings of
Pl. 102 surface textures, as can be seen in the study of *The Hare* and *The Large Piece of Turf.* Dürer's ability to put the same intensive effort as was required for a portrait or a large composition into the depiction of an apparently insignificant object raises these works far above the level of realistic nature studies. They seem to exude something of the spirit of Ficino and are reminiscent of his description in *Theologia Platonica* of how Apelles painted a field or flowers and

110 *St. Eustace.* 1500–2. Engraving. 35.7 × 26. Kupferstichkabinett SMPK, Berlin. ▷

St. Eustace is Dürer's largest engraving. A multitude of single features is brought together in an impressive composition which successfully conveys the stillness of the miraculous event. Unfortunately this effect is slightly marred by the dogs lined up in the foreground as if on a page from a pattern-book. The ground itself is shown in rare detail; the plants around the tree in particular remind one that Dürer did his separate studies of plants and animals (Pls. 98, 100, 102) at the same time. The engraved lines are extraordinarily fine and regular, yet follow the outlines and curves of shapes in a supple way and establish a richly varied network of light and dark.

heathen philosopher could conceive of drawing this parallel between Job and Socrates. Job's wife, rather a minor figure in the Bible and in Christian iconography from early times onwards, becomes the embodiment of female spite in Dürer's version of the scene. She needed a counterbalance, and in a Christian altarpiece this could only be provided by the Virgin Mary who presumably was the central figure of the inside panels.[141]

Pl. 107   The *Adoration of the Magi,* painted in 1504 for Frederick of Saxony, marks a peak in Dürer's painting and is comparable to *Adam and Eve* among the engravings and the *Green Passion* among the drawings. The picture has rightly been called "the first absolutely clear painting in German art".[142] Dürer achieved a perfect compositional balance in which the

111   *King Death on Horseback.* 1505. Charcoal. 21×26.6. Department of Prints and Drawings, British Museum, London.

This quickly, yet unhesitatingly sketched charcoal drawing of Death riding along is one of the most moving *memento mori* representations in art. Dürer may have been driven to draw this haunting image by a recurrence of the plague in Nuremberg in the summer or early autumn of 1505 (cf. Pl. 99).

shapes and colours of the landscape, the architectural ruins and figures in the background are a harmonious foil to the group of figures in the foreground.[143] Dürer's theoretical study of the proportions of the human figure and of horses and of the construction of perspective (which is often underestimated by art historians only interested in stylistic developments) played an important part in making this painting a composition of almost classical balance.

Dürer's steady development towards artistic maturity which had begun in 1500 was suddenly interrupted in the summer of 1505 by a new outbreak of the plague. He was working on a winged altarpiece, showing the half-length figure of the *Salvator mundi* on the centre panel (A. 83) and two standing saints on the wings (A. 84, 85). It remained unfinished as he left town, fearing the epidemic.

Pl. 111 Before he left he made a quick charcoal sketch of *King Death,* a moving expression of his stark horror at the ele-

mental force of the plague's random killing. But the recurrence of the plague alone does not explain this drawing; rather, death and mortality were a central preoccupation of both the ordinary man and the artist of the time. From his stay in Basle onwards Dürer repeatedly took up and reformulated these two themes; whether he depicted the *Joys of the World* (cf. p. 77) or the *Walk* where Death lies in wait Pl. 53 behind a tree, he continually found new and striking ways of presenting his idea. The allegory of mortality is conveyed in a particularly impressive manner in Dürer's first dated engraving, *The Coat of Arms with a Skull* of 1503.[144] Pl. 109

VI. Italy: 1505–7

Venice · Bologna · Florence · Rome

In the autumn of 1505 many inhabitants of Nuremberg were driven out of the city by the plague, as they had been during the late summer of 1494. The situation was the same as it had been eleven years earlier: Dürer had reached a point in his career where occasional contacts with outside developments (cf. p. 48) were no longer sufficient for him to solve the artistic and theoretical problems which occupied him. Only direct contact with Italian artists and scholars could give him the support he needed. Dürer once again seized the opportunity and set out for the south, leaving his wife, mother and fifteen-year-old brother Hans—who trained as a painter under him—behind in Nuremberg. It is very likely that he stopped at Augsburg and drew portraits of the brothers Ulrich and Georg Fugger. It is even possible that he was commissioned there to paint a picture for the altar of the German congregation at the church of S. Bartolomeo in Venice. Dürer probably went on by way of Salzburg and Carinthia where he wanted to see a classical statue of a youth which had just been discovered.[145] And it may have been there that he drew the *Peasant Woman from the Windische Mark.*

Pl. 112

We know a great deal about Dürer's second stay in Venice from letters he wrote to his friend Pirckheimer during the eighteen months he was away.[146] Dürer was not unknown in Venice; here as elsewhere his graphic work had made him famous. In fact, it was so assiduously copied by local artists that Dürer complained in one of his letters that on the one hand the painters "copied his things", yet on the other, maintained that he was not "classical" in his art.[147] Indeed, he does not seem to have got on well at first with his Venetian colleagues, with the exception of old Giovanni Bellini. He was warned of possible attempts by other painters to poison him; he was also called in front of the *Signoria* three times and forced to pay four ducats into their guild funds, because he wanted to work in their city.[148] Dürer in his turn had gone before the court to lodge a complaint against Marcantonio Raimondi who had not only copied his engravings and woodcuts, but had added Dürer's monogram as well. This complaint may be regarded as the first lawsuit in history concerning copyright. The court decision did not bar the young Italian engraver from copying, but he was forbidden to use Dürer's monogram on his copies.[149]

Dürer appears to have taken most of his money with him when he left Nuremberg; as a result he worried about the family he left behind. In letters he repeatedly asked his friend Pirckheimer to provide financial help for his family. He even solicitously asked him to ensure that his brother was employed in Wolgemut's workshop while he, Dürer, was away. In return, Dürer tried to satisfy Pirckheimer's wishes concerning Oriental carpets, new publications of printed books in Greek, pictures, precious stones, ornamental feathers and paper. Apart from the financial problems at home and his strained relationship with the local painters, Dürer seems to have led an unconstrained and pleasant life in Venice. At all events he felt like a gentleman[150] who could afford to live at Peter Pender's inn near S. Bartolomeo, where German princes customarily took lodgings.[151] When work on his large altarpiece was finished he even tried to take dancing lessons.[152] During these months he was in constant contact with the Nuremberg merchants working in Venice and also succeeded in establishing relations with the Venetian nobility.[153] His moment of supreme social and artistic recognition came when Doge Leonardo Loredan and the Patriarch Antonio Suriano came to his workshop to look at the painting *Feast of the Rose Garlands*, which was almost completed. On the same occasion he was reputedly offered 200 florins annually to enter the service of the Venetian state.[154] Such treatment explains Dürer's heartfelt sigh in his last letter from Venice: "O how I shall yearn for the sun. Here I am a gentleman, at home a parasite."[155]

This statement very clearly reveals the difference in the way artists were regarded north and south of the Alps. At home in Nuremberg, Dürer was an "honest" artisan, but in spite of his growing wealth he remained among the "poor", for he had to live by the labour of his own hands and could not therefore become a member of the ruling patriciate.[156] In Italy, on the other hand, where the families of many of the rulers had risen to princely power from humble social beginnings, artists might not have been treated quite as equals, but many of their peculiarities were regarded with indulgence, and their creative power was freely acknowledged and respected. In Nuremberg a social gap separated Dürer, as the son of a skilled artisan, from the sons of higher

families, even if he had known them from childhood or gone to school with them. Dürer, who was well aware of his own achievements, found this oppressive. In Venice there were no comparable distinctions.

The high esteem in which his art was held in Venice is reflected in the great number of requests for pictures he received. To his regret he had to turn down commissions amounting to "about 200 ducats" (c. 325 florins),[157] since his work on *Feast of the Rose Garlands,* for which he was to Pl. 114 get 110 florins, demanded all his time. But he had totally underestimated the time the picture would take. The panel was supposed to be installed on the altar one month after Easter, in mid-May.[158] But a rash on his hands, which often afflicts painters because they handle turpentine and similar substances, stopped him from working. He did not start on the design and the preliminary studies until the beginning of February, 1506, but hoped none the less to finish the work by Whitsuntide, at the beginning of June.[159] But not until 23 September did he write to Pirckheimer that the painting was completed.

Dürer's picture has been called *Feast of the Rose Garlands* Pls. 114–15 since the nineteenth century, although this festival was only introduced in 1716 and cannot therefore be the theme of Dürer's painting. Even though the title is incorrect, it suits the composition very well, because a picture has rarely managed to convey such an atmosphere of festivity by means of formal arrangement and colour. The serene, festive mood that emanates from the finely balanced colours (and can still be felt today in spite of damage to the paint) may without exaggeration be interpreted as an expression of the serenity, which at times borders on exuberance, that is found in Dürer's letters from Venice. The composition is reminiscent of Stephan Lochner's *Adoration of the Magi* in the council chapel in Cologne; it is dominated in the foreground by the enthroned Madonna and Child and the large kneeling figures of the pope and emperor. These figures are arranged in a triangle according to a High Renaissance pattern; the remaining lesser figures are grouped around them more or less symmetrically, ecclesiastics to the left, laymen to the right. The two supreme representatives of Christianity, both members of the Brotherhood of the

112 *Peasant Woman from the Windische Mark.* 1505. Pen. 39×27. Department of Prints and Drawings, British Museum, London.

Dürer's inscription, *una vilana windisch,* implies that the sitter was a woman from the Windische Mark, an area extending on both sides of the Karawanken (eastern Alps) with inhabitants of mixed Italian-Slav descent. There is some evidence that Dürer travelled to Venice in 1505 via Carinthia and the Friuli region. A second drawing on parchment is in a private collection in Italy.

113 *Portrait of a Young Venetian Woman.* 1505. Oil. 32.5×24.5. Kunsthistorisches Museum, Vienna.   ▷

This painting and that of the *Fürlegerin* (Pl. 63) are Dürer's best female portraits. The portrait of the young Venetian woman is dated 1505 and was Dürer's first work after his arrival in Venice. It is unfinished, as the bow and the unmodelled sleeve on the left show.

123

114 *Feast of the Rose Garlands*. 1506. Oil. 162 × 194.5. Národni Galeri, Prague.

115 Detail of Pl. 114. ▷

This painting shows the Virgin Mary, the Christ Child and St. Dominic distributing rose garlands to the Christian world. On the left the clerics kneel behind the Pope; on the right the laity behind the Emperor Maximilian. The man in the blue cloak immediately behind the Emperor is probably Georg Fugger, the donor of the altarpiece. On the extreme right the artist can be seen holding a sheet of paper bearing a Latin inscription and his signature. Several other figures are portraits of real people, but of the many only Burkhard von Speyer (seen on the left) can be identified with reasonable certainty, as another portrait of him by Dürer exists. The striking features of a man on the extreme right also draw the observer's attention. He holds an angle iron in his hand, and is therefore generally thought to represent the architect Hieronymus of Augsburg.

Rosary founded in Cologne in 1475, are receiving rose garlands from the hands of the Madonna and the infant Jesus. Other believers are being given rose garlands by St. Dominic, founder of the rosary prayer, and by small angels hovering in the air; the garlands symbolize the avowal of a willingly undertaken imitation of Christ by those who receive them. The individuality of some of the faces, among

them those of the German King Maximilian and members of the German community in Venice as well as that of the artist himself,[160] must have been particularly impressive to contemporary viewers.

As soon as Dürer had finished this important work, which convinced even his ill-disposed Venetian colleagues of his ability as a painter,[161] he was again inundated with commissions for portraits. Late in 1505 he had painted the portrait Pl. 113 of a young Venetian woman. He now painted two male por-

116 *St. Dominic.* 1506. Brush on blue paper. 41.6×28.8. Graphische Sammlung Albertina, Vienna.

Dürer was commissioned to paint an altarpiece for S. Bartolomeo in Venice, the church of the German community. He may have received this commission even before he reached Venice, possibly during a stay in Augsburg. He made a large number of individual studies for the composition. Most of these studies, including that of St. Dominic, are executed in a technique commonly used in Venice: that of black and white brush drawings on blue paper.

traits (A. 96–8) and one female (A. 95) within the space of a month. Dürer himself estimated that he had to refuse commissions worth approximately 2500 florins.[162] It is very likely that many wanted their likenesses painted by the German master because they had seen his *Feast of the Rose Garlands* and his excellent portraits. Apart from commissioned work, Dürer also painted the *Madonna with the* Pl. 117 *Siskin* which he later took back with him to Nuremberg. He had also made a number of preliminary studies for a second composition. These studies, like most of his Venice drawings, were executed in black-and-white washes on blue Venetian paper. This was a Venetian technique which he handled with perfect ease, far surpassing its inventors. In spite of his large work-load in Venice, Dürer still found time to continue his studies of the proportions of the human body. The beautiful *Female Nude seen from the Back* on Pl. 122 blue paper reflects such theoretical studies, as do a number of studies dated 1506 which Dürer may have done with the two paintings of *Adam* and *Eve* of 1507 already in mind. Pls. 123–4

Dürer, always eager for new experiences,[163] wrote to Pirckheimer on 18 August 1506 that he planned to join the retinue of King Maximilian, who was going to Rome in the autumn to attend the coronation of the emperor.[164] Dürer's decision was based not merely on a wish to be present at this solemn occasion, nor on his understandable interest in acquainting himself with classical art in Rome, nor on the desire to go as a pilgrim and procure indulgences in the Eternal City. Rather, he seems to have planned this journey primarily for financial reasons. He says in his diary, in connection with other financial losses: "And someone has died in Rome which means that I have lost my assets. Moreover, being in the thirteenth year of my marriage, I have paid a large debt which I incurred in Venice."[165] As the thirteenth year of Dürer's marriage extended from July, 1506 to July, 1507, his intended journey to Rome must have been connected with the death of the person mentioned,

117 *The Madonna with the Siskin.* 1506. Oil. 91×76. Gemäldegalerie SMPK, Berlin. ▷

This painting in Berlin is closely related stylistically to *Feast of the Rose Garlands* and was probably painted at the same time or very shortly afterwards. The subject, as well as the composition and colours, make it Dürer's most Italianate picture. The Madonna receives a bunch of lilies of the valley *(convallaria maialis)* from the infant St. John the Baptist; these are a symbol of her virginity. She has closed the book containing the prophecy of the incarnation of the Redeemer, since it has been fulfilled by the birth of Christ. Christ will redeem the souls of sinful mankind, symbolized by the siskin, through His death on the Cross, which is alluded to by the staff in the shape of a cross held by the small angel.

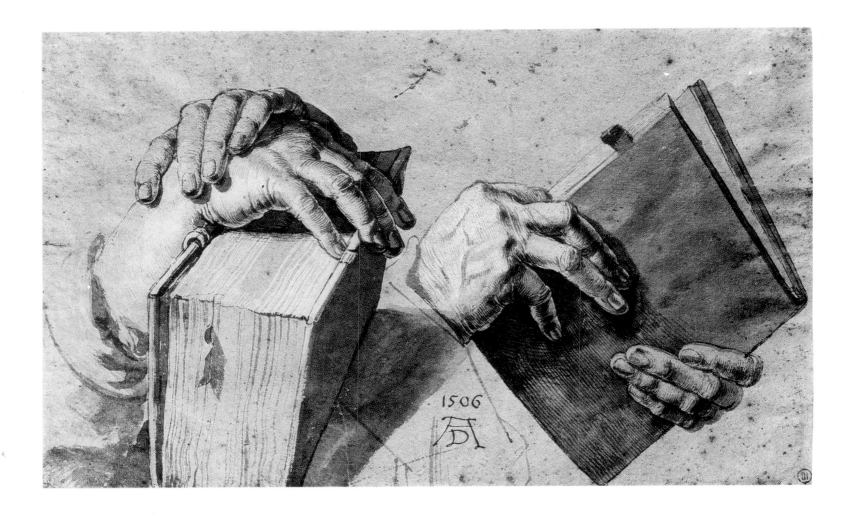

who had presumably sold graphic works there for him.[166] There had been an outbreak of the plague in Rome during the summer of 1506, in which a number of Germans had died.[167]

Dürer's plan to join the king's retinue had to be abandoned as the Venetians would not allow Maximilian to cross their territory with an army.[168] But Dürer did not give up his plans altogether, and in mid-October, after he had finished his work in Venice, he wrote to Pirckheimer that in about ten days' time he would ride to Bologna because someone there had agreed to teach him "the secret of perspective".[169] He did in fact go to Bologna even though French troops were advancing on the city from the north and an army under Pope Julius II from the south. They took the city on 10 November. In Bologna the German artist was given a ceremonial reception by the local painters who, with southern exuberance, hailed him as the new Apelles, and claimed that now that they had seen him they could die with an easier mind. We know this from the eye-witness account of Dürer's young compatriot, Christoph Scheurl.[170]

The name of the mathematician, Fra Luca Pacioli, is often mentioned in connection with the instruction in perspective Dürer had hoped to obtain. Pacioli was a fellow country-man, a pupil of Piero della Francesca and friend of Leonardo. He had been active in Florence for some time when Dürer came to Bologna. It is not known whether Dürer was instructed by Scipione del Ferro who taught mathematics in Bologna from 1496 to 1526,[171] or whether he went to see Pacioli in Florence. In fact, there is doubt as to whether he received any instruction at all, for there is no hint of a more thorough knowledge of perspective in his work in the years before 1510.[172] On the evidence of

119 *Christ among the Doctors* (Opus quinque dierum). 1506. Oil. 65 × 80. Thyssen-Bornemisza Collection, Lugano-Castagnola.

This strange painting by Dürer consists almost exclusively of heads, hands and books. At some unknown period owners must have considered the format of the panel too narrow for the multitude of figures represented, and added a strip of wood a few centimetres wide at the top; however, this strip was removed some years ago. The piece of paper protruding like a bookmarker from the book on the left bears the remnants of an originally more extensive signature (cf. p. 132). It contained a reference to the picture having been painted in Rome; this has been confirmed by a drawing owned by a Paris gallery in 1940, and by a second picture which appeared at a Berlin auction in 1978 which shows the original state before the strip was added at the top.

120 *Portrait of a Young Man.* 1507. Oil. 35 × 29. Kunsthistorisches Museum, Vienna. ▷

121 *Vanitas* (*verso* of Pl. 120). ▷▷

This painted panel showing a young man on the front and an ugly old woman on the back was painted early in 1507 and is Dürer's last work executed in Venice. The witch-like old hag was formerly thought to be an allegory of avarice, because she holds a sack of money, and popular speculation had it that Dürer painted this figure on the back because his patron proved to be stingy when it came to paying. However, this image of promiscuity and wastefulness represents the futility of all human actions (Vanitas).

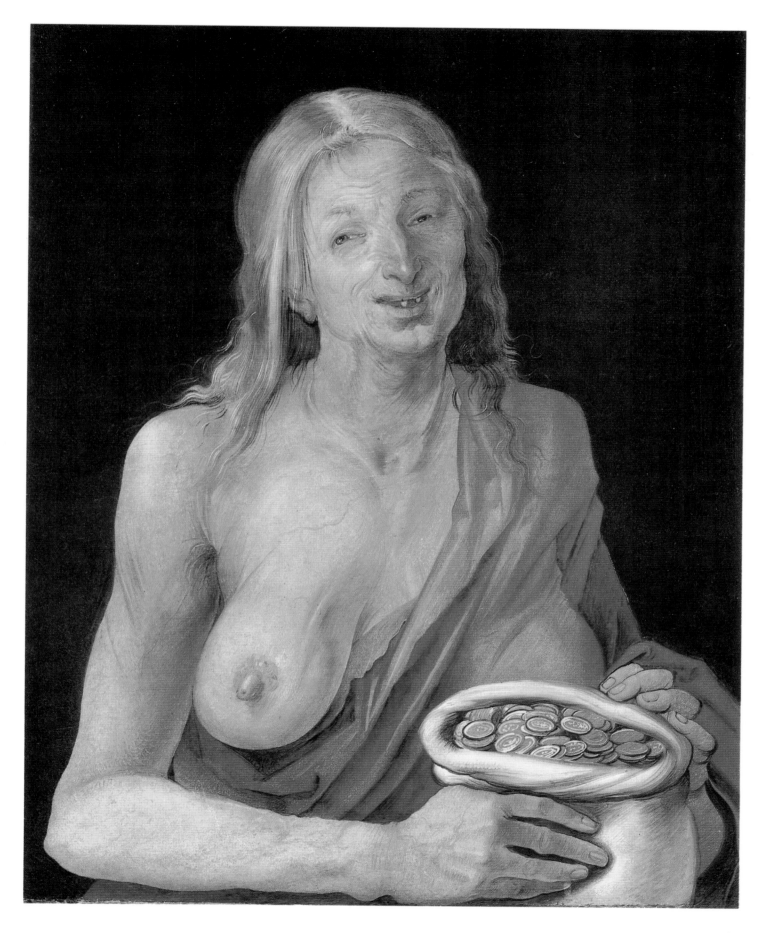

existing drawings and sketches, some of them with inscriptions in Bolognese dialect, these lessons dealt mainly with problems in architecture and geometry,[173] but not with perspective.[174]

Dürer then rode on south and stayed in Florence for a short time. It must have been there that he first saw the works of Leonardo and the young Raphael which had such a decisive influence on his own work. Leonardo was then in Milan, but his pupils and his workshop remained in Florence. Dürer's tracings of studies of human anatomy by Leonardo were presumably made at this time.[175] And it is almost certain that he also saw caricatures by Leonardo, because there is a definite echo of them in his painting *Christ among the Doctors,* completed shortly afterwards. Raphael's altarpiece of the coronation of the Virgin which he painted in about 1503 for S. Francesco in Perugia had a great impact on Dürer. This is clearly reflected in the altarpiece he painted for Jakob Heller in 1508–9.[176]

Although winter was closing in, Dürer seems to have gone on to Rome[177] to settle business concerns arising from the death of his agent. Rome, after the schism, was a revived but by no means lively city, and no match for Florence, let alone Venice. The overall area of the city was still enclosed by a wall nearly nineteen km long which, although partially rebuilt, had originally been constructed in the third century. The city itself had been naturally divided by the Tiber into three distinct settlements: city life had its centre in an area between river and forum which was enclosed by a bend of the Tiber; on the opposite bank was Trastevere, inhabited predominantly by artisans; north of it was the Borgo, which had its own wall, the location of St. Peter's and the Vatican, where the popes had resided since 1420. These three settlements occupied scarcely a quarter of the area of the classical city of Rome. The remaining land, which was covered with high heaps of rubble, was taken up by vineyards and gardens of the citizens of Rome. In Dürer's time the former capital of the Imperium Romanum had slightly fewer inhabitants than Nuremberg.

The popes and high-ranking clerics as well as affluent merchants had recently made attempts to revive Rome's splendour, but their large new palaces served only to emphasize the miserable state of the majority of mediæval houses. The best artists in the country had been summoned to Rome to design these new buildings and their decorations, because there were only a few, mostly mediocre, artists in the city itself. But the classic period of the revived Eternal City had not yet begun. It is true that in 1506 Bramante had finished his plans for the new basilica of St. Peter,

but when Dürer arrived in Rome neither Bramante's nephew, the young Raphael from Urbino, nor Michelangelo from Florence had created those large fresco cycles which were to become the supreme achievement of a new era in art.

The classical sculptures which had been excavated up to that time usually found their way into the palaces of prelates and aristocrats. A copy of the Hercules Lysippus was in the palazzo of Cardinal Francesco Piccolomini,[178] and a statue of Apollo, excavated in the late fifteenth century, in the newly erected Belvedere on the Vatican Hill in 1503. Apart from the statues of the Dioscuri on the Monte Cavallo, which were difficult to remove because of their enormous size, almost all remnants of classical Roman statues had disappeared from the streets and squares of Rome. It is therefore not surprising that there are hardly any echoes of classical art in Dürer's later works.

The forum, once the centre of the Roman Empire, had become a pasture for cattle. Its western perimeter was dominated by two huge towers built around 1200, the *Torre delle Milizie* and the *Torre dei Conti.* Petrarch had praised the *Torre dei Conti* as a truly miraculous work, and the two imposing buildings seem to have made a lasting impression on Dürer. When he was working on designs for the tombs of Georg and Ulrich Fugger in 1510, he added one of the towers and the surrounding buildings in the background of one of the drawings. There are other reminders of Rome in these drawings. The relief designs closely echo the composition of early Renaissance tombs which Dürer could have seen only in Rome. Particularly the principal church of the Dominican Order, S. Maria sopra Minerva near the Pantheon, had many fine examples of such tombs.[179]

The main testimony to Dürer's stay in Rome is his painting *Christ among the Doctors,* which he proudly signed: *1506/A.D./F.ROMAE/opus quinque dierum.* The reference to five days can only apply to the execution of the painting; Dürer must have planned the composition and made a number of studies while he was still in Venice. The panel is one of the principal examples of the category of painting which Dürer called "common painting".[180]

Dürer appears to have been back in Venice early in 1507 at the latest, because he painted another portrait, that of a

122 *Female Nude Seen from the Back.* 1506. Brush on blue paper. 38.1 × 22.3. Kupferstichkabinett SMPK, Berlin.   ▷

Dürer showed a great interest in the problem of the ideal human body on both his first and second visit to Venice. This drawing on blue Venetian paper of a female nude seen from the back, presumably drawn from a living model, testifies to this interest.

132

Pls. 120–1 *Young Man* with a repulsive figure of *Vanitas* on the back, before he set off for Nuremberg. He seems to have left Venice in early February, because he passed Augsburg by the middle of the month.[181] The routes across the Alps, which were not without danger even in summer when the weather was good, were hazardous during winter, even though roads and passes were kept as free of snow as possible by well-organized groups of local people.[182] Travellers usually took eight to ten days to cover the 700-kilometre route from Venice to Nuremberg, but during winter it would have taken about two weeks, so that Dürer presumably arrived back in his home town around 20 February.

VII. Maturity: 1507–12

Principal Paintings · Civic Honours · Manual on Painting

Dürer's Nuremberg workshop had not been entirely idle while he was in Italy. Before Dürer's departure, the Elector Frederick the Wise, Dürer's patron for many years, had commissioned a winged altarpiece showing a Crucifixion and a multitude of figures. Before leaving, Dürer had made careful brush designs on green primed paper for the central panel and the four wings (W. 320–323); but had left the actual execution to Hans Schäufelein, the oldest member of his workshop. Hans von Kulmbach and Hans Baldung also seem to have remained in the workshop for some time. Only Dürer's brother Hans, whom he would have liked to have taken to Italy, was sent to Michael Wolgemut to continue his training.[183]

Dürer's neighbour, Sebald Schreyer, who had fled to Schwäbisch-Gmünd with his wife in 1505 because of the plague, may also have commissioned an extensive altarpiece from Dürer's workshop while the master was away.[184] This would explain why Schreyer paid Dürer seven florins "for his default" early in 1508 and gave gifts to Dürer's wife Agnes and one of his journeymen as well.[185] The existing parts of the altarpiece, which Schreyer donated to the principal church of Schwäbisch-Gmünd, do not show Dürer's hand, however. The panels were presumably painted by the same journeyman who was to later help Dürer on the *Heller Altarpiece*.[186]

Another indication that the workshop continued to function on a limited scale is that Dürer's wife Agnes went to the Easter fair at Frankfurt/Main in 1506 to sell her husband's woodcuts and engravings.[187] Dürer's mother also sold his graphic work at the fair, held every year in Nuremberg at the time when the sacred relics were on public display. These sales may have helped to improve the family's financial situation. However, Dürer also seems to have brought back a considerable sum of money earned in Italy, even though he had always complained about his lack of fortune. On 8 May 1507 he was able to cancel the yearly mortgage of four florins on the house he had inherited from his father by making one single payment of 116 florins.[188]

It is not known when Dürer received his next major commissions; scholars generally believe that the small portrait of a girl (A. 102, in Berlin), painted in 1507, was an uncommissioned work. However, the two Madrid pictures of *Adam* and *Eve*, also dated 1507, seem to have been commissioned. It has sometimes been suggested that Dürer painted these panels for the Nuremberg council as part of a decorative scheme for the town hall,[189] but there is no adequate proof of this. A report of 1516 by the Bohemian Humanist Jan Dubravius, on the other hand, may well refer to the Madrid panels. It states that a few years before, he had seen a panel of Adam and Eve painted by Dürer in the possession of Bishop Johann V of Breslau. Bishop Johann V (1466–1520), a member of the Thurzo family from Zips, was related by marriage (through his brother Georg who died in 1521) to the Fugger family. Johann Thurzo, an enlightened patron of the arts and of Humanist studies,[190] bought a picture of the Virgin from Dürer in 1508, but it was not until 1511 that he arranged for payment to be made through Wolfgang Hoffmann, the Nuremberg factor of the Fugger family.[191] If it was really Johann Thurzo who commissioned Dürer to paint the Adam and Eve panels, he must have ordered them in 1506 at the latest (as has already been mentioned) while Dürer was still in Italy. However, the panels must not have been executed until early in 1507 in Nuremberg. If, in spite of its rich variety of plants and animals, the engraving of 1504 appears a little like an illustration from a pattern-book, in the later panels Dürer succeeded, despite the monochrome background, in depicting a couple full of life and beauty, who bear no trace of the system of proportions on which they are constructed. The assimilation of Italian influences is hardly noticeable.[192]

Dürer appears to have received two other commissions while he was still at work on these two panels. The execu-

Pls. 123–

Pl. 87

tion of these commissions took over two years of such intensive work—only interrupted by a fever in 1507[193]—that he could undertake little else. The first patron seems once again to have been the Elector of Saxony. Despite having Lucas Cranach in his service, he ordered a picture from Dürer for the relic chamber of the palace church in Wittenberg. (Cranach had become the Elector's highly-paid court painter around 1505.) At about the same time, Jakob Heller of Frankfurt/Main appears to have given Dürer a commission for an extensive altarpiece.[194] This is confirmed by the fact that in August, 1507 Dürer apologized to him for not having begun work because he had not yet finished his painting for the Elector.[195] The painting to which he referred, a composition with a multitude of small figures and a richly varied landscape, represents the martyrdom of ten thousand Christian soldiers together with their leader Achatius on Mount Ararat. It occupied the artist well into 1508. On hearing that Konrad Celtis, a friend of the Elector as well as of Dürer, had died in Vienna on 2 February 1508, Dürer was able to insert the figure of his friend beside his own in the painting. The Humanist and the artist, who represent platonic friendship as described by Ficino,[196] are shown contemplating the sufferings of the martyrs. The two figures fit into the context of the picture only if they are interpreted in this manner. The many scenes of martyrdom show that Dürer had been inspired by the iconography of works he had seen on his travels through the Lower Rhine region.[197]

While Dürer was completing the panel for Frederick the Wise, Jakob Heller urged him to start work on his altarpiece. Since there is a drawing of 1503 showing the subject of the centre panel, a coronation of the Virgin, and Heller was becoming impatient, some scholars believe that Dürer received the commission before his second journey to Italy.[198] But the drawing of 1503 is more likely to have been connected with the woodcuts for the *Life of the Virgin,* or it might have been a design for the embroidery of a cope.[199] Dürer delegated work on the wings of the *Heller Altarpiece* (A. 111–14) entirely, or at least predominantly, to journeymen whose names are not known, but who must have been in the workshop even before Dürer's return to Nuremberg. He himself painted the centre panel showing the coronation of the Virgin and took great pains with the composition as well as the execution. It is a handsome, unified composition reminiscent of Italian High Renaissance art. Dürer was justly proud of his achievement and incorporated a full-length portrait of himself in the middle ground, holding a tablet with an extensive inscription and his signature. As in the *Adam* and *Eve* panels and the *Martyrdom of the Ten*

123–4 *Adam* and *Eve.* 1507. Oil. 209×83 each. Museo del Prado, Madrid. ▷

Dürer's studies of the proportions of the human body, resumed in Italy and continued after his return to Nuremberg, find artistic expression (as they had done in 1504) in a representation of Adam and Eve. In contrast to the earlier work, Dürer now created two panels, each showing one life-size figure. Both figures are again influenced by Italian art. Dürer must have started work on these panels shortly after his return.

Thousand, Dürer signed himself "alemanus", meaning Albrecht Dürer the German. He might have come across this unusual term in Celtis's writings or in Italy where Germans were sometimes called "Alemani", in imitation of the French term. Dürer apparently only used this version of his signature on pictures for patrons who did not live in Nuremberg, which also contradicts the argument that the *Adam* and *Eve* were originally meant for the Nuremberg town hall.

After lengthy negotiation by letter, Dürer finally succeeded in getting Heller, the rich Frankfurt merchant, to pay him 200 florins for his altarpiece, rather than 130 florins as had originally been agreed. This was still a modest price for this extensive work, compared with the 280 florins which Frederick the Wise had paid for his much smaller panel. In a letter of 26 August 1509, Dürer told Jakob Heller that he had finally delivered the carefully packed altar panels to Hans Imhoff who would be responsible for their transport to Frankfurt. He also gave instructions on how to erect the work so as to minimize damage.

Dürer's next important commission came in 1508 from Matthäus Landauer, a nephew of Sebald Schreyer, who had made his money in the metal trade. Landauer ordered an altarpiece for the chapel of All Saints at a refuge for old artisans which he had founded. Dürer immediately produced a design which, even at that stage, incorporated all Pl. 130

125 *The Martyrdom of the Ten Thousand Christians.* 1508. Oil. 99×87. Kunsthistorisches Museum, Vienna. See p. 138.

126 Detail of Pl. 125. See p. 139.

Shortly after his return from the south Dürer was commissioned by the Elector Frederick the Wise of Saxony, who had been his patron many times before, to paint a picture of the martyrdom of the ten thousand Christians on Mount Ararat. The picture was to be hung in the relic chamber of the palace church in Wittenberg which contained a huge collection of relics amassed by the prince, including some of the ten thousand martyrs. In the centre of the picture are the figures of Dürer and Konrad Celtis (cf. Pl. 45) who had died in Vienna shortly before the painting was completed.

136

the major elements of the finished panel and frame of the painting *All Saints,* completed in 1511. Painting and frame form an iconographic as well as a pictorial unit. The Trinity around which the saints are crowded is shown as the "throne of grace", a favourite mode of representation since the twelfth century. It combines the Maiestas Domini with the Crucifixion. Cross and Maiestas — as is made clear in the sermon for Good Friday — symbolically refer to the Last Judgement, which is carved in the lunette of the frame in Dürer's design. The side of the damned is symbolized, as was common, by the mouth of Hell, while the side of the elect is represented by the sun instead of the more usual gates of Heaven. The sun may be interpreted as *sol iustitiae* or, as in Neoplatonic philosophy, as an image of God.[200]

Pl. 133 A small, delicately coloured picture of the *Virgin and Child* (now in Vienna) bears the date of 1512. The only

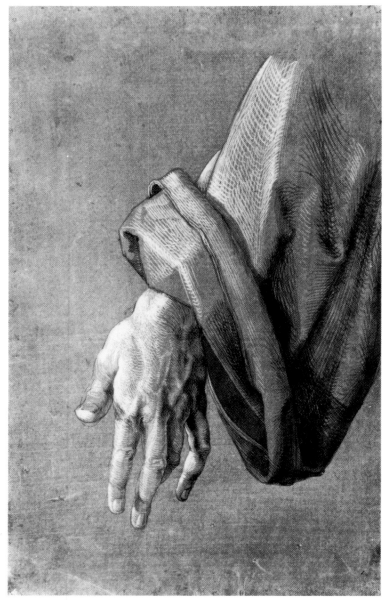

128 *Study of the Left Hand of an Apostle (Heller Altarpiece),* 1508. Brush on green primed paper. 31.7 × 19.8. Graphische Sammlung Albertina, Vienna.

127 *Study of Christ's Draperies (Heller Altarpiece).* 1508. Brush on green primed paper. 25.6 × 19.6. Cabinet des Dessins, Musée du Louvre, Paris.

129 Copy of the *Heller Altarpiece* by Jobst Harrich. C. 1614. Historisches Museum, Frankfurt-on-Main. ▷

The altarpiece painted for the Frankfurt merchant Jakob Heller was Dürer's main work during this period, but only the wings, which are painted on both sides, survive. The centre panel showing the coronation of the Virgin was destroyed in a fire in the Munich Residence in 1729. We have only Jobst Harrich's copy of 1614 to give us some impression of what this magnificent Italianate composition must have been like. Fortunately eighteen brush drawings, studies for the centre panel, survive in various collections. However, they can only give us an imperfect impression of the extreme care with which Dürer prepared his paintings. Apart from studies of the heads of the apostles he concentrated on draperies and hands. Almost all of these studies are dated 1508 and signed with Dürer's monogram.

140

142

◁ 130 Design for the *All Saints* painting *(Landauer Altarpiece)*. 1508. Pen and coloured washes. 39.1 × 26.3. Musée Condé, Chantilly.

Dürer appears to have designed the altarpiece, commissioned by Matthäus Landauer, while he was still working on the *Heller Altarpiece*. The new altarpiece was destined for the chapel of the old people's home which had been endowed by Landauer. This drawing in Chantilly, which is dated 1508, is no design in the true sense of the word, but rather a "presentation", a kind of *modello* which was shown to the patron so that he could comment on it. It shows how the whole completed work, including the frame, was to look. Picture and frame are essentially the same as in the completed altarpiece, but a number of details were changed, at times quite radically (cf. Pls. 131, 132).

documented commission the city of Nuremberg ever gave to Dürer also falls into the period from 1510 to 1512. It was Pl. 135 for two larger than life half-length figures of Charlemagne Pl. 136 and the Emperor Sigismund, intended as part of the decoration of the relic chamber in the Schopper house facing the market place. Every year on the Friday after Easter, scaffolding was erected in front of this building and from there the sacred treasures, i.e. the robes, insignia and relics used during the coronations of kings and emperors, were shown by bishops to the faithful. On the evening before this event the sacred relics were moved to the Schopper house from the church of the Hospital of the Holy Spirit and kept in the relic chamber under heavy guard. Dürer made several Pl. 134 studies of parts of the actual coronation robes for the picture of Charlemagne, while he seems to have modelled the figure of Sigismund on a contemporary portrait. The rigidly formal character of the two panels is somewhat softened by the animation of the faces.

Dürer's paintings of 1507 to 1512 fall into two distinct formal categories. The first includes paintings of average size Pls. 125, 130 showing a multitude of figures, such as *Martyrdom of the Ten Thousand* or *All Saints*, which mark the end of a stylistic phase in the artist's œuvre. In direct contrast are large paintings with one or more figures, beginning with the Pls. 123–4 *Adam* and *Eve* panels and the centre panel of the *Heller* Pls. 228–9 *Altarpiece* and the *Four Apostles*, which all reflect the style of the Italian High Renaissance. We know from Melanchthon[201] that Dürer himself was aware of this development from complex to simple pictures.

The financial situation of the Dürer family had become reasonably settled by the time Dürer returned home from Italy; in the ensuing year and a half it improved markedly. Deeds dated 14 June 1509 marked the completion of Pl. 137 Dürer's purchase of a house near the Tiergärtner gate which was part of the estate of the astronomer Bernhard Walther who had died in 1504.[202] The selling price was 275 florins,

and a month later Dürer paid another seventy-eight florins, one pound and four shillings to cancel a yearly mortgage.[203] Moreover, not only had Dürer's financial situation improved, but his social standing as well. He seems to have been an original member of a group of Humanists who regularly visited the patrician inn from 1497–8.[204] At Easter 1509 Dürer was even elected a *Genannter* of the Greater Council. This meant that he was respected enough to be considered a member of the upper level of the non-patrician burgher class. Furthermore, not only was he well-established and honoured at home, he was also famous in Italy. During these years, he was in contact with Raphael for instance, sending him in Rome his self-portrait painted on fine canvas,[205] while Raphael in turn sent a number of his studies to Nuremberg.

The relatively small number of woodcuts and engravings Dürer executed after his return from the south show how much his time was taken up by commissions for paintings. In 1507 he designed only one engraving (B. 14), and in 1508 four small, dated prints, including two compositions for the Pl. 139 *Engraved Passion*. Woodcuts of this period comprise *The Six Knots* (B. 140–5), based on Italian engravings, and two or three lesser prints. Dürer's output of graphic works remained very modest throughout 1509, the year he was working on the *Heller Altarpiece*. He did the engraving of a *Man of Sorrows* (B. 3), two woodcuts of *Christ before Herod* (B. 32) and *Christ Carrying the Cross* (B. 37) for the *Small Woodcut Passion*. A few of the undated designs for this cycle may also have been executed during this year.

131 *Landauer Altarpiece*. 1511. Oil. 144 × 131. Carved, painted and gilded frame. Kunsthistorisches Museum, Vienna. ▷

132 Detail of Pl. 131. ▷▷

In 1501 Matthäus Landauer, a nephew of Sebald Schreyer, who had become rich trading in ores, endowed an old people's home for twelve artisans impoverished through no fault of their own. This foundation naturally included a chapel; it was dedicated to All Saints. Landauer commissioned Albrecht Dürer to paint the *All Saints Altarpiece*. As the "presentation" of 1508 (Pl. 130) shows, Dürer designed the picture and the frame as a visual and iconographic unit. The frame acts like a gateway, above which the carved figure of Christ, the Judge of the World, sits enthroned; through this gateway the "community of the saints" can be seen above a sunny landscape, crowding round the Trinity. According to an inscription on the plinth of the frame the work was completed in 1511. When the picture was sold to the Emperor Rudolf II in 1585 the frame remained in Nuremberg; today it is kept in the Germanisches Nationalmuseum. The frame is carved in the complicated manner of the German Renaissance and contrasts with Dürer's classically simple forms.

With the exception of the *Knots,* these twenty or so graphic works all have a small format.

Pl. 131 The execution of the *Landauer Altarpiece* and the portraits of the two emperors does not appear to have taken nearly as much of Dürer's time as earlier paintings. From 1510 onwards he had enough time to turn to graphic works again. An artist like Dürer, whose imagination was "full of figures within" and who could always invent new compositions, found it unbearable to be tied down for years by a single commission for a painting. Dürer preferred graphic work, not because he rejected painting in general, but because he felt the need to give his imagination free rein. Only graphic techniques enabled him to give concrete expression to his manifold ideas, unhampered by the wishes of patrons and with relatively quick results.

The graphic works of 1510–12 show very clearly how Dürer was brimming with ideas, once free of large commissions for paintings. For instance, he designed many different exemplary versions of one of his central themes, Christ's Passion. In 1510 he completed the two large woodcut cycles
Pls. 140–1 started earlier: he made four designs for the *Large Passion*
Pl. 138 and two for the *Life of the Virgin.* Both cycles were published as books in 1511, supplemented by new title vignettes and Latin verses by the Benedictine monk Benedikt Schwalbe (Chelidonius) of the monastery of St. Egidius in Nuremberg, who had been educated in the Humanist tradition. The *Apocalypse,* too, was reprinted, after another woodcut had been added as the title-page (B. 60). Dürer, who published his own books, was the first German publisher to be granted a special printing privilege by the emperor which protected him from the publication of pirated editions of his works.[206]

While completing the large books Dürer also created the
Pls. 142–3 remaining thirty-five woodcuts for the *Small Passion* which was published in book form later in 1511, similarly
Pl. 144 accompanied by Chelidonius's verses. Another fourteen woodcuts, including masterpieces like the *Mass of St.*
Pl. 145 *Gregory* (B. 123) and the *Trinity,* testify to the artist's inexhaustible creative imagination and capacity for work.

Compared to the woodcuts, the number of engravings at first remained small. *Christ on the Cross* from the *Engraved Passion* (B. 13) and *Virgin with the Pear* (B. 41) are dated 1511. In 1512 Dürer designed the remaining ten engravings
Pls. 146–7 for the *Passion* cycle. His renewed interest in graphic work is also reflected in experiments with dry-point etching, a technique he had not previously used. However, the soft, painterly effect produced with the dry point does not seem to have satisfied Dürer, for he gave up the technique after

three attempts, of which *St. Jerome* is the most important. It
Pl. 149 is unfortunate that Dürer turned away from dry-point etching so quickly without having fully explored its possibilities. This technique, rather than traditional woodcut and engraving, would have made it easier for him to convey light effects, which was one of his foremost aims during this period, especially in the graphic works.

Dürer's attempts to represent natural or supernatural light effects are so marked in the graphic works of these years that Panofsky even thought he detected the influence of Grünewald, an artist diametrically opposed to Dürer.[207] At about this time Master Mathis painted two standing wings as a supplement to the *Heller Altarpiece* and also, for the same patron, a *Transfiguration* which was much admired for its light effects. However there is nothing to indicate that Dürer knew Grünewald or had seen any of his paintings before 1520. Even when Dürer stayed in Frankfurt/Main in 1520, on his way to the Netherlands, he mentioned neither the name nor the works of Master Mathis. The "luminarist" art of both painters must be seen rather as a general stylistic phenomenon of the time, particularly since Albrecht Altdorfer was also simultaneously pursuing very similar aims in his paintings and graphic works.

Dürer belonged to the European artistic élite not only in the capacity of painter and designer of woodcuts and engravings, but also as a draughtsman. He had not only mastered the Venetian technique of drawing with the brush on coloured or colour-primed paper, as the studies for the *Heller Altarpiece* show, but all other techniques known to his contemporaries, including pen drawings—from quick sketches like the *Rest on the Flight into Egypt* of 1511 to
Pl. 148 detailed compositions and careful pen and wash studies—
Pls. 150–1 and loosely drawn charcoal portraits. Moreover, after an
Pls. 152–3 interval of approximately ten years, Dürer took up landscape drawing again. It is very likely that the small group of
Pl. 154 pen drawings of views in the vicinity of Nuremberg, executed around 1510–11 (W. 478–81), reflects Dürer's newly acquired knowledge of perspective (cf. p. 148).

Among the many drawings done between 1507 and 1512, the designs for three-dimensional works for execution by

133 *The Virgin and Child.* 1512. Oil. 49×37. Kunsthistorisches Museum, Vienna.

This painting in Vienna is one of Dürer's most harmonious representations of the Virgin, both in colours and composition. The twisted body of the Child is no invention of Dürer's, but was a favourite motif in painting; it first appears in a small panel by the Master of Flémalle, and Dürer himself had already used it in an early drawing (W. 142).

other artists deserve special attention. These include the knight's tomb for the Vischer workshop (W. 489), two Pls. 155–6 reliefs for the tombs of Georg Fugger (who died in 1506) and Ulrich Fugger (who died in 1510), the chandelier made Pl. 158 of antlers which was later executed by Veit Stoss, and several other works. Perhaps the most important designs done between 1510 and 1512 for sculptures were the drawings for statues of King Arthur and King Theodoric, which have unfortunately been lost, and a study for a figure of Emperor Charlemagne[208] for the tomb of Emperor Maximilian in Innsbruck;[209] our only information on this latter project comes from a letter by Lazarus Spengler.

The designs for the Fugger tomb reliefs raise the question of Dürer's relationship with that family. On the evidence of

134 *Imperial Robes of Charlemagne.* 1510. Pen and wash. 41.5 × 18.5. Graphische Sammlung Albertina, Vienna.

preliminary studies which Dürer drew on paper bearing the Fugger trademark, a trident with a small circle, it may be supposed that he had enjoyed the brothers' confidence for some time, especially as Georg had lived in Nuremberg from 1484 to 1500 and had married Regina Imhoff, the daughter of a Nuremberg patrician. Georg was presumably also the donor of *Feast of the Rose Garlands;*[210] Dürer included a posthumous portrait of him in this painting as the man at prayer in a blue cloak, holding a rosary. Georg had had his portrait painted by Giovanni Bellini in 1475, and it may therefore have been he who arranged the necessary contacts for Dürer in Venice. The friendly relationship between Dürer and Georg Fugger seems later to have extended to Jakob the Rich, the youngest of the three brothers.

The question arises as to whether Dürer, a former goldsmith, ever executed the sculptures he designed. A letter dated 6 April 1509, from Anton Tucher to the Elector Frederick of Saxony,[211] mentions a (lost) "image of a woman" in a box. It is often thought to refer to a small relief of a female nude seen from the back (Metropolitan Museum, New York),[212] which bears Dürer's monogram and is dated 1509. The figure shows such close similarities to Dürer's art that one may assume he designed it. This is also true of five medallions produced between 1508 and 1514, the Pirckheimer medallion of 1517 and the medallion for Charles V commissioned by the city of Nuremberg in 1521. However, there is no proof that Dürer worked as a sculptor. It is not yet known who created these small sculptures with such perfection.

During the years 1507 to 1512 Dürer seems to have dedicated much of his time to the study of perspective. The lessons which he had hoped to receive in Bologna seem to have been a failure, since after his return he translated, with Pirckheimer's help, an outline of Euclid's *Perspectiva naturalis* which he had bought in Venice.[213] Moreover, his works before 1510 contain no evidence of a thorough knowledge of how to construct views in perspective. This may mean that Dürer's subsequent progress in this area is connected with the publication of a handbook on perspective which appeared in Nuremberg in 1509. The Nuremberg publisher Jörg Glockendon had reprinted the book *De artificali perspectiva* by Jean Pèlerin (Latin name: Viator; *c.* 1445–1523), a second edition of which had been published in Toul in 1504. Glockendon added a short commentary in German, using the woodcuts of the 1504 edition. But the German text is so general that a reader not already familiar with the subject could never learn the necessary construction methods. Yet it seems that Dürer based his first

135 *The Emperor Charlemagne. C.* 1512. Oil. 190×89. Germanisches Nationalmuseum, Nuremberg.

136 *The Emperor Sigismund. C.* 1512. Oil. 189×90. Germanisches Nationalmuseum, Nuremberg.

These three pictures of the Emperors Charlemagne and Sigismund were the first official commission which Dürer received from the Nuremberg Council. They were to be hung in the relic chamber of the Schoppersches

Haus in the market place. Since 1424 the coronation insignia of the German emperors and the relics associated with the ceremony were annually kept in this room for one night from Thursday to Friday after Easter. They were then shown to a large crowd of pilgrims and curious onlookers from scaffolding erected in front of the house in a ceremony called the "showing of the relics". Dürer's paintings replaced two earlier panels of about 1430; they must have been finished in 1513, since the Emperor Maximilian admired them that year. The dated studies of the imperial robes, which Dürer may have made in Nuremberg, suggest that the artist received the commission for the panels in 1510.

149

precisely constructed drawings,[214] one of which is dated 1509,[215] on these illustrations.

It is very likely that at this time Dürer also gained access to the library of Bernhard Walther who had just died and whose house Dürer had recently purchased. Among the astronomer's books was a copy of Leon Battista Alberti's *Trattato della pittura* which had originally come from the estate of Regiomontanus.[216] Pirckheimer, who had been commissioned by the council in 1512 to catalogue all

137 *Dürer's House near the Tiergärtner Gate.* Built *c.* 1450. Denkmals-archiv, Hauptamt für Hochbauwesen, Nuremberg.

In 1509 Dürer, who had lived in his father's house on the road Unter der Vesten since 1475, bought the house of the merchant Bernhard Walther for 275 gold florins following the latter's death. The contract, dated 14 June 1509, was drawn up by the imperial mayor, the knight Hans von Obernitz. As early as 25 August 1509 Dürer cancelled a mortgage on the house by paying seventy-eight gold florins. Walther had been an assistant of Regiomontanus and continued to work as an astronomer in his own right after Regiomontanus's death. In order to be able to observe the stars better he had an open wooden loggia added to the attic of the house on the Zisselgasse (now Albrecht-Dürer-Strasse) near the Tiergärtner gate; this loggia is still a feature of the building today.

Walther's books so that they could be sold, may have shown his friend the library. Dürer does not seem to have been much influenced by Alberti's theory of perspective, but clearly knew other aspects of the handbook.

Dürer's negative experiences in Italy and the lack of books on the theoretical principles of painting made him once again take up the plan for a handbook on painting. He had thought of it before going to Italy, but from 1508 onwards it gradually took a more concrete shape. On the basis of incomplete notes by the artist, Rupprich[217] reconstructed the planned sequence of the work, which originally was to have had the title *Nourishment for Young Painters (Speis der Malerknaben)*. According to this reconstruction the handbook was to have been in three parts. The first was to have dealt with the spiritual and practical training of an apprentice and was to have given a detailed exposition of the spiritual and material benefits of painting.[218] The second part was to have consisted of a discourse on practical matters, such as the theory of the proportions of man, the horse and architecture, and a detailed account of the theories of perspective, light and colour. The third part was to have discussed where a painter should live and how much he should charge, and would have then given thanks to the Creator.

Dürer did not confine himself merely to planning the programme of his work, but started to write his ideas as early as 1508–9 while continuing with his studies on proportion. In one of the earliest drafts of the preface he deals with the problem of beauty in a section entitled "Of beauty".[219] Dürer admits in the second sentence that "I do not know what beauty is," but tries none the less to define the concept. For him, as for Alberti, it comprised the natural beauty of the body as well as the harmony achieved in a work of art. Dürer also follows Alberti in thinking that a conception of what is beautiful can only develop through experience (Dürer talks of practice). He believed that perfect beauty is not found in any living being, but only in certain individual parts; these parts must be brought together in a work of art.[220] Finally, Dürer acknowledges that God is the only true judge of beauty.

In a draft of the introduction dated 1512, Dürer defined the function of painting as follows: "For the art of painting is used in the service of the church and shows the suffering of Christ, and it also preserves the image of men after their death."[221] This idea had been expressed in a similar way by Alberti at the beginning of the second book of his *Trattato*.[222] But Alberti put portrait-painting first and painting in the service of religion second, and used examples of statues of classical gods to expound his theme. Dürer's emphasis on the central importance of Christ's Passion reflected not only his own feelings and the subject matter of his works, but also the general religious atmosphere in Germany before the Reformation.

138 *The Death of the Virgin.* 1510. Woodcut for the *Life of the Virgin.* 29.3 × 20.6. Kupferstichkabinett SMPK, Berlin.

In 1510 Dürer designed several compositions in order to complete the unfinished cycle of the *Life of the Virgin.* He designed a frontispiece and two further woodcuts, of which the *Death of the Virgin* is the most impressive. Dürer took over Schongauer's compositional device of positioning the bed of the dying Virgin at right angles to the picture plane, which fitted his upright format very well. The apostles are grouped around the dying Virgin in a loosely symmetrical arrangement. Superfluous details are omitted, and all shapes are simple and generous, making the picture a typical High Renaissance composition. After he had finished the two woodcuts, Dürer published the sequence in book form accompanied by Latin verses written by Benedikt Chelidonius.

139 *St. George on Horseback.* 1505—8. Engraving. 11 × 8.6. Kupferstichkabinett SMPK, Berlin.

St. George was especially revered during the late Middle Ages, as evidenced by the numerous representations of his fight with the dragon. Dürer also followed this popular iconographic representation in one of his woodcuts. In his two engravings (B. 53, 54), however, he shows the saint after the fight, calmly holding the banner of the Cross. The present engraving (B. 54) was originally dated 1505, but Dürer altered the date to 1508 after his return from Italy.

140 *Christ Being Taken Prisoner.* 1510. Woodcut for the *Large Passion.* 39.4 × 28. Kupferstichkabinett SMPK, Berlin.   ▷

141 *The Resurrection.* 1510. Woodcut for the *Large Passion.* 39.1 × 27.7. Kupferstichkabinett SMPK, Berlin.   ▷▷

In 1510 Dürer completed this Passion cycle, for which he had created seven large woodcuts between *circa* 1496 and 1498 (cf. Pl. 46), by adding four more designs: the *Last Supper, Christ Being Taken Prisoner, Christ in Limbo* and the *Resurrection.* The theme of a celestial apparition witnessed by humans on earth preoccupied Dürer during the years 1509 to 1511; it is found in the centre panel of the *Heller Altarpiece* (Pl. 129), for instance, or the *Life of the Virgin* (Pls. 90, 92). Formally, Dürer's versions rank with the classical works of Italian painting, and surpass them in the intensity of feeling they convey.

151

142 *The Annunciation.* 1509–11. Woodcut for the *Small Passion*.
12.8 × 9.8. Kupferstichkabinett SMPK, Berlin.

143 *Christ as a Gardener.* 1509–11. Woodcut for the *Small Passion*.
12.7 × 9.7. Kupferstichkabinett SMPK, Berlin.

The *Small Passion* comprises thirty-six representations and a frontispiece
and is Dürer's most extensive woodcut cycle of Christ's Passion. In fact,
the artist did not confine himself to the events of the Passion proper. He
started the sequence with two representations of the *Fall of Man* (B. 17,
18) – the reason that mankind had to be redeemed by Christ's Passion –
and pictures of the *Annunciation* (B. 19) and the *Birth of Christ* (B. 20).
The Passion proper, which starts with *Christ Taking Leave of His Mother*
(B. 21), consists of twenty-four woodcuts. The remaining eight woodcuts
narrate the events from the *Resurrection* to the *Last Judgement*. In
designing this sequence between 1509 and 1511, Dürer was particularly
preoccupied with the problem of light, both supernatural light and the
natural rays of the rising sun. The *Small Passion* was published as a book
with a text by Benedikt Chelidonius. His Latin verses are addressed to the
educated contemporary public, whereas Dürer's woodcuts link the text of
the Gospels with popular late Gothic pictorial traditions.

144 *St. Jerome in his Cell.* 1511. Woodcut. 23.5 × 16. Kupferstichkabinett SMPK, Berlin.   ▷

St. Jerome, the learned Father of the Church who had translated the Bible
from Greek into Latin, was a favourite saint of Humanist scholars. It is
therefore not surprising that Dürer depicted the saint many times, either
in his study or as a penitent. A comparison between the Basle frontispiece
of 1492 (Pl. 15) and this woodcut of 1511 illustrates the development of
Dürer's work from the late Gothic picture made by a journeyman to the
balanced composition designed by a mature artist. It also explains why
scholars have found it difficult to believe that the Basle woodcut and the
woodcut of the same theme made almost thirty years later, were products
of the same hand and mind.

146 *Ecce Homo. 1512. Engraved Passion.* 11.7×7.5. Kupferstich-kabinett SMPK, Berlin.

◁ 145 *The Trinity. 1511. Woodcut.* 39.2×28.4. Kupferstichkabinett SMPK, Berlin.

"...for a good painter is full of figures within...", and if he could live forever he would still invent ever new things. This characterization of the painter's creative talent by Dürer is typical of the Renaissance; mediæval artists considered it their duty to repeat their models, which had become established over the centuries, as faithfully as possible. Compared with the composition of the Trinity in the *Landauer Altarpiece* (Pls. 131, 132) Dürer's woodcut of the *Trinity* of 1511 seems like an illustration of his own words. This *Trinity* is Dürer's most accomplished woodcut; he (and his cutter) succeeded in drawing lines which are almost as fine as those in an engraving.

147 *Christ in Limbo. 1512. Engraved Passion.* 11.7×7.5. Kupferstich-kabinett SMPK, Berlin.

Immediately after finishing his commissions for the large paintings, Dürer again turned to graphic work, almost as if to underline his own words to Jakob Heller in Frankfurt, that he could earn more from graphic work than from painting large pictures. By 1512 he had not only completed his two large woodcut sequences, but had also designed the thirty-six sheets of the *Small Passion* and the sixteen compositions for the *Engraved Passion*. These compositions are dominated by a few large figures and structured according to subtle gradations of light and shade. The strongest highlights are often on minor figures; none the less, composition as well as story are nearly always focussed on Christ.

157

149 *Penitent St. Jerome.* 1512. Dry-point etching. 20.8 × 18.5. Rijks-prentencabinet, Amsterdam.

In 1512 Dürer etched three compositons with the dry-point. This was a new technique for him, in which the metal plate could be worked more easily than in the case of engravings; moreover, the artist did not have to take such care to make the hatchings regular. In dry-point etchings the drawing produces metal shavings on the plate along the furrows, and if this "burr" is left, the printed etchings will be dark and velvety in tone; if the burr is removed, good prints will look like delicate pen drawings. Judging by surviving prints, Dürer experimented with both methods. Neither appears to have satisfied him, however, for he gave up the technique of dry-point etching after these few experiments.

Around the same time, Dürer compared the beauty of classical gods with that of Christ and the saints: "Just as they [the classical artists] used the dimensions of the most beautiful male figure to represent their god Apollo, so will we use the same for the Lord Christ who is the most beautiful in all the world. And as they used Venus as the most beautiful woman so will we portray the same delicate figure of the most pure Virgin Mary, the mother of God. And we will turn Hercules into Samson, and we will do likewise with all the other figures."[223]

These remarks and those previously quoted embody more important ideas than is apparent at first glance. When Dürer compares the outward appearance of Christ with that of Apollo he transfers Neoplatonic ideas to the theory of painting: just as Ficino and Pico della Mirandola had called Plato the Attic Moses or Dürer himself had shown a figure of Job-Socrates in the *Jabach Altarpiece*, he transferred the proportions of Apollo to the figure of Christ. The impression Dürer's ideas must have made on his contemporaries may be guessed from a friendly admonition that Sixtus Tucher, the learned provost of St. Lorenz, had once given to Konrad Celtis. He had advised him to give up "the vile fables of Diana, Venus, Jupiter ... who are even at this moment being tortured in the flames of Hell".[225]

Dürer evidently did not come into contact with ideas of this kind merely through Celtis's teaching or his contemporary reading of Ficino's *De vita triplici*, but must have been familiar with the thought processes and philosophy of Neoplatonism for some time. Pirckheimer seems to have played a more important role as a mediator only after Celtis's death. He had copied Ficino's commentary to Plato's *Symposium* by hand for his father when he was a student. Ficino's interpretation of Plato's theory of beauty influenced Dürer, though possibly only in later years when he formu-

◁148 *The Holy Family Resting on the Flight into Egypt.* 1511. Pen. 27.7 × 20.7. Kupferstichkabinett SMPK, Berlin.

Dürer, who even today is usually thought to have painted every single hair, proves in this sketch that he was not always a "stickler" for detail, but had mastered the art of omission, which, according to the definition of a late nineteenth-century painter, is a central feature of drawings. There seem to be no superfluous strokes of the pen in Dürer's quick sketch, and each line, including those of the monogram and date, has its definite place. A comparison with the elaborately drawn woodcut of the same year illustrates the range of Dürer's talent as a draughtsman.

150 *The Holy Family in a Hall.* 1509. Pen and coloured washes. 42.2 × 28.3. Öffentliche Kunstsammlung, Kupferstichkabinett, Basle. ▷

Dürer was fascinated with the theme of the Holy Family throughout his life and represented it in ever new versions. The setting in this drawing is a splendid Renaissance loggia, like those which Dürer had seen in Italy. This noble setting, which even includes a servants' bell, is more appropriate to the Queen of Heaven and her Son and the angels playing musical instruments than to the Lord's foster-father Joseph, who had not been worshipped as a saint until the fifteenth century. In this picture he seems to have drunk too much of the heavenly potion in the large jug and has gone to sleep, resting his head on the table. The drawing was made at a time when Dürer was once more intensely preoccupied with the problems of perspective, and here applied the insight gained in his studies.

151 *Wing of a Roller*. 1512. Watercolour and gouache on vellum. 19.7 × 20 (enlarged). Graphische Sammlung Albertina, Vienna.

Dürer's reputation as a painter of great detail and precision is largely based on his animal studies; and indeed this study of a roller's wing (in Vienna), though less well known than the *Hare* (Pl. 100), is a masterpiece of detailed observation from nature. The rendering of the shimmering colours of the feathers is perfect. The fact that the picture was painted on vellum implies that Dürer regarded this study from nature as a work of art in its own right and perhaps intended to sell it or give it away as a present. Collectors and connoisseurs in Dürer's time and long afterwards very much admired "feats" of this kind.

161

152 *Portrait of Konrad Verkell.* 1508. Charcoal. 29.5 × 21.6. Department of Prints and Drawings, British Museum, London.

This head with its sharply beaked nose, alert eyes and thin lips is an enigmatic work. It is not known whether "conrat verkell" is a real name or a derisive nickname, as no man of this name is documented. The old-fashioned, turban-like headgear, which looks almost like part of a carnival costume, is another strange feature. The same applies to the worm's-eye view of the head, which is unusual for Dürer's work. In spite of all these uncertainties, this charcoal drawing is one of Dürer's most impressive portraits.

153 *Portrait of Andreas Dürer.* C. 1512. Charcoal. 20 × 17. Mrs. Alexander Morgan, The Pierpont Morgan Library, New York.

This drawing of about 1512 is one of the most important rediscoveries since 1945. The sitter has correctly been identified as Dürer's brother Andreas (Endres). Andreas had obviously inherited his mother's eye defect (cf. Pl. 179). In contrast to the silver-point drawing of 1514, which shows Andreas Dürer in his everyday clothes, the New York drawing shows him wearing a fur-trimmed cloak; this characterizes him as a respected, and presumably affluent burgher, who worked in his father's house as a goldsmith.

lated his own "aesthetic excursus" in his theory of proportions.[226]

Dürer noted the differences in appearance of the various classical gods because he knew their iconography and also because he must have been familiar with the theory of the four basic human "complexions".[227] This theory of the bodily shape of the four temperaments (sanguine, choleric, phlegmatic and melancholic), which had originally been expounded in classical medical science, was one of the starting-points for the theory of proportions which Dürer was writing at the time.[228] He refers to "physicians" as his authority, but one need not go back to Albertus Magnus and the Arab Rhazes to confirm this, as Rupprich has done. In this context as in others Dürer was presumably influenced by the physician and philosopher Ficino, who had commented in detail on the classical theory of the temperaments in his *De vita triplici.* This work had appeared in 1505 and 1508 in a German translation by Johann Adelphus Muling, and Dürer may have consulted one of these editions for his

154 *View of Heroldsberg.* 1510. Pen. 21.1×26.3. Musée Bonnat, Bayonne.

About 1510 Dürer took up landscape views again, a subject he had not touched for over a decade. Three of these drawings were done in silverpoint. The view of Heroldsberg, however, is a pen drawing. Martin Geuder, a brother-in-law of Willibald Pirckheimer, owned a manor house in Heroldsberg. This is likely to be the tall, double-gabled building to the left of the church.

comments on the rules of health to be observed in the training of apprentice painters.[229]

Ficino's *De vita triplici* seems also to have been the source for Dürer's famous statement of 1512 (or at least for its second part): "For a good painter is full of figures within. And if it were possible that he lived for ever, his inner ideas, of which Plato writes, would always give him something new to express through his works."[230]

This passage from Dürer's first drafts of his handbook on painting may give the impression that the planned work was entirely derived from Italian sources. But the impressive overall programme for the work, comprising discussions on the practical as well as the theoretical and ethical aspects of art, goes far beyond anything Italian theoreticians of art—with the exception of Leonardo da Vinci—had put forth in over a century. Dürer's thoughts are among the

155 *Samson Fighting the Philistines*. 1510. Pen and brush on green primed paper. 31.3 × 15.9. Kupferstichkabinett SMPK, Berlin.

To the left above the main scene of this painstakingly executed and finely drawn work, two further events of Samson's life are shown: Samson's fight with the lion and Samson holding the gates of Gaza. A preliminary drawing (W. 484, now lost) depicted these scenes in reverse sequence, so that Samson carrying off the wings of the city gate of Gaza was shown in the foreground. In a further preliminary study (W. 488, in Milan) this conception is changed, and all the essential elements of the fight with the Philistines and the two subsidiary scenes are identical with the final version. The Berlin chiaroscuro drawing depicts a corpse on a bier and several mourning putti and satyrs beneath the representation of Samson. A corresponding picture depicting the *Resurrection* is in the Germanisches Nationalmuseum in Nuremberg. The two drawings were designs for the tombs of Ulrich (1441–1510) and Georg Fugger (1453–1506) in the church of St. Ulrich in Augsburg; they were intended as models for reliefs to be executed by a sculptor.

◁ 156 *The Resurrection.* 1510. Pen and brush on grey-black primed paper. 32 × 16.5. Graphische Sammlung Albertina, Vienna.

This drawing in Vienna is a copy — drawn by Dürer himself — of the design for the tomb of Ulrich Fugger. In the corresponding pen drawing in Nuremberg a corpse is shown below the main picture, as in the Berlin drawing of *Samson Fighting the Philistines* (Pl. 155).

157 *Chandelier Made from Antlers.* C. 1513. Pen and wash. 16.8 × 21.3. Wesenberg Galerie, Konstanz.

158 *Chandelier made from Antlers.* Germanisches Nationalmuseum, Nuremberg.

Chandeliers which combined carved figures and antlers were a late Gothic German invention; they clearly reflect the love of bizarre shapes typical of this period. According to the inscription on the drawing, which was added by a grandson of Johann Neudörffer, Dürer was commissioned by the Nuremberg Council to design the antler chandelier as a model for Veit Stoss. The chandelier was intended for the regimental chamber in the Nuremberg town hall; it is now kept in the Germanisches Nationalmuseum in Nuremberg.

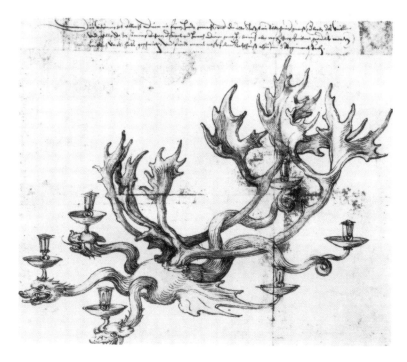

most important comments on art in his time, and his achievement is impressive even when he depends on Italian sources, for there were hardly any corresponding German terms, except for a few mathematical concepts, which could have facilitated his translations. Only a careful philological study could establish how much his friend Pirckheimer helped him in his efforts. In any case, Dürer must be regarded as one of the originators of modern scientific German prose.[231] His poems, too, testify to his linguistic abilities.[232] Except for a poem to Lazarus Spengler, all have religious themes and may be regarded as a typical expression of lay piety in the pre-Reformation era.[233]

VIII. The Emperor Maximilian: 1512–17

Triumphal Arch and Prayer-book · Master Engravings and Graphic Experiments

The Emperor Maximilian visited Nuremberg on 4 February 1512 and remained until the middle of the month. This was Maximilian's last stay in the city and he established a contact with Dürer which was to keep the artist busy for a number of years. But as the imperial printing privilege manifests, contact between the art-loving emperor and the artist must have been made as early as 1510–11; the president of the Tyrolean Raitkammer, Peter Rummel, may have been the go-between.[233a] As Maximilian was only very rarely in direct contact with the artists who worked for him, he may have approached Dürer by way of the Nuremberg Council, or perhaps through Willibald Pirckheimer, whom he had known since the Swiss War of 1499, or through his own historiographer Johannes Stabius.

The Emperor Maximilian, history's "last knight", was a man of many interests who conformed more to the image of the universally educated courtier, as his contemporary Count Baldassare Castiglione described him, than to the ideal of a mediæval ruler. He was not only a military commander, jouster and huntsman, but had also mastered the problems of his administration and chancery; he could speak and write a number of foreign languages, including Latin and French, and even knew enough about various craft techniques to introduce new and improved designs in the fields of armoury and gun manufacture.

His striving for personal fame and the glorification of his family was a true Renaissance aim; what was unusual, however, was that he did not leave it to his historiographer to describe his glorious deeds, but himself composed and edited an extensive plan for his autobiographical writings. In the *Theuerdank,* derived from allegorical mediæval verse epics, he describes the journey he made for the purpose of courting Mary of Burgundy. The *Weiskunig,* a combination of historical and fictional narrative, describes his life and that of his father Frederick III. The *Freydal* was to be a partly factual, partly fictional account of Maximilian's adventures at the lists and the feasts he arranged. The plan

of Maximilian's writings, drawn up in 1512 by the emperor's private secretary Marx Treitzsauerwein, contained more than twenty projected titles.[234]

The emperor employed scholars such as Konrad Peutinger and Johannes Stabius for the preliminary work on his many literary projects. The actual writing was left to secretaries whose activities were constantly checked by Maximilian. Furthermore, the emperor was equally determined that the projected publications should be well produced. The Augsburg printer Johann Schönsperger, who had entered the emperor's service in December 1508, was commissioned to cast two new types, the so-called prayer-book type and the *Theuerdank* type. Dürer, together with the calligrapher Johann Neudörffer and the type-caster Hieronymus Andreae, helped to improve this new type face, the so-called *Fraktur,*[235] which had been developed in the imperial chancery.

Not only did the emperor want the type face of his books to reflect the imperial dignity of their author, he wished them to be lavishly illustrated as well, and for this purpose engaged artists like Burgkmair, Schäufelein, Beck and Dürer.

Dürer's first commission from the emperor was for drawings to illustrate a book on fencing. The explanatory text was written by the painter himself, his friend Pirckheimer and an unknown author.[236] Subsequently, the two friends collaborated on the two-part manuscript of Horapollon's *Hieroglyphs.* In accordance with the emperor's wishes, Pirckheimer translated the Greek text into Latin and Dürer made pen drawings to illustrate it. Pirckheimer presented the work to the emperor in Linz in 1514.[236a]

The most magnificent and at the same time idiosyncratic project among the one thousand and more woodcuts made for Maximilian in the following years was undoubtedly *The Triumph,* planned as a series of more than 130 large illustrated sheets with short explanations. The idea of a triumphal procession goes back to the triumphal entries into

159 Detail of the *Triumphal Arch.*

Rome enjoyed by victorious Roman commanders; but in Maximilian's mind the concept merged with the memory of the "Entrées solennelles" which he and his wife, Mary of Burgundy, had experienced in the Netherlands. The last pictures of the woodcut sequence, showing the baggage train, confirm that Maximilian was thinking of a real procession. Notes dictated by Maximilian to Marx Treitzsauerwein[237] in 1512 only mention a *Triumphal Chariot,* but it is obvious that this term is meant to cover the triumphal procession proper, including both the imperial chariot and the *Triumphal Arch.*[238] Out of the complete sequence, Dürer was commissioned for the *Triumphal Arch,* Pl. 160 the *Triumphal Chariot,* several bearers of trophies and Pls. 164, 16 twenty-five to thirty other groups of figures in the procession. His contribution was larger than that of the other artists involved,[239] and the parts he designed or supervised were also the most important thematically.

As with all Maximilian's other projects, the painters commissioned to make the drawings for the wood blocks had to follow the coloured designs supplied by Jörg Kölderer, Albrecht Altdorfer and their associates. Dürer's earliest drawing for the project (W. 671) is much more fluent in style than Altdorfer's model, but Dürer faithfully copied the iconographic details of Altdorfer's parchment paintings.

As the master of a workshop, Dürer did not execute all the works commissioned by the emperor. He left a large part for Hans Springinklee and Wolf Traut, two journeymen working for him at the time; they designed the twenty triumphal carriages and the royal couple. Springinklee, who was about twenty years old, was also Dürer's main associate on the monumental work *Triumphal Arch.* Dürer also employed the calligrapher Johann Neudörffer, who was then about eighteen years old, for the numerous inscriptions; this is confirmed by comparison with other examples of Neudörffer's script. The actual cutting of the wood blocks, including the inscriptions, was performed by Hieronymus Andreae, known as Formschneider (block-cutter). Johannes Stabius, the emperor's historiographer and astronomer, was responsible for the overall supervision of the project. It can be assumed that Dürer and Stabius had known each other since 1504, when Stabius had published in Nuremberg two of his writings, for which Dürer's pupil, Hans von Kulmbach, had designed the woodcut illustrations.[240]

The *Triumphal Arch* is the largest woodcut ever made. It was printed from 190 separate wood blocks and then glued together. Next to Dürer and his workshop, Albrecht Altdorfer was the main collaborator on this immense project. He designed the scenes from the Emperor's private life which are shown in the two corner towers. Dürer was obliged to follow a miniature painting by the Innsbruck court painter Jörg Kölderer which served as an overall model for the architecture of the paper building; Dürer added the sumptuous and fanciful ornament as well as a number of individual figures. However, he must also have been responsible for supervising the technical details of the whole project, since this was the only way that architecture and pictorial scenes could be coordinated. The overall plan for the structure had been devised by the court historiographer Johannes Stabius; he had been commissioned by the Emperor and worked under Maximilian's constant supervision. Stabius also wrote the lengthy explanation underneath the picture proper. The *Triumphal Arch,* a hybrid containing elements based on classical triumphal arches, late Gothic decorated façades and Renaissance forms, was part of the *Triumphal Procession of Maximilian,* for which Hans Burgkmair in Augsburg had designed most of the woodcuts and Dürer designed a *Triumphal Chariot* (cf. Pl. 164) between 1518 and 1522.

160 *The Triumphal Arch of the Emperor Maximilian.* 1515. Woodcut. 3.409 × 2.922 m. Department of Prints and Drawings, British Museum, London.   ▷

169

The *Triumphal Arch* is made up of 192 wood blocks of varying formats; including Stabius's explanatory text, it covers a surface of over ten square metres. Transposing Kölderer's designs not only taxed Dürer's ability as an artist but also represented a considerable achievement in organization and manual execution. Dürer managed this difficult task by drawing the right-hand half of the actual architectural frame of his imaginary "building" and then letting his journeymen draw a mirror image of it for the left-hand side. The half-length figures of Roman emperors on the left, the portraits of princes related to the House of Hapsburg, and four scenes from the emperor's life were created by Dürer himself.

Two sketches in Dresden (W.673–4) and one in London (W.675) are all that survive of the preliminary drawings. The *Hieroglyphic Portrait of the Emperor* for the niche in the cupola over the arch is also generally thought to be based on a design by Dürer; he created it according to an idea of Pirckheimer's deriving from Horapollon's *Hieroglyphs*.[241] The two flanking towers designed by Altdorfer—except for one scene by Dürer—and the portrait of the emperor seem to have been among the last works executed before trial printing started.

By mid-1515, after three years of work, all the essential parts of the *Triumphal Arch* seem to have been transferred to wood blocks; most of them appear to have been cut by Hieronymus Andreae, since he received a honorarium from the emperor in June, 1515.[242] Dürer, on the other hand, had worked without pay until then, as is confirmed by a letter to Christoph Kress dated 30 July 1515.[243] The emperor (who was then in Landau) had asked the Nuremberg Council as early as 12 December 1512 to exempt Dürer from paying taxes,[244] since he was working in the emperor's service, but the council had advised the artist to waive his claim.[245] On Stabius's recommendation Maximilian eventually, in September, 1515, promised the painter an annual pension of

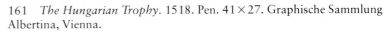

161 *The Hungarian Trophy*. 1518. Pen. 41×27. Graphische Sammlung Albertina, Vienna.

As well as the huge woodcut of the *Triumphal Arch* (Pls. 159, 160) and the *Triumphal Chariot of the Emperor Maximilian* (consisting of eight separate sheets) Dürer designed a number of horsemen carrying trophies and a horse-drawn carriage also laden with trophies; these were the enemy's weapons seized in the course of various campaigns. There are two versions of each of these figures of horsemen: a preliminary sketch and a carefully executed, slightly altered drawing coloured with washes. These final versions, which were submitted to the Emperor for inspection, may have been executed by journeymen employed in Dürer's workshop.

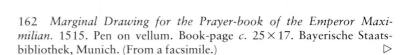

162 *Marginal Drawing for the Prayer-book of the Emperor Maximilian*. 1515. Pen on vellum. Book-page *c.* 25×17. Bayerische Staatsbibliothek, Munich. (From a facsimile.)   ▷

The drawings in the margin of the Emperor Maximilian's prayer-book are generally acknowledged to be among the best of Dürer's ornamental graphic works. Johann Schönsperger printed a small edition of the book in Augsburg in 1513, and renowned German artists were sent a number of quires each and asked to illustrate the page margins. The Augsburg Humanist Konrad Peutinger was responsible for Dürer receiving the main share of these illustrations (at the beginning of the book). Apart from Dürer, Cranach, Burgkmair, Baldung, Altdorfer and several unknown artists also designed illustrations. Dürer invented a special kind of decoration for the pages of this book; it is half-way between ornamental book-illumination of the traditional kind and illustrations of the actual text. His drawings provide imaginative and humorous explanations of the prayers and hymns printed in the book. The drawing illustrated here, for instance, accompanies a plea for protection against the lure of evil; it shows the fox as the tempter who lures the chickens by playing an enticing melody on his flute.

tua Agla Anañzapta te
tragramaton: que sunt lau
danda: glorificanda: tremen
da: et adoranda: nunc et Per
infinita secula seculorũ Amẽ·
Pater Noster·

O Iesu vera libertas an
gelorum: mundi fabri
tator: ꝫ omniũ bonoꝛ auctor:
via salutis eterne: verus osten
sor· Memento comprehensio
nis et temptationis tue: quan
do iudei tanquã leones fero
cissimi iŋ templo te circũste

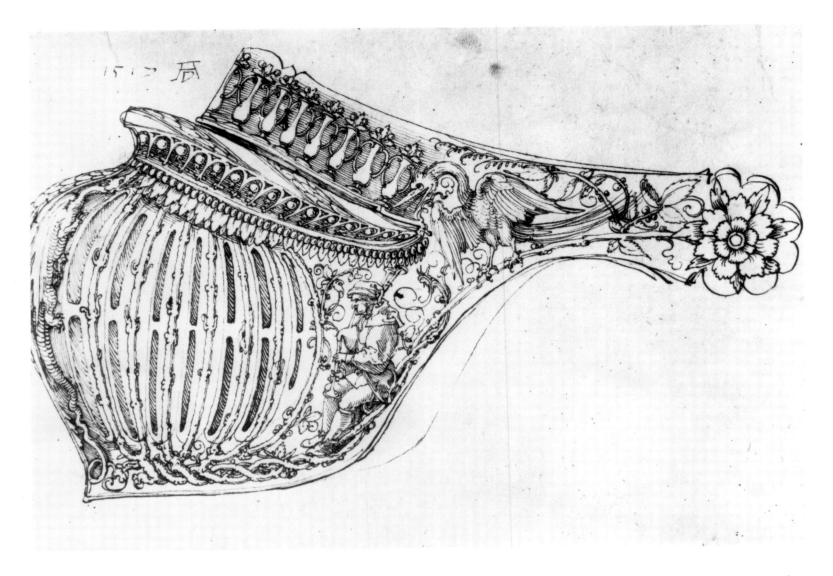

100 florins for the rest of his life. It was to be allocated by the City of Nuremberg from taxes due to the emperor,[246] but appears to have been paid very irregularly.[247]

It is very likely that by the autumn of 1515 Dürer was already at work on the next project for his imperial patron, drawings for the margins of a prayer-book[247a] which the emperor had designated either for his own use or for the Order of the Knights of St. George, founded by Frederick III. The court printer Schönsperger had been commissioned around 1508 to produce the prayer-book. On 3 January 1514 he delivered the first ten copies, printed on parchment in the new type face, to the Augsburg Humanist Konrad Peutinger. Peutinger, on an order from the emperor, sent one copy to various artists' workshops to have the page margins illustrated in the manner of illuminated manuscripts.[248] The book had 157 pages, and Dürer was again the main contributor, responsible for the decoration of fifty-six pages. The remaining pages were illustrated by Lucas

163 *Ornamental Visor.* 1517. Pen. 19.4×27.5. Graphische Sammlung Albertina, Vienna.

Among the numerous works which Dürer executed for the Emperor are four designs for decorations of various parts of a suit of armour. They are usually thought to be for a suit of armour which Maximilian commissioned in 1515 from Koloman Helmschmied in Augsburg, the most famous armourer of his time. Dürer's drawings may well have been designs for the decoration of this silver-coated suit of armour, which was never delivered to the Emperor because he never had enough money to pay for the costly work done by the armourer. Dürer's designs are similar to his drawings for the margins of the prayer-book in that they show him as a master of humorous, playfully decorative linear art.

Cranach, Hans Baldung, Jörg Breu, Hans Burgkmair and Albrecht Altdorfer and one of his assistants.

Dürer's forty-five drawings in red, green and purple ink decorating the second, third and fourth quires are inspired by late mediæval illuminations, but transformed into the purely graphic style of pen drawings. It is doubtful whether

164 *The Large Triumphal Chariot*. 1518. Pen and wash. 46×2530. Graphische Sammlung Albertina, Vienna.

The *Triumphal Chariot* was to be the centrepiece of the Emperor Maximilian's *Triumph* consisting of *Triumphal Arch* (Pls. 159, 160) and *Procession*. Pirckheimer had drawn up the programme on which Dürer's design of the chariot is based. Maximilian, in his imperial robes, sits enthroned on the sumptuous chariot; his two wives, his son Philip and daughter Margaret, his two grandsons and four granddaughters sit in front of him. The chariot is drawn by six pairs of horses in ornate harness; they are led by women in classical dress who symbolize the virtues of the Emperor.

Dürer thought they might later be turned into woodcuts. In the ornaments he skilfully combines the intertwining foliage of German late Gothic art with elements of Italian Renaissance decoration. A comparison of the pages decorated by Dürer with those by the other masters clearly demonstrates his superiority as an artist: his ornaments are the work of an inspired draughtsman, theirs are attempts to match his model.

The pages decorated by Dürer are usually dominated by a large figure in the outer margin. These include Christ, the Virgin, angels and saints, a physician, several burghers, peasants and mercenaries. Surprisingly, Hercules appears

twice, and there is even a Red Indian, an inhabitant of the newly discovered American continent. The figures are linked to small, mostly humorous scenes in the lower margin by the use of elegantly intertwining foliage through which romp many symbolic animals. Since many of these illustrations concern rather profane subjects, it has long been thought that they were mostly products of Dürer's vivid imagination and that direct reference to the text of prayers, hymns and psalms was exceptional. However, it is now known that although Dürer's margin drawings are not literal illustrations of the text,[249] they do refer to it by means of allegories and symbols. They are also inspired by the Bible and by Horapollon's *Hieroglyphs,* as well as by the prayer-book itself; yet in spite of this close connection with literary sources the margin drawings remain admirably light and free, making Dürer's achievement all the more remarkable.

Similarly free are designs for etched decorations on an imperial suit of armour which are dated 1517. Five Pl. 163

165 *The "Tightened Race"*. C. 1516–17. Woodcut for the *Freydal*. 22.3×24.3. Kupferstichkabinett SMPK, Berlin.

Among the many literary projects which Emperor Maximilian planned to have written for him according to his own detailed instructions, the *Freydal* was particularly dear to his heart. Like the book on tournaments written by Duke René the Good of Anjou in the mid-fifteenth century, the *Freydal* was intended as a manual of the rules on how to organize the jousts between riders. Maximilian, who was a passionate jouster, also wanted to give a survey of the different types of combat, some of which he himself had invented; these were to be explained both in the text and through illustrations. Dürer drew five woodcut illustrations for this manual, which was never published. In the *"Tightened Race"* the combatants fought in only partial armour (without greave and cuisse) and with sharp-edged lance; the tilting shield, the so-called *Stechtartsche*, was screwed (tightened) to the actual cuirass. Dürer's illustration shows the last phase of combat.

woodcuts for the *Freydal* may be even earlier. In the period up to the spring of 1518, Dürer designed the 2.50 m-long coloured drawing of the *Triumphal Chariot,* based on Pirckheimer's suggestions,[250] the six bearers of trophies on horseback (W.690) and some imaginative figurines for a court dress (W.686–9).

The Emperor Maximilian's commissions clearly dominated Dürer's output during these years, yet did not monopolize him to the extent that the large number of works he delivered to the emperor would seem to suggest. In 1513 Dürer appears to have completed no paintings at all, only two woodcuts of little importance (B. 106, P. 205) and three engravings, though one of them was the masterpiece *Knight, Death and Devil.* Therefore, it seems very likely that most of the work on the *Triumphal Arch* was done during this year. 1514 seems to have left Dürer rather more time for his own projects. His main works were the eight engravings of *St. Jerome in his Study, Melencolia I,* the *Madonna by the Wall* (B. 40), the *Madonna on the Crescent Moon*

Pl. 165

Pl. 164

Pl. 168

Pl. 169–70

166–7 *Knight on Horseback (recto* and *verso).* C. 1512–13. Pen. 23.9 × 17.3. Biblioteca Ambrosiana, Milan.

168 *Knight, Death and the Devil.* 1513. Engraving. 25 × 19. Kupferstichkabinett SMPK, Berlin. ▷

The years 1513–14 marked the peak of Dürer's achievement as a graphic artist. *Knight, Death and the Devil* is the first of the so-called master engravings. Dürer based his picture on two studies of about 1500, the *Horseman* (Pl. 73) and a study of rocks (W. 111). He adopted the figure of the horseman in armour almost without alteration, but made several changes in the horse. He experimented with representations of the horse's movement in a drawing which is now in Milan. He based the animal on his studies of the proportions of horses, begun in 1502, and constructed it according to a system of proportions which owes much to Leonardo. As in his studies of the proportions of the human body (Pls. 84, 85), he traced the design through to the back of the sheet, and then added the dog which symbolizes faithfulness. The tracing, in mirror image, could be transferred on to the copperplate without any difficulty.

Pl. 171
Pl. 172 (B. 33), *St. Thomas* (B. 48), *St. Paul*, the *Bagpipe Player* (B. 91) and *Peasant Couple Dancing*. One of the two representations of the Madonna, the *Madonna by the Wall* (B. 40), has a rich architectural landscape unusual for Dürer's small engravings. The two apostles form the beginning of a series that was not taken up again until 1523 and was never completed.

Pl. 47 Almost two decades separate Dürer's *Three Peasants Talking* from *Peasant Couple Dancing* and *Bagpipe Player*, but neither the early nor the late portrayals disclose whether Dürer's attitude toward peasants was positive or negative; rather, it seems to have been ambivalent. On the one hand he, like all city dwellers of his time, smiled pityingly at the awkward country people; on the other, one senses his sympathy for them and their hard way of life, from which their coarse and primitive dances gave them only very occasional respite.

The great Dürer monographs, from Thausing's to Panofsky's, usually discuss Dürer's works for the emperor in a separate chapter, thereby setting them clearly apart from other pictures executed during these years. This obscures the fact that Dürer's engravings of these years were outstanding, in spite of the works for Maximilian which doubtlessly took up a great deal of his time. He created the three so-called master engravings of *Knight, Death and Devil* (1513), *St. Jerome in his Study* and *Melencolia I* (both 1514). The term "master engravings" chiefly refers to the technical mastery of their execution, but it has always been felt that these engravings also represent an exceptional artistic and intellectual achievement, not only among Dürer's own works, but in the context of German art in general. There have been many scholarly attempts to discover one comprehensive idea underlying all three compositions, even though Dürer himself clearly did not think of them as a unit, as is indicated by many comments in his diary of the journey Pl. 168 to the Netherlands. "The Rider", as he calls *Knight, Death and Devil,* is always mentioned separately when he talks of Pl. 169–70 selling or donating his pictures, while *St. Jerome* and *Melencolia I* are mentioned together several times.[251]

Early Dürer scholars often assumed that "the Rider" is a symbol of the Christian knight as described in the *Enchiridion militis Christiani* (Handbook of the Christian Knight) by Erasmus of Rotterdam which was first published in 1504.[252] This is no longer generally accepted, because the composition is so straightforward that no literary source is needed to explain it. The origins of the engraving lie Pl. 73 elsewhere. As is proven by preliminary drawings in Vienna Pls. 166–7 and Milan, the composition is based on Dürer's studies of

the proportions of the horse, which he resumed after his return from Italy. Influences evident in the engraving can be traced back to Leonardo, to the equestrian monument of Colleoni in Venice and also to impressions Dürer gathered in Florence.[253] Unfortunately, due to theft, only one of the studies is still extant;[254] the pages of the Dresden sketchbook, dated 1517, are only tracings made from drawings by Leonardo.

St. Jerome in his Study can also be understood without any commentary. Because of his erudition, the saint was considered a kind of patron of the Humanists and is portrayed working on his translation of the Bible. The late Gothic room which he shares with the lion and dog is considered Dürer's first architectural interior constructed in exact perspective according to Alberti's method.[255] More important is Dürer's success in conveying the different textures of wood, masonry, fur and plants solely by means of drawn lines. The representation of light effects, as in the circular shadows on the embrasure of the window glazed with bull's-eye panes, was admired by Erasmus of Rotterdam.[256]

Although Dürer gave his third master engraving the explicit title *Melencolia I*, inscribed on the wings of a bat, it is difficult to understand the picture without some explanation.

Its meaning is once more deeply rooted in Neoplatonic philosophy.[257] In his *De vita triplici*, published in 1489, Marsilio Ficino examined the influence of the planet Saturn on human melancholy. He linked Aristotle's remark, that intellectual men were often melancholy, with Plato's concept of the "furor divinus" (divine fury/madness) and came to

169 *St. Jerome in his Study*. 1514. Engraving. 24.7 × 18.8. Kupferstichkabinett SMPK, Berlin.

The last of the master engravings has a different aim from the two earlier ones. It emphasizes surface textures: the soft fur of the animals, the rough, crumbling masonry, the lively grain of the wooden ceiling. At the height of his powers Dürer attempted a detailed rendering of an interior, a feat which he had attempted once before, in 1492, in a woodcut of the same theme (Pl. 15). In the later work he explored the possibilities of engraving in a way that has never been surpassed. The most wonderful feature of this engraving is the rendering of the light pouring through the bull's-eye window panes and casting delicate shadows on mullions and walls. The bright aureole round the head of the saint, who is absorbed in his work, vies with the natural sunlight; this aureole is the area of greatest brightness in the composition. Looking at this engraving, it is easy to understand Erasmus's praise of Dürer: he said that Dürer was greater than Apelles, because he could represent even immaterial subjects purely by means of black lines, without recourse to colour.

176

the conclusion that melancholy was a positive characteristic in theologians and other learned men.[258] Ficino's ideas were further developed in *De occulta philosophia,* a treatise written by the young German physician Heinrich von Nettesheim around 1510. He distinguished three levels of creative melancholy. The lowest level was that possessed by artists and artisans, the next that of scholars and statesmen, and the highest level that of true theologians. This manuscript was passed around among Franconian Humanists and became the basis of Dürer's engraving. He expands the concept of Saturnian melancholy by linking it with the discipline of geometry.

The principal figure is female: she symbolizes Saturnian melancholy by the angle of her head, which lies in shadow and rests on her clenched fist. Her purse and key ring are symbols of the riches and power of Saturn's children. The emaciated dog, writing putto, bat and the comet, which can be seen to have caused a flood, also have their place in this context. The scales, hourglass and magic square of numbers are symbols originally found in representations of "geometria", but are here used to refer to the art of measurement which Saturn's children possess. The three objects correspond to the three basic qualities of science mentioned in the Bible: weight, measure and number. Measure and number also define proportion which in turn determines all art. The tools lying around on the ground, the unfinished building with the ladder against it, as well as the sphere, millstone and polyhedron, all symbolize human qualities linked with the art of measurement; the most comprehensive symbol in this context is the compasses held by the figure of Melancholy. Dürer's engraving is thus an allegory of the creative melancholy of the artist and may be interpreted as a symbolic self-portrait.

As Dürer often gave away the engraving of *Melencolia I* together with that of *St. Jerome,* it does indeed seem likely that he regarded the two prints as complementary works. And the learned Father of the Church, Jerome, who had translated the Bible from the original Hebrew and Greek into Latin, appeared to conform to Agrippa von Nettesheim's definition of a true theologian more than any other figure in the history of the Church. Moreover, St. Jerome had at times lived as a hermit, and hermits were considered to be children of Saturn and therefore also subject to melancholy. However, the knight who is shown in the earliest master engraving, pursuing his goal in spite of death and the devil, has no place among melancholiacs.

Throughout 1515 Dürer seems to have been primarily occupied with preparing the first copies of the *Triumphal*

Arch for printing and with the illustrations for the prayerbook. He accomplished very little apart from the works commissioned by the emperor, but the few he did create are interesting because they show that he was constantly experimenting with new techniques. Two prints dated 1515 (B. 19, 22), for instance, were etchings on iron plates, a new technique at that time. His first work employing this technique was perhaps the etching *The Desperate Man* (B. 70).[259] Two further etchings on iron plates were completed in 1516, and in 1518 he made the well-known etching *The Cannon,* in which he himself appears in Turkish dress.

Pls. 173–4

Pl. 177

Dürer's woodcuts of these years are often closely connected with Humanist science. In 1515, for instance, he designed two large woodcuts showing the exact positions of the constellations of the northern and southern hemispheres. He did these woodcuts in collaboration with Johannes Stabius and the Nuremberg astronomer Konrad Heinfogel (who died in 1517), a pupil of Bernhard Walther. It is obvious that the artist was as interested in the science of astronomy, which had been practised in Nuremberg since the days of Regiomontanus, as in Ficino's astrological and philosophical speculations. There is a third and equally important woodcut of this time which depicts a *Map of the World.*[260] The subject had been suggested by Stabius and, like the two woodcuts of the constellations, was dedicated to the Bishop of Gurk, Cardinal Matthäus Lang von Wellenburg. It shows the eastern hemisphere of the globe with most of Europe, East Africa and Arabia, as well as those parts of the Indochinese peninsula which had been discovered by Vasco da Gama and other Portuguese seafarers in 1497–8. Dürer's representation is a considerable feat of technical

Pl. 175

Pl. 176

170 *Melencolia I.* 1514. Engraving. 23.9 × 16.8. Kupferstichkabinett SMPK, Berlin.

Since classical times melancholia has been interpreted as a depressed state of mind which takes away all enthusiasm for work. On the other hand, Aristotle had observed that talented and creative people in particular are often melancholics. The Florentine philosopher Marsilio Ficino linked this dual aspect of melancholia with the astrological doctrine of the dual nature of the planet Saturn whose influence on human beings may bring them either bad luck or good luck and wealth. This doctrine forms the basis of Dürer's engraving. The large, seated figure of winged genius symbolizes melancholia. The bat represents the negative forces of Saturnine melancholia; the industriously writing putto the positive forces. The hourglass, magic square of numbers and the scales reflect divine creation, which is ordered according to measure, number and weight. The number I behind the word Melencolia must be interpreted as a reference to the lowest kind of melancholia, which characterizes artists. The great variety of tools refer to art, as do the polyhedron and the sphere, which are at the same time linked with geometry, the basis of all art.

179

171 *The Apostle Paul.* 1514. Engraving. 11.9×7.5. Kupferstichkabinett SMPK, Berlin.

In 1514 Dürer started a series of engravings in small format. The first two published prints were those of the Apostles Paul and Thomas. The series was not continued until 1523 with the Apostles Bartholomew (Pl. 230) and Simon, and was finished in 1526 with the Apostle Philip (Pl. 231).

172 *Peasant Couple Dancing.* 1514. Engraving. 11.8×7.5. Kupferstichkabinett SMPK, Berlin.

Dürer had designed several small engravings of country folk before 1500 (cf. Pl. 47); the *Peasant Couple Dancing* of 1514 takes up the subject once more. Pictures of dancing or celebrating country folk had been popular in the visual arts since the fifteenth century; such pictures belong in the same context as the numerous, often rather coarse peasant and Shrovetide plays. However, Dürer's pictures of peasants should not be looked at only from the point of view of cultural history and the development of the genre, but should be recognized as visual representations of theoretical subjects, in this case of the "fat, peasant-like" type of the human body which is described at the beginning of Dürer's treatise on human proportions.

draughtsmanship, even though he may not have constructed the correctly foreshortened grid of parallels and meridians, which form a basis for this woodcut, unaided. It has been suggested that he worked with the help of a glass-panel device for drawing perspective, and used a three-dimensional model made by the cartographer and globe-maker Erhard Etzlaub.

The Portuguese had brought two animals back to Europe from India which were to become famous in the history of art: an elephant and the first rhinoceros to be seen in Europe. The Portuguese king gave both animals to Pope Leo X as a present, but only the elephant survived the second sea voyage; the ship carrying the rhinoceros sank in a storm in the Mediterranean. But a faithful likeness had earlier been taken of the animal which Dürer obtained, and his own woodcut version made the animal world-famous.[261] Pl. 178

Dürer completed very few paintings during the years he worked intensively for the emperor. Of three small paintings dated 1514, the most important was *Christ Wearing the*

173 *Veronica's Sudarium.* 1516. Iron etching. 18.5 × 13.4. Kupferstich-kabinett SMPK, Berlin.

Iron etching, a technique originally developed by armourers for the decoration of pieces of armour, was discovered as a medium for pictures about 1510. Dürer tried out this new, experimental graphic technique in five etchings completed between 1515 and 1518. His etching shows an angel holding Veronica's veil on which Christ's face and crown of thorns were supposed to be indelibly imprinted. This is an original and unusual composition, since representations of the subject generally depicted St. Veronica holding the veil or just the veil itself.

174. *Abduction on a Unicorn.* 1516. Iron etching. 30.8 × 21.3. Kupferstichkabinett SMPK, Berlin.

The precise subject of this iron etching showing the abduction of a woman is as yet unknown. The imaginary animal implies that the subject was taken from a mythological tale. This could have been a German legend or a classical myth, although this is not very likely, since the unicorn is unknown in Greek or Roman mythology.

Crown of Thorns (A. 126 K); unfortunately only copies of it now exist. The expressive power of Christ's head, which can be sensed even in the copies, links it, both from an artistic and a human point of view, with one of Dürer's best-known and most impressive works, the portrait of his mother of the same year. Barbara Dürer, who was then sixty-three years old, presents a profoundly disturbing image of human decline. The ruthless objectivity with which she is portrayed implies that it was a private portrait, because in contemporary art such ugliness and the effects of age were still considered expressions of evil forces, as is shown by a comparison with the painting *Vanitas.* Dürer's mother died two months after he had drawn her, and in his diary he wrote a short, moving account of her life and character, as he had done in 1502 when his father died.[262]

While Dürer does not appear to have completed any pictures in 1515, he painted five the following year, including two of heads of the apostles *Philip* (A. 128) and *Jacob.* The great care with which he rendered the curly hair

Pl. 179

Pl. 121

and beards of the two apostles is reminiscent of the calligraphic style of the drawings in the margins of the prayerbook. Apart from these two idealized portraits Dürer Pl. 182 painted a *Portrait of Michael Wolgemut* and also a *Portrait* Pl. 181 *of an Unknown Clergyman* (A. 123), in which the sitter is

175 *The Northern Firmament*. 1515. Woodcut. 43 × 43. Kupferstichkabinett SMPK, Berlin.

176 *Map of the World* (eastern hemisphere). 1515. Woodcut. 65×86. Kupferstichkabinett SMPK, Berlin.

Dürer had collaborated with Johannes Stabius, the Humanist adviser of the Emperor Maximilian, on the *Triumphal Arch* (Pls. 159, 160). He collaborated with him on three other works, the map of the world and the northern and southern firmaments. These were scientific representations dedicated to Cardinal Matthäus Lang von Wellenburg. The two pictures of the firmament are based on two maps of the two celestial spheres, which had been designed in 1503 in Nuremberg by the astronomer Konrad Heinfogel; the figures representing the signs of the zodiac shown on these maps may have been drawn by the astronomer himself. Stabius presumably based the map of the world on the first globe, made in 1493 by Martin Behaim in Nuremberg. The woodcut illustrates how intensively Dürer must have studied stereometry and perspective, which made it possible to represent the globe as a three-dimensional image on the picture plane. The depiction of India and Indochina, done according to information by Stabius which was even then no longer up-to-date, is less convincing.

believed to have been the Swiss reformer, Huldreich Zwingli. Dürer drew and painted Bishop Georg III during a stay in Bamberg in October, 1517 (A. 134K). The artist, who stayed with an acquaintance, Dr. Lorenz Beheim, a canon,[263] was evidently unprepared for the church dignitary's commission and had to borrow the necessary painting tools from the episcopal court painter, Hans Wolff.[264]

Less than three weeks after Dürer's return from Bamberg, the Nuremberg citizens heard the news that on the eve of All Saints Day (31 October 1517) Dr. Martin Luther, a monk of the Order of Augustinian Hermits, had posted on the door of the palace and university church in Wittenberg ninety-five theses condemning the sale of indulgences. Luther was not

183

177 *The Cannon.* 1518. Iron etching. 21.7×32.2. Kupferstichkabinett SMPK, Berlin.

The Cannon, Dürer's last iron etching, is almost a pure landscape. The gun, which gave the picture its title, and the group of figures in the foreground appear more like secondary features than the principal actors who determine the subject of the picture. The figures near the right-hand margin are shown to belong to different nationalities by their costume. The man in front is Dürer himself, in Turkish dress; the figure wearing a tall hat may well be a Byzantine, and the man with bow and sabre wears a Hungarian costume. The figure on the extreme right, wearing old-fashioned pointed shoes, can only be identified in a general way as West European. They all appear to be looking at the Nuremberg cannon which is tended to by a mercenary. The landscape depicts the village of Kirchehrenbach near Forchheim and the Ehrenburg hills behind it.

entirely unknown to Dürer nor to the group of Nuremberg citizens, among them Anton Tucher, Hieronymus Holzschuher, Kaspar Nützel, Hieronymus Ebner, Lazarus Spengler, and Christoph Scheurl,[265] who had become friendly with Johann von Staupitz, the head of Luther's religious order. Staupitz, the vicar-general, told them about Luther's kindness and learning and also about his work. The circle around Staupitz, which Scheurl called "Sodalitas Staupiziana", had formed after Staupitz preached during the Advent of 1516, before such a large crowd that the Augustinian church in Nuremberg proved too small to hold the faithful who had come to hear him.[267] He had told his astounded congregation that all sins were negligible in the face of God's immense and forgiving mercy.[268] To understand the impact of Staupitz's sermons it must be remembered that preachers at this time commonly prophesied that people would be punished in Hell, not just for their sins but above all for breaking church rules, and that their listeners

did not take this as an empty threat but believed such a fate really awaited them.[269] This also explains why Dürer tried to express his gratitude and love for Staupitz by making him almost daily presents of woodcuts and engravings.[270] The

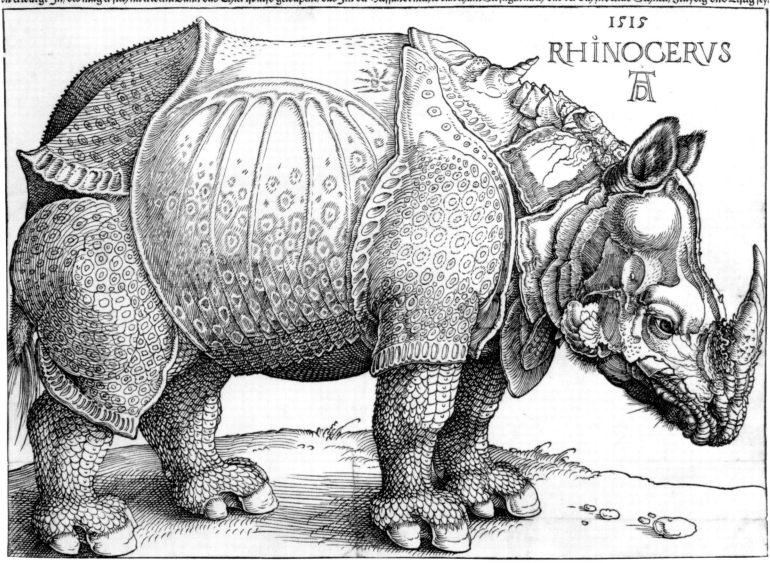

Nach Christus geburt.1513. Jar. Adi. j. May. Hat man dem grosmechtigen Künig von Portugall Emanuell gen Lysabona pracht auß India/ein sollich lebendig Thier. Das nennen sie Rhinocerus. Das ist hye mit aller seiner gestalt Abcondertfet. Es hat ein farb wie ein gesprecklete Schildtkrot. Und ist vō dicken Schalen vberlegt fast fest. Und ist in der grös als der Helfandt Aber nydertrechtiger von paynen/vnd fast werhafftig. Es hat ein scharff starck Horn vorn auff der nasen/Das begyndt es albeg zu werzen wo es bey staynen ist. Das dosig Thier ist des Helf fantz todt feyndt/Der Helffandt furcht es fast vbel/dann wo es In ankumbt/so laufft Im das Thier mit dem kopff zwischen dye fordern payn/vnd reyst den Helffandt vnden am pauch auff vō erwürgt In/des mag er sich nit erwern.Dann das Thier ist also gewapent/das Im der Helffandt nichts kan thün. Sie sagen auch das der Rhynocerus Schnell/Fraydig vnd Listig sey.

1515
RHINOCERVS

178 *The Rhinoceros*. 1515. Woodcut. 21.1×30. Kupferstichkabinett SMPK, Berlin.

In 1515 Portuguese sailors had brought the first rhinoceros and an Indian elephant to Lisbon. King Manuel I ("the Happy") of Portugal gave both animals to Pope Leo X as a present. But only the elephant, which was later painted by Raphael, reached Rome; the ship carrying the rhinoceros was shipwrecked and sank in the Mediterranean, taking the rare animal with it. The text accompanying the picture tells the tale of a fight between the two animals, which had been arranged at the royal court, which the rhinoceros won. From this time onwards the rhinoceros was believed to be the strongest and most courageous animal in existence, since even the much larger elephant ran away from it. Dürer's source for this very faithful rendering of the animal and the account of the fight is not known.

other members of the group, who met Staupitz at social gatherings at the Augustinian monastery or during his absence, at the house of one of their number,[271] also believed that it was he who would "deliver Israel". The members of the "Sodalitas" therefore initially thought that Luther's public posting of the theses was nothing but the courageous action of a disciple of Staupitz.

Dürer had decided as early as 1513 to tackle the theory of proportions before the other sections planned for his manual on painting.[272] In his drafts he mentions several times that certain circles considered such studies useless, even wicked.[273] Dürer opposed such restrictive claims which were also made against poetry,[274] pointing out that these

186

180 *The Apostle Jacob.* 1516. Oil. 46×38. Gallerie degli Uffizi, Florence.

Two heads of apostles painted on canvas (both now in Florence) are dated 1516. They form part of a series of pictures of the twelve apostles which Dürer planned but never completed. Written sources dating from the late sixteenth and early seventeenth century mention two other paintings in this series. The two paintings in Florence are masterpieces of the detailed rendering for which Dürer was famous for among his contemporaries and later collectors. The head of Jacob illustrates Dürer's realism of detail particularly clearly.

◁ 179 *The Artist's Mother.* 1514. Charcoal. 42.1×30.3. Kupferstichkabinett SMPK, Berlin.

According to the two inscriptions on this drawing, one inserted at the time the drawing was made, and the other (written in ink) added later, Dürer drew this portrait of his mother on 19 March 1514, almost two months before her death. The picture of this woman, exhausted by many illnesses and by eighteen births, is one of the most deeply moving portraits ever made. Its characterization is all the more extraordinary if one remembers that before Dürer's time artists only depicted old age and ugliness as symbols of death or evil. Dürer's moving account, in the *Gedenkbuch,* of his mother's death shows that neither are intended in this picture. For her son this portrait of Barbara Dürer was a purely private document, yet it was to influence other artists, as there are many pictures of ugly old women by Dürer's pupils.

studies satisfied a general thirst for knowledge.[275] Strangely enough, no one has yet been able to establish who these people were who despised the arts and science; at first one is reminded of the iconoclasts who were to wreak havoc ten years later. However, around 1513 critics like these were more likely to be found among the orthodox and conservative clergy who were suspicious of any branch of science or art which did not conform to the narrow framework of traditional worship. They may even have been the Dominican monks from Cologne who carried on a literary feud with Reuchlin during these years because they had burnt Hebrew literature. The slightly ironic words "O dear holy gentlemen and fathers" with which Dürer addresses such critics[276] also imply that he had clerical philistines in mind. However, he may equally have been thinking of iconoclastic Hussite sectarians in Franconia.[277]

Dürer continued working on his theory of proportions in spite of these attacks on science and art, which were hardly directed against him personally. After his return from the south, he simplified his original procedure for determining the measurements and contours of the human figure by means of circles and arcs drawn with compasses, and combined this simplified version with a numerical definition of the various parts of the human body.[278] His figures, which had been shown in slight movement in the early studies, were now drawn stiffly erect, in front, back and side views clearly showing their method of construction as well as their proportions.[279] Dürer started with the head, because its measurements (seen from the three views as well as from above) had to be determined first,[280] since according to his system, the proportions of the rest of the body depended on

181 *Portrait of an Unknown Clergyman.* 1516. Oil. 41.5×33. Kress Collection, National Gallery of Art, Washington. ▷

This man in clerical dress was traditionally believed to be Johann Dorsch, vicar of St. Johann. More recently it has been thought that this is a portrait of Huldreich Zwingli, who later was the Zurich reformer. However, there is no evidence of any contact between painter and reformer before 1519, nor do existing portraits of Zwingli confirm this identification.

182 *Portrait of Michael Wolgemut.* 1517. Oil. 29×27. Germanisches Nationalmuseum, Nuremberg. ▷▷

It is very likely that an earlier version, painted on parchment, preceded this panel, now in Nuremberg. Dürer added an inscription to the Nuremberg portrait of his eighty-two-year-old teacher identifying the sitter. He later added the date of Wolgemut's death, as he had done in the portrait of his mother (Pl. 179). This implies that the picture was in Dürer's possession at the time.

187

Das her albrecht durer ab contrafet hot
seine lermeister, bider gobemus, im Jor
1516 vnd er was 82 Jor
vnd hat gelebt pis das man
zelet 1519 Jor do ist er ferschidë
an sant endres dag fru er dy
sun auff ging

1516

the size of the head. By 1513 at the latest he had developed the system sufficiently to be able to express each part of the male and female body as a fraction of its overall length; he had thus advanced from purely geometric construction to arithmetic measurement.

Dürer did not stop at this arithmetic system of measurement which he had developed, but from about 1515 supplemented it with the geometric method of "Exempeda" which Leon Battista Alberti had put forward in his treatise *De statua*. Alberti used a measuring rod of the same length as the figure to be measured. He divided this rod into 600 equal parts and read off the various proportions, which were not identical with real measurements. Dürer adapted Alberti's method by taking a length of six feet (*c.* 1.70 m) as the basic measurement and dividing it, like Alberti, into 600 parts by means of inches *(Zoll)*, "parts" *(Teil)* and "small parts" *(Trümlein)*.

Dürer did not seek to establish an ideal set of measurements for the male and female body, but instead described several figure types (such as tall and thin, slim, muscular and stocky) all of which had harmonious proportions. This method, which he developed independently, surpassed any system established by the Italians, on whom Dürer had originally modelled himself. Dürer's method may be regarded as an early form of anthropometry, a discipline which developed only much later.[281] One sees how Dürer's starting-point, the different temperaments which are directly expressed in outward appearance, was brought to fruition.

IX. New Directions in Dürer's Art: 1518–20

Portraiture · Travels · The Reformation

The two-year interval between the spring of 1518, when Dürer sent the coloured drawing of the *Triumphal Chariot* to the emperor, and the summer of 1520, when he left for the Netherlands, seems to have been a time of reflection for him. After several hectic years, when one commission from the emperor had followed another in quick succession, Dürer once again had the time to work in a more leisurely way. However, only a few works dating from this two-year period have survived. It seems almost as if the creative energy of the artist, who was not yet fifty, had temporarily dried up. It is more likely, however, that work on the final version of his theory of proportions and the drawings which were to illustrate it kept him so occupied that he had little time for other works. When he left for the Netherlands he had finished the fair copy of the first two books of the theory of proportions.[282]

This very intense preoccupation with theoretical problems necessarily affected Dürer's art as well. Even after his return from Italy, he had cut down the number of figures in his pictures as far as the commissions allowed, thereby attaining an effect of monumentality rare in earlier German art. Yet, at the same time he had continued to paint in a refined calligraphic style, as is shown as late as 1516 in the heads of the Apostles. It was this style which, according to an anecdote in Joachim Camerarius's preface to his Latin translation of the *Four Books on Human Proportions*, had already been admired by the elderly Giovanni Bellini.

From about 1518 onwards, however, Dürer's striving for simpler compositions became even more pronounced. At this time he was particularly interested in conveying an impression of space, achieved solely through the extreme plasticity of his figures, which were mostly half-length or only head and shoulders. He concentrated on the most expressive parts, the head and the hands, stressing their individuality and thereby making even his pictures with religious subjects seem like portraits. We know, for instance, that the artist's wife was the model for the half-length figure of St. Anne in the panel painting *The Virgin and Child with St. Anne*, painted in 1519 for Leonard Tucher.

In complete contrast to this devotional picture is a painting of the *Suicide of Lucretia* (A. 137), in which the figure of the classical heroine was based on one of the figures Dürer used to exemplify proportions. Preliminary studies indicate that this painting had been planned as early as 1508, but was not executed until a full decade later. The whole of this full-length nude, including the inclined head, was constructed according to Dürer's system. He tried in vain to convey something of the tragic greatness of the Roman heroine through her expression, but the everyday details of the background make the heroic pose even more implausible.

It is not surprising that Dürer turned to the depiction of single figures. From the very beginning, he had been a supreme portraitist, both as a painter and a draughtsman.

183 *Portrait of a Man*. 1518. Charcoal. 37 × 27.6. Department of Prints and Drawings, British Museum, London. ▷

The delicately etched features of the man in this London drawing belong to Dürer's friend Lazarus Spengler, clerk to the Nuremberg Council. This is presumably the drawing on which a portrait painting of the same year, now lost and known only through two minor copies, was based.

184 *The Virgin and Child with St. Anne*. 1519. Oil. 60 × 49. Benjamin Altman Foundation, Metropolitan Museum of Art, New York. ▷▷

The belief that St. Anne, the mother of the Virgin Mary, had also experienced an immaculate conception had found wide acceptance since the last quarter of the fifteenth century. This made St. Anne one of the important saints and she was revered throughout Europe. In painting, the emergence of this new cult was reflected in a compositional type showing a group of three figures: St. Anne, the Virgin Mary, and the Infant Jesus. The figures in Dürer's picture appear like portraits. This is confirmed by a study for St. Anne, who clearly bears the features of Dürer's wife. The Infant Jesus is shown asleep, a presentiment of death. A painful premonition of the future fate of the Child is movingly conveyed in the features of the youthful Virgin. St. Anne, who is also aware of the suffering to come, consolingly puts her hand on her daughter's shoulder.

191

192

There is, however, a definite attempt in these later paintings to do justice both to his theoretical ideals and to the individual features of the sitter, regardless of whether it was the portrait of a fellow-citizen or an idealized picture of a saint or classical heroine.[283] Thus, in all his paintings after 1518 Dürer applied the knowledge gained in his *Self-Portrait* of 1500, an experiment which he could never repeat.

The majority of the paintings executed during these two years were purely portraits; most of them, and certainly the most important, were connected with Dürer's stay in Augsburg. The painter, the city councillor Kaspar Nützel and his friend Lazarus Spengler, clerk to the council, had been sent as representatives of Nuremberg to the Diet which took place in Augsburg from June to September, 1518. The princes and prelates who gathered in the city, led by the emperor and the arch-chancellor, Archbishop Albrecht of Mainz, were eager to have their portraits executed by the most famous painter of their time. Dürer made drawings of prominent politicians (W. 568, 570), the Augsburg

185 *Portrait of the Emperor Maximilian*. 1518. Charcoal. 38.1×31.9. Graphische Sammlung Albertina, Vienna.

186 *Portrait of the Emperor Maximilian*. 1519. Coloured and gilded woodcut. 41.4×31.9. Staatsbibliothek, Bamberg.

In the summer of 1518, Dürer, Kaspar Nützel and Lazarus Spengler (Pl. 183) went to the Diet of Augsburg as representatives of the City of Nuremberg. On this occasion the Emperor had his portrait drawn by Dürer in the Emperor's room at the bishop's palace. Dürer's drawing gives a good impression of the friendly, but somewhat restless character of the ageing Maximilian. Three portraits of the monarch are based on this sketch: a woodcut and two paintings, now in Nuremberg and Vienna (Pl. 187). At the upper margin of the woodcut is a scroll with an inscription modelled on imperial coins of classical Rome. The epithet *divus* (divine) may well imply that the Emperor was already dead when Dürer designed this woodcut, since the Roman Caesars—whose successors the emperors of the Holy Roman Empire of the German Nation considered themselves to be—were only called *divus* after their death. It is likely that this woodcut was designed when Dürer heard of Maximilian's death; some copies are gilded and coloured, making them look like paintings.

187 *Portrait of the Emperor Maximilian*. 1519. Oil. 73×62. Kunsthistorisches Museum, Vienna.
▷

194

POTENTISSIMVS · MAXIMVS · ET · INVICTISSIMVS · CÆSAR · MAXIMILIANVS
QVI · CVNCTOS · SVI · TEMPORIS · REGES · ET · PRINCIPES · IVSTICIA · PRVDENCIA
MAGNANIMITATE · LIBERALITATE · PRÆCIPVE · VERO · BELLICA · LAVDE · ET
ANIMI · FORTIDVDINE · SVPERAVIT · NATVS · EST · ANNO · SALVTIS · HVMANÆ
M · CCCC · LIX · DIE · MARCII · IX · VIXIT · ANNOS · LIX · MENSES · IX · DIES · XXV
DECESSIT · VERO · ANNO · M · D · XIX · MENSIS · IANVARII · DIE · XII · QVEM · DEVS
OPT · MAX · IN · NVMERVM · VIVENCIVM · REFERRE · VELIT ·

195

188 *The Small Cardinal.* 1519. Engraving. 14.8 × 9.7. Kupferstich-kabinett SMPK, Berlin.

This engraving of 1519 is called the "Small Cardinal" to distinguish it from the portrait engraving of the same sitter, Albrecht of Brandenburg, made in 1523. Dürer had portrayed the church dignitary during the Diet of Augsburg in 1518. Albrecht (1490–1545), who was then not yet thirty years old, was the Elector and Archbishop of Mainz as well as Arch-chancellor of the German Empire, Archbishop of Magdeburg and Administrator of the Halberstadt diocese. When Albrecht made attempts to become a cardinal in 1517, he had to pay the Papal Court a "pallium tax" of 50,000 florins. The Fugger bank had advanced this huge sum and as a result shared the receipts from indulgences granted by the Pope. The priest Tetzel's method of selling indulgences induced Luther to write his ninety-five theses. The cardinal's ambition may thus be regarded as the indirect cause of the Reformation. The inscriptions on the engraving read: "Albrecht by the grace of God cardinal priest of the Holy Roman Church with the titular church of St. Chrysogonus, Archbishop of Mainz and Magdeburg, Elector and Primate of the Empire, Administrator of [the diocese of] Halberstadt, Margrave of Brandenburg.—This is what his eyes, cheeks and mouth looked like."

189 *The Madonna with the Infant Jesus in Swaddling Clothes.* 1520. Engraving. 14.4 × 9.7. Kupferstichkabinett SMPK, Berlin.

This is one of two small engravings of the Madonna made in 1520. The picture of Mary holding the sleeping child on her lap appears almost like a genre scene, but the sleeping child was generally regarded as a symbolic representation of the dead Christ (cf. Pl. 184). This interpretation is enforced by the swaddling clothes which make the infant resemble a mummy. The Madonna seems to have a premonition that she will hold her Son, who will then have died on the Cross, in the same way as she now holds the newly born infant.

190 *The Madonna and Child Sitting on a Grassy Bank.* 1519. Pen. 30.5 × 21.4. By gracious permission of Her Majesty Queen Elizabeth II; Royal Library, Windsor Castle. ▷

The subject of the Madonna and Child is the most frequently recurring theme in Dürer's work. He constantly invented new compositions for the subject. This drawing in Windsor shows a variation of the central group of figures in *Feast of the Rose Garlands* of 1506 (Pl. 114). The composition is both graceful and monumental, making the drawing a masterpiece of the High Renaissance.

1519

191 *Peasants at the Market.* 1519. Engraving. 11.6×7.3. Kupferstich-kabinett SMPK, Berlin.

This work reflects Dürer's studies of human proportions even more clearly than the engraving of *Peasant Couple Dancing* (Pl. 172). The man's head, for instance, is very reminiscent of the head which appears on the upper right of sheet Q 4 of Dürer's theory of proportions. The awkward, comical effect which predominates in the picture of the dancing couple has been replaced here by a certain sympathy for the poverty of the hard-working country folk.

merchant Jakob Fugger (W. 571), the richest man of his time, of his fellow-painter from Augsburg, Hans Burgkmair

Pl. 183 (W. 569), and presumably also of his friends Lazarus Spengler and Kaspar Nützel (W. 565).[283a] Most of these portrait drawings were almost certainly intended as preliminary studies for paintings to be executed later. While still in Augsburg, Dürer did a painting of Jakob Fugger. The portrait was done in tempera on canvas (A. 143); the more durable panel version (A. 144K) was not painted until 1520 when Dürer was back in Nuremberg.

Dürer's study of the head of the 59-year-old emperor Pl. 185 shows a man who was clearly ageing and in indifferent health, yet also conveys much of the monarch's benevolent charm. Three works are based on this study: a picture on canvas (A. 145), presumably executed while Dürer was still in Augsburg, a portrait panel painted early in 1519, and a Pls. 187, 186 woodcut. The two painted versions differ in technique and colour, but the formal arrangement is almost identical. Dürer attempted to create a representative portrait of a ruler without falling back on the usual device of showing the king in his full regalia. In his picture, the imperial coat of arms with the crown of the House of Hapsburg and the chain of the Order of the Golden Fleece are merely heraldic symbols of the sitter's rank. The true impact of the portrait depends on the formal arrangement and the vivid characterization. The half-length figure is shaped roughly like an equilateral triangle and is reminiscent of Dürer's early portraits. The forearms and hands, which hold a pomegranate, a symbol chosen by the emperor, form the base of the triangle. Dürer's characterization of the emperor in these two works differs considerably from the method he employed in any of the other portraits he painted. Neither picture shows the aggressive liveliness typical of Dürer's portraits. The emperor, who was in fact a lively man, appears rather withdrawn; this was presumably intended as an expression of his dignity and majesty.[284] Dürer attempted a kind of "state portrait" in both these works, while his woodcut portrayal ensured that the memory of the emperor, who died in Wels on 12 January 1519, was kept alive. It is the first monumental woodcut portrait in European art.

Strangely enough, the idea of making engravings from portraits does not seem to have come from Dürer. The goldsmith Israhel van Meckenem of Bocholt in Westphalia had already produced portrait engravings around 1500, and Lucas Cranach had done so in 1509 and 1510. Albrecht of Brandenburg, a vain man who had been made a cardinal by the papal legate in Augsburg on 1 August 1518, had his portrait drawn by Dürer immediately afterwards so that the artist could make an engraving of him in his new rank. This portrait, the so-called *Small Cardinal*, engraved in 1519, is Pl. 188 very similar in composition to the two painted portraits of the late emperor. All three carry a coat of arms as well as an inscription listing the sitter's titles at the top of the picture. However, the curtain behind the cardinal and the inscribed plate underneath the portrait proper are new elements.

Dürer made six other small engravings during the years before his journey to the Netherlands. Among these are two pictures of the Virgin, dated 1520, which he mentions Pls. 189–90 several times in his diary. The engravings, like his other works of the period, are of single figures; only *Peasants at the Market* has two. By now, however, the figures are no longer depicted in front of a neutral background but rather as part of a frequently detailed landscape. A particularly good example is *St. Anthony*, who is shown sitting outside the gates of a town absorbed in his reading. Among the few woodcuts of these years, *St. Sebaldus* (B. app. 21) and the *Virgin as Queen of the Angels* deserve mention, because they are two of the last compositions incorporating a multitude of figures which Dürer designed before going to the Netherlands.

On 8 September 1518, while the Diet was still in progress in Augsburg, the emperor wrote to the Nuremberg Council to make a single payment of 200 florins to Dürer out of the city taxes.[285] However, a letter, dated 27 April 1519, which Dürer wrote to the council makes it clear that the artist had not yet received the money promised to him, although the emperor's letter had contained a receipt for the sum payable. Dürer asked for the money to be paid straightaway, and at the same time offered his house as a surety in case the successor to Maximilian, who had died in January, would not acknowledge the claim.[286] Finally, in 1519 and 1520, Dürer received a back payment of 500 florins from the Nuremberg Council.

It is possible that the reason Dürer tried so hard to obtain the 200 florins was an illness which caused him serious concern. On 18 January 1519 Pirckheimer wrote to Thomas Venatorius in Kornburg that his friend did not feel at all well.[287] But the artist's indisposition does not appear to have been particularly serious or protracted, since it did not stop him from planning long journeys. A letter written on 29 March by Lorenz Behaim to Pirckheimer mentions that Dürer toyed with the idea of going to England or Spain.[288] The reasons for these plans appear to have been financial, for Behaim advised the painter to be content with what he presently possessed since he had no direct heirs, and to spend his days quietly worshipping God. The two distant destinations may well have had some connection with the two candidates whom Maximilian had put forward at the Augsburg Diet as possible successors; these were King Henry VIII of England and Maximilian's grandson, Charles of Burgundy, who had become ruler of Spain in September, 1518.

Even though Dürer gave up the plan to visit England and Spain, he could not altogether suppress the urge to travel, an urge which Lorenz Behaim had predicted in his horoscope of Dürer as early as 1507.[289] Dürer joined Willibald Pirckheimer and Martin Tucher who went to Zurich for negotiations in late April, 1519. The three Nuremberg

192 *St. Anthony outside the City Gates.* 1519. Engraving. 9.6 × 14.3. Kupferstichkabinett SMPK, Berlin.

The monk sitting on the ground outside the walls of a town, who appears to be completely absorbed in his reading, can only be identified as St. Anthony by the shape of the cross on a staff and by the bell. Dürer's engraving is totally independent of the traditional iconographic representation of this saint who was widely revered in the late Middle Ages. For the town Dürer used a view from the drawing *Pupila Augusta* (Pl. 50) of 1496–7.

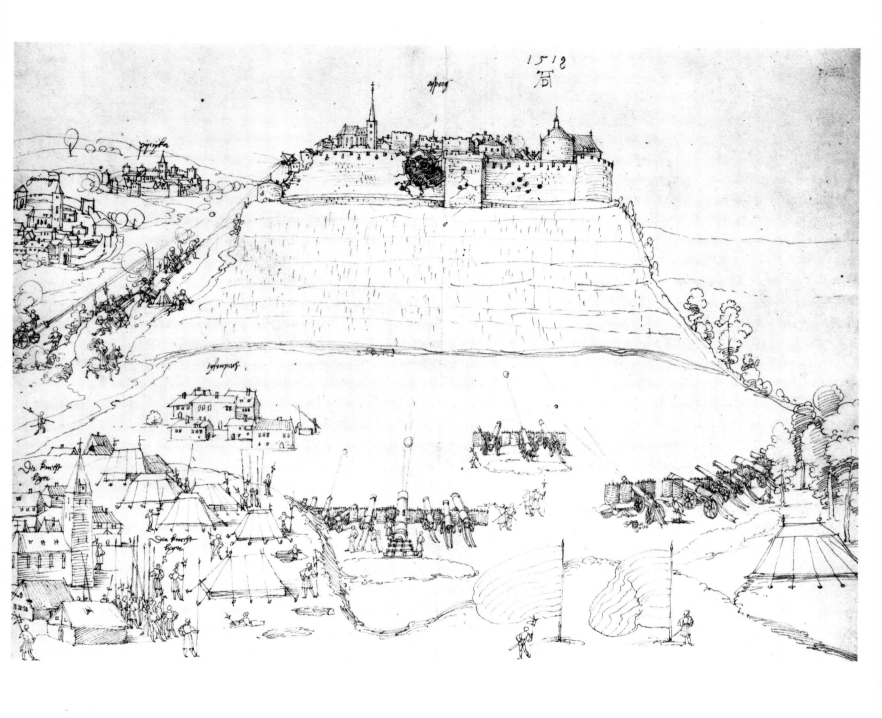

194 *Siege of the Fortress of Hohenasperg.* 1519. Pen. 31.2×43.6. Kupferstichkabinett SMPK, Berlin.

◁ 193 *The Virgin as Queen of the Angels.* 1518. Woodcut. 30.1×21.2. Kupferstichkabinett SMPK, Berlin.

Dürer's style from about 1508 to 1516–17 was partly determined by the commissions he received in these years. It is characterized by an attention to detail, and yet at the same time is strongly decorative. However, from about 1518 onwards his shapes become larger, draperies become simpler, and there are hardly any of the details which Dürer had shown with such loving care in earlier pictures. Simple parallel hatchings replace lines curving in many directions. The woodcut of the *Virgin as Queen of the Angels* marks this change to Dürer's mature style.

This drawing was made on a journey to Zurich which Dürer undertook with Pirckheimer and Martin Tucher in May, 1519. It shows the siege of the Württemberg fortress of Hohenasperg near Ludwigsburg by troops of the Swabian League under Georg von Frundsberg. The defenders surrendered after a ten-day siege, on 26 May 1519, the last of the duke's occupying forces to do so. Dürer's drawing of the encirclement of the fortress was scarcely an on-the-spot work; it is more likely that it was completed later, based on memory and several quick sketches. This is confirmed by the draughtsmanship, which is very neat in parts, as well as the careful inscriptions of the names of local villages, such as *pyetyka* (Bietigheim), *grünign* (Grüningen) and *tyfenpach* (Tiefenbach).

201

citizens travelled through Württemberg where Duke Ulrich had been at war with the troops of the Swabian Confederation for several weeks. Most of the towns and princely castles had already been conquered and the duke had fled. When the Nuremberg travellers rode through the immediate vicinity, only the fortress of Hohenasperg was still resisting the besieging army under the mercenaries' leader, Georg von Frundsberg. Dürer made a quick sketch recording the

Pl. 194 already heavily damaged fortress and the camp of the besieging army. Behaim's relief at the safe return of the travellers is understandable, since the journey through areas thick with mercenaries appears to have been dangerous.[290]

Little is known about the artist's life during the next twelve months up to his departure for the Netherlands. He and his wife were invited to the wedding of Dr. Christoph Scheurl and Katharina Fütterer, which took place on 29 August 1519.[291] The Portuguese nobleman Rui Fernandes de Almada stayed in Nuremberg for about a week in September, before going on to Augsburg, Ulm and Munich on a diplomatic mission for his king.[292] Judging by the friendly relationship Dürer later had with this man in Antwerp, it seems likely that they had already met in Nuremberg. An even more important event for Dürer was the death of 85-year-old Michael Wolgemut on 30 November. Dürer added a note about his former teacher's death to

Pl. 182 the portrait of Wolgemut which he had painted in 1516.

Luther's public display of his theses, which was the usual procedure and signified a general challenge for a learned disputation on a subject, had met with an unexpectedly strong response throughout Germany. The theses had been translated by Kaspar Nützel and published in Nuremberg as early as November, 1517.[293] In 1518 Lazarus Spengler, who was later to become the most important supporter of the Reformation in Nuremberg, anonymously published his *Schutzrede* in Augsburg. It was a speech in defence of Luther, but as his authorship soon became known, he was threatened with excommunication. Both Dürer and Pirckheimer welcomed the progress of the church reforms for which people had longed for a century. Dürer himself compiled a list of Luther's writings, entering sixteen titles between 1518 and 1520, which shows how eagerly he tried to keep up to date with the developments of the new teaching. The impact Luther's work made on Dürer personally is seen in a letter written to Georg Spalatin, early in 1520, in which Dürer asks Spalatin to thank his long-standing patron, the Elector Frederick the Wise, for sending him some of the writings of Luther "who has helped me out of great fears". These few words express what a large part of the German population must have felt. There was a general feeling of tremendous liberation, which we in the twentieth century can hardly recapture, as there is no longer the interest in religious, let alone theological problems.

X. The Journey to the Netherlands: 1520–1

Height of Fame · Illness · Plans

Dürer set out on his journey to the Netherlands on Thursday, 12 July 1520, accompanied by his wife and their maid Susanna. There was yet another outbreak of the plague in Nuremberg when they left.[294] Dürer may have subjected his wife Agnes to the journey, despite its rigours and dangers,[295] because he could not foresee how long he would be away, or possibly because he himself needed constant attention due to ill-health.[296] Dürer's reason for making the journey was his wish to have the pension promised him by the late emperor confirmed by Maximilian's grandson, Charles of Burgundy. The latter had been elected German emperor in Frankfurt/Main on 18 July 1519, but had not returned to the Netherlands from his Spanish kingdoms until 1 June 1520.

Dürer and his wife and maid first went by carriage to Bamberg, which they reached in two stages. Bishop Georg Schenk of Limburg, whose portrait Dürer had painted in 1517, thanked Dürer for a present (consisting of a picture of the Virgin and a considerable number of woodcuts and engravings)[297] by providing the artist with three letters of recommendation and a customs permit which exempted the travellers from paying duty at many of the numerous customs posts on the Main and Rhine. From Bamberg Dürer travelled down the Main by boat, while his extensive luggage went overland to Frankfurt, at the cost of six florins for haulage. This surprisingly high fee was probably due to the transport of paintings and a large number of graphic works, including prints by Hans Schäufelein and Hans Baldung, which Dürer took with him.[298] The graphic works were presumably packed in barrels to protect them against damp, as was the custom. In Frankfurt, Jakob Heller sent Dürer some wine at his inn; from there the three travellers went by boat to Cologne via Mainz, arriving on 25 July. Here Dürer visited his cousin, the goldsmith Niklas Unger, son of Dürer's uncle Ladislaus. Hieronymus Fugger, for whose father Dürer had designed a tomb ten years earlier, also sent him some wine; indeed, wine was a gift which Dürer received from well-wishers quite frequently on his journey. After five days the travellers continued their journey overland to Antwerp where on 3 August they arrived at the inn of Jobst Planckfelt on the Wolstraat.

Antwerp was a flourishing city at that time. Since the middle of the fifteenth century trade had increasingly switched to this Brabant city on the river Schelde because the harbour approach to Bruges, the old trading metropolis of the southern Netherlands, had silted up more and more, so that the large, three-masted sailing ships could only reach the harbour with difficulty. The wide Schelde estuary provided easy access to Antwerp and its extensive harbour; Dürer made one of his most inspired pen drawings of the harbour at the southern end of the city. Antwerp, which contemporary travellers called "the flower of the earth" or "the home for all peoples", had approximately the same number of inhabitants as Nuremberg.[299] All the European nations had trading stations there. Among the south German merchants, the Fugger family and many Nuremberg trading companies were represented, and the Hanseatic League had moved their office from Bruges to this city on the Schelde. The English stored their wool and their sought-after cloth in Antwerp, and even strangely mediæval-looking Irish – inhabitants of "farther-England" (W. 825), as Dürer wrote – could be seen here. In the streets one might have met the wives of Prague burghers (W. 751)[299a] and rich Livonian women in their bizarre dresses. And, of course, there were Spaniards, French, Italians and Portuguese. Dürer came into contact, to a greater or lesser extent, with people of all these nationalities. Among the Italians, he was particularly friendly with the brothers Gherardo, Tommaso and Vicentino Bombelli from Genoa. The painter Tommaso Vincidoro went to see Dürer when he visited Antwerp on his way to Brussels, where he was to deliver Raphael's cartoons for the tapestries of the Sixtine Chapel in the Vatican to the carpet weaver Pieter Aelst. Tommaso gave a ring to the Nuremberg artist whom he revered. Dürer was also in close

Pl. 195

Pl. 196

Pl. 197

Pls. 155–6

203

Whilst in Antwerp Dürer, his wife and maid lived at the inn "Engelenborch", owned by Jobst Planckfelt (Joos Blanckvelt in the Netherlandish version) on the Wolstraat, also called Engelsche Straat. It was situated in the best quarter of the town, between the market and the harbour, where the English merchants had warehouses for their wool, and the Hanseatic merchants (e.g. Bernhard von Reesen) conducted their business. According to the diary which Dürer kept during his stay in the Netherlands he appears to have rented a whole suite of rooms from Planckfelt, including a living-room, bedroom and kitchen. Several entries in the diary show that Dürer was on friendly terms with his host, which is confirmed by this Frankfurt drawing. It was presumably a preliminary study for the portrait in oils which Dürer painted of Planckfelt. Unfortunately neither the drawing nor the picture of Planckfelt's wife have survived. At the end of his stay, Dürer gave the double portrait to the couple as payment.

contact with three Portuguese friends, João Brandão, Rui Fernandes de Almada and Francisco Pesão.

Dürer and his wife had rented a small separate suite of rooms at Jobst Planckfelt's inn "Engelenborch", so that Agnes and the maid could live and run their household independent of the rest of the inn.[300] Scholars have often found it strange that Dürer either had his meals alone in the inn's public room or with friends and acquaintances elsewhere, while his wife and maid had to provide their own.[301] But at that time even the wives of well-to-do burghers only appeared in public when their housewifely duties made it necessary, and then only if they were accompanied. Furthermore, the public room of an inn was not a place which a respectable woman could enter without a compelling reason. It is therefore likely that the maid Susanna had been taken on the journey not only to be a servant to Dürer's wife Agnes, but also to be her companion when necessary.

The extent to which Dürer's fame had spread was demonstrated to him from the very beginning of his stay in Antwerp. Bernhard Stecher, the factor of the Fugger family, invited him to dinner on the very first evening, which also indicates how close Dürer's relationship with the Augsburg merchants must have been. The next morning, Planckfelt took the painter to see the mayor, Arnold van Liere, who lived in a large house built in 1516.[302] It is not known whether Dürer drew the late Gothic turret of this extensive group of buildings (W. 774) on that occasion or later. An even greater honour for Dürer was an invitation for the evening of the third day for himself, his wife and his maid to the painters' Guild Hall, "De bonte Mantel", on the main market place. There they were given a banquet by the Antwerp painters, whose most important representatives were Quentin Massys, Joos van Cleve and Joachim Patenier. Late at night the guests of honour were seen home by torchlight.

Even in those early days Dürer made several new acquaintances, among them the Munich astronomer Nikolaus Kratzer, who was in the service of Henry VIII of England and had come to Antwerp to visit Erasmus of Rotterdam. Erasmus had lived in Louvain since 1517, but had moved to Antwerp where Dürer made his acquaintance and did his portrait (W. 805).

The friendly reception he received in Antwerp did not, however, make Dürer forget the aim of his journey. As early as August he went with Tommaso Bombelli to Mechelen, where he met the sculptor Konrad Meit from Worms, who was in the service of Margaret of Austria, the daughter of Emperor Maximilian and Governor of the Netherlands.

From Mechelen, Dürer went on to Brussels where the newly elected German emperor Charles V resided in the palace of the former dukes of Burgundy. In this palace on the Couden hill, Dürer submitted a petition which one of the German government officials had drafted for him to the king's

secretary, Jakob de Banissis.[303] De Banissis had been Latin secretary to the previous emperor and perhaps knew Dürer from that time; he was also a friend of Pirckheimer's.[304] He immediately passed the petition to the king's aunt, Margaret of Austria, who had the artist called before her and assured him that she would plead with her nephew Charles on his behalf. Jakob de Banissis then invited Dürer for a meal, and during the last days of August drafted an approval to be signed by the king.[305]

While he was waiting, Dürer looked at the sights of Brussels. In the town hall he saw Rogier van der Weyden's famous paintings representing justice, and in the house of Duke Engelbert of Nassau he cast his eyes on a painting by Hugo van der Goes. In his diary he referred with great admiration to the precious objects which Hernando Cortez

196 *Antwerp Harbour*. 1520. Pen. 21.3 × 28.3. Graphische Sammlung Albertina, Vienna.

This view of a part of the flourishing trading city of Antwerp fronting the river Schelde is one of Dürer's most important landscapes because of its clear composition and simple lines. Dürer drew this view near the southern end of the city, by the "Eeckhof", a house owned by the Antwerp Painters' Guild; it was situated next to the tower with the high pointed roof. The view is to the west, across river boats and the Schelde; beyond the river is the range of hills known as "Hofd van Vlanderen".

The drawing is inscribed at the top: "This is how the rich ladies look in eiffland". Dürer's critics, even recent ones, have repeatedly voiced the opinion that Dürer copied this drawing, as well as two others (W. 826–8) and his picture of Irishmen (W. 825), from foreign pictorial models which he saw in Antwerp. However, this view ignores several aspects: firstly the quality of the conspicuously signed drawing; secondly Dürer's interest, from an early date, in all kinds of costumes; and thirdly the fact that Antwerp even at that time was a harbour visited by ships from all parts of Europe. It should also be remembered that both Dürer's early costume studies (Pls. 38, 73, 97) and the studies of the Livonian ladies and the Irishmen are pen and wash drawings. The four costume studies may not have been drawn directly from the models, but may well be based on sketches made by Dürer himself.

had several conversations with Dürer on this occasion and again in the spring of 1521 in the house of Petrus Aegidius. He found that although the painter had not had a scholarly education, he was surprisingly knowledgeable about questions of religion and philosophy and was also conversant with contemporary writings on mathematics and astronomy.[308]

Back in Antwerp, Dürer witnessed the ceremonial entry of King Charles V into the town. Triumphal arches had been erected for the occasion and young people from Antwerp enacted allegorical scenes beneath them. Dürer bought the Latin description of the ceremonial architecture by Petrus Aegidius.[309] He also admired some prehistoric bones said to have come from the legendary giant Brabo. The list of names of Dürer's acquaintances at that time is impressive: there were the Herren von Rogendorf, for whom he drew the family coat of arms on a wood block, the king's secretary, Jakob de Banissis, to whom he gave a picture as a present, Captain Felix Hungersberg, whose portrait he drew twice (W. 749, 819), Hans Ebner from Nuremberg, Rui Fernandes and the Bruges painter Jan Provost. Dürer made charcoal drawings of many of these men, but none exist today. The artist generously gave many of his graphic works away, but he was also interested in selling his prints so that he could meet part of the cost of his stay from the proceeds.

On 4 October Dürer went to Aachen where the coronation of the twenty-year-old Charles of Spain was shortly to take place; his aim was to obtain at long last the hoped-for confirmation that his pension would be continued. As always, he visited the sights of the city while he was waiting. He made a silver-point drawing of the cathedral,[310] where Pl. 199 he was particularly interested in the well-proportioned late classical columns of the interior; he also drew the town hall (W. 764) where he asked to see the great hall. Together with

had sent King Charles from Mexico, which he had just conquered. These objects had presumably been shown to Dürer in the Brussels palace. From an upper window of this residence, which was situated on a steep hill, Dürer made a sketch of the tilt-yard, the Clutink Pond and the zoological gardens below him (W. 822).[306] The court painter of the Governor, Barent van Orley, also invited Dürer for a meal; among those present were the treasurer, Jan de Marnix, the master of the king's household, Jehan de Metenye, and Gillis van Busleyden. In spite of the numerous sightseeing excursions and visits, Dürer had more than enough time to make charcoal drawings of many of the people he met, including his host, Barent van Orley (W. 810). He drew Erasmus of Rotterdam for the second time, in the presence of Nikolaus Kratzer.[307] Dürer later based his portrait Pl. 222 engraving of Erasmus on this drawing, now lost. Erasmus

198 *The Imperial Herald Kaspar Sturm.* 1520. Silver-point. 12.7 × 18.9.
Musée Condé, Chantilly.

Dürer inscribed this drawing at the top: "1520. CASPER STURM. 45
YEARS OLD. Drawn in Aachen." Underneath it is the word "toll"
(customs). Kaspar Sturm, born around 1475 in Oppenheim, was created
Imperial Herald by Charles V four days after his coronation, on
27 October 1520, and received the official title of "Germany". As Dürer
had left Aachen on the previous day, this portrait must have been drawn
between 7 October, the date of Dürer's arrival in Aachen, and his departure. Sturm, who died in 1548 in Nuremberg, published several books of
armoury as well as a number of accounts of his occupation. His most
famous official duties consisted in escorting Luther to the Diet of Worms
in 1521 and being present at the siege of Franz von Sickingen in his Castle
Landstuhl in 1523. Dürer presumably added the landscape background
on 14 or 15 November, during his return journey to Antwerp. It shows
the customs house either in Lobith or in the small town of Tiel.

199 *Aachen Cathedral.* 1520. Silver-point. 12.6 × 17.7. Department of
Prints and Drawings, British Museum, London.

The drawing is inscribed by Dürer on the top right: "The Minster in ach
[Aachen]". As he had done in earlier years, Dürer chose a high view-point
for his drawing of the cathedral. The rising ground of the palace courtyard is bordered by the building of the cathedral brewery. The impressive
architecture of the cathedral rises above the low houses at the north end
of the courtyard; the Carolingian west end can be seen on the extreme
right, Charlemagne's octagon in the centre, and Charles IV's choir on the
right.

several Nuremberg acquaintances such as Paulus Topler, Martin Pfinzing (W. 761), Hans Ebner and the "older mayor" Leonhard Groland, who had accompanied the coronation regalia to Aachen, he visited the thermal baths or spent his time drinking and gambling. At this time he also made a portrait drawing in his sketchbook of the imperial herald Kaspar Sturm (W. 765).[311] Dürer was among the spectators when Charles V was crowned German king in the cathedral on 23 October. As he still had not received any official information about his pension, he had to follow the court to Jülich, where he bought himself spectacles,[312] and then to Cologne. On 12 November 1520, he finally received the long-awaited document which assured him that his pension would be continued.[313]

Dürer stayed in Cologne for several weeks and took the opportunity to go and see Stephan Lochner's *Altarpiece of the Three Magi* in the chapel of the town hall. He also found

200 *View of Bergen op Zoom*. 1520. Silver-point. 13.3 × 19.4. Musée Condé, Chantilly.

Inscribed at the top: "In pergen". On 3 December 1520 Dürer hired a horse and, together with several Nuremberg friends, rode to Zeeland, to look at a whale which had been washed ashore in the Schelde estuary near Zierickzee. The first stop on this journey was Bergen op Zoom; here Dürer drew a view of the town, including the church which was being built, and a view of the building site itself (W. 722). The view shown in this drawing was used by Dürer for the background of his large, unfinished engraving of a Crucifixion with a multitude of figures, executed around 1523.

201 *Rui Fernandes de Almada*. 1520–1. Brush on grey-purple primed paper. 37.3 × 27.1. Kupferstichkabinett SMPK, Berlin. ▷

Rui Fernandes de Almada (*c.* 1465/70–1546/48) was a Portuguese diplomat and representative of his king in Antwerp. He was in frequent contact with Dürer while the artist was in the Netherlands. The drawing is executed in a technique which Dürer first used around this time. It is the preliminary study for the (much damaged) portrait painting of Almada now in the possession of the Isabella Stewart Gardner Museum in Boston, Mass.

time to design a woodcut with a coat of arms for Lorenz Staiber (St. 1520/26 and B. 167), who was married to a relative of Dürer's wife. As in Antwerp, while in Cologne he kept himself informed of events concerning Luther. It was in Cologne, if not earlier, that he must have heard from Leonhard Groland, of whose son he had just done a portrait,[314] that his friends Pirckheimer and Spengler, together with Luther, had been threatened with excommunication by the pope. The council had sent notice of this event to Groland and Niklas Haller on 20 October.[315] There is no mention of it in Dürer's diary, but it might have been because of these new developments that Dürer bought the *Condemnatio Lutheri* and one of Luther's tracts in Cologne.[316] He returned to the Netherlands by a roundabout route, going by boat down the Rhine to Tiel, then down the Meuse to Bommel, then overland to Antwerp by way of s'Hertogenbosch.

At the beginning of December, in spite of it being so late in the year, Dürer and several Nuremberg acquaintances once again set off on a journey, this time to see a giant whale which had been washed ashore in a storm near Zierickzee in Zeeland. The travellers were almost shipwrecked when they landed at Arnemuiden on the island of Walcheren. On 10 December they went across to Zierickzee but by then the whale had been washed back into the sea again. On the way Pl. 200 the tireless artist had drawn a view of Bergen op Zoom (W. 768) and of the choir of its principal church which was then being built (W. 772); he also did portraits of his travelling companions and their hosts (W. 770/1).

Dürer and his wife stayed in Antwerp throughout the winter, until April, 1521. He had enough free time to work during these months, in spite of his busy social life. 1518 and 1519 had not been productive years, but the different surroundings may well have given him fresh impetus to paint[317] and new ideas for graphic works. According to his diary, the pictures which he gave away in Antwerp early on and later in Aachen (A. 150–3) appear to have been works brought with him from Nuremberg; but now he did a lot of painting in Planckfelt's house and in the Eeckhoff, the painters' house on the banks of the Schelde.[317a] In his diary, Dürer mentions as many as twelve pictures before the end of March, 1521. Among them were a portrait of a duke, Pl. 202 unfortunately lost, and a portrait of Bernhard von Reesen from Danzig,[318] which today is one of the treasures of the Dresden gallery. Dürer also painted his friend Rui Fernandes de Almada (A. 164) with whom he exchanged gifts on several occasions; the portrait was presumably based on the Pl. 201 brush drawing Dürer had mentioned previously.[319] He also

gave the most important work of these months, his painting of *St. Jerome*, to the Portuguese nobleman. A note in Pl. 205 Dürer's diary to the effect that he paid an old man three stivers for sitting for a drawing[320] presumably refers to a preliminary study for this picture—probably the large drawing of the head of a ninety-five-year-old man which is now in the Albertina in Vienna. As is shown by other brush drawings on colour-primed paper done during this year, Pl. 204 now in Vienna (W. 790–2) and Berlin (W. 789), Dürer made careful preparations for the painting of *St. Jerome*. The panel seems to have created a sensation among the Netherlandish painters who probably saw it later in Almada's private chapel; no other picture by Dürer was as frequently copied by Netherlandish painters. On 10 November 1520 Rui Fernandes wrote from Antwerp to King Manuel of Portugal that he was about to ship home, by the caravel Santa Ana, art objects obtained in Germany, and that these included life-size pictures of Adam and Eve. It is doubtful, however, whether he was referring to Dürer's paintings of 1507.[321]

Seven large pen drawings in landscape format for a *Passion*, dated 1520 and 1521 (W. 793–9), also appear to have been executed during the quiet winter months. They testify to Dürer's renewed interest in the problem of compositions with a multitude of figures. The choice of a landscape format reflects not only a stylistic change, but also a new emphasis on epic narrative.[322] Dürer made two different versions of the Stations of the Cross, *The Agony in the Garden* (W. 797, 798) and *Christ Carrying the Cross*, and Pl. 206 even three versions of the *Entombment* (W. 795, 796, 799). It seems reasonable to suppose that the rougher drawings, in which the figures' gestures are more agitated and their facial expressions more dramatic, are the earlier attempts, while the more developed and tranquil compositions represent the second stage of the artist's thoughts on the subject. There is hardly any overt drama in these drawings yet they do not

202 *Portrait of Bernhard von Reesen.* 1521. Oil. 45.5.×31.5. Gemäldegalerie, Dresden.

Only one of the various people whom Dürer painted and mentioned in his diary of the journey to the Netherlands can be linked with an existing painting dating from that time. The man in this Dresden painting of 1521 holds a letter in his hand which bears the inscription: "to pernh... at ..."; this has been linked—rightly, one must suppose—with Dürer's entry of March, 1521, where he says that he has painted a man called Bernhard von Resten. The sitter has recently been identified as the merchant Bernhard von Reesen from Danzig, who died in October, 1521 (when he was thirty years old) from the plague. His name implies that his family had moved to Danzig from Rees on the Lower Rhine.

210

lack tension. Rather, Dürer tried to express dramatic action by formal means. In *Christ Carrying the Cross* (W. 793), for instance, the many accentuated verticals made up of human figures and architectural elements are contrasted with the slightly oblique posture of Christ and the people surrounding him; this ensures that Christ's figure is effortlessly set off from the mass of people pushing forward through the gate. In *The Agony in the Garden*, Dürer rejected the figure stretching his arms upwards in passionate protest in favour of a Christ quietly submitting to God's will by lying prone on the ground in the foreground of the picture — a composition in the Nuremberg tradition. The growing emphasis on epic elements and the choice of a landscape format reflect the influence of Netherlandish art, particularly of the works of Lucas van Leyden, who had made a number of engravings of biblical scenes in landscape format between 1509 and 1519. One of Lucas's favourite motifs was a single large tree trunk or a small group of trees roughly in the centre of his compositions which served to accentuate the action. Dürer used this device in his *Entombments,* and varied the idea in *Christ Carrying the Cross* by placing the Cross almost vertically. In the *Agony in the Garden,* on the other hand, the trees serve to emphasize the group of sleeping disciples and thus balance the composition. The *Entombment* reflects the influence of Raphael, who had painted the subject in 1500, as well as that of Netherlandish artists. Dürer seems to have intended his drawings as designs for woodcuts to be published later; this is confirmed by a wood-

204 *Ninety-Three-Year-Old Man.* 1521. Brush on dark purple primed paper. 42×28.2. Graphische Sammlung Albertina, Vienna.

Inscribed at the top by Dürer: "This man was ninety-three years old and still healthy and strong in antorff (Antwerp)." This very beautiful drawing, which is probably based on a study from nature, was Dürer's source for the picture of *St. Jerome,* which he painted in Antwerp (Pl. 205).

203 *Small Reading Desk.* 1521. Brush, heightened with white, on purple primed paper. 19.8×28. Graphische Sammlung Albertina, Vienna.

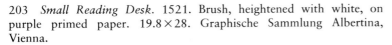

205 *St. Jerome.* 1521. Oil. 59.5×48.5. Museo del Arte Antigua, Lisbon.   ▷

The painting showing the half-length figure of St. Jerome, which Dürer mentions in his diary, is the only free composition to survive from the years 1520 and 1521. Four preliminary studies for the painting (W. 789–92, cf. Pl. 203) are still in existence, as well as the brush drawing of the head of a ninety-three-year-old man (Pl. 204). Dürer gave the completed panel to his Portuguese friend and patron, Rui Fernandes de Almada, as a present. Even during its excecution, Dürer's composition exerted a strong influence on his Netherlandish colleagues who copied it at once.

cut of the *Last Supper* which he made in 1523 and that has roughly the same dimensions as the earlier version. The drawings are mentioned in Dürer's diary a few days after his fiftieth birthday.[323]

As this private record shows, the famous artist was called upon to exercise his talent in widely varying fields. For instance, he had to become an architect for the personal physician of Margaret of Austria. He designed a house for him, but unfortunately neither the design nor the finished building have survived. This is greatly to be regretted as it was Dürer's only documented architectural commission. For the governor herself Dürer made two drawings on vellum which, judging by the estimated price of thirty florins, must have been of outstanding quality.[324] For the Fugger factors and the three Bombelli brothers Dürer designed masks and

206 *Christ Carrying the Cross*. 1520. Pen. 21×28.5. Gallerie degli Uffizi, Florence.

There is an alternative version of this drawing, also in the Uffizi. Dürer is believed to have prepared a new, woodcut cycle of the Passion while he was staying in Antwerp. Although none of these designs were executed, Dürer based a grisaille painting of 1527 (Pl. 233) on this drawing.

207 *Portrait of the Treasurer Lorenz Sterck*. 1521. Oil. 50×36. Museo del Prado, Madrid. ▷

The date on this panel is almost illegible and has been interpreted as both 1521 and 1524. The formal arrangement of this impressive portrait suggests the earlier date, since it differs markedly from Dürer's portraits after 1522. The portraits which Dürer painted in the Netherlands still show the sitters as almost half-length figures, an arrangement Dürer had long preferred (cf. Pl. 222; in contrast Pls. 219, 220, 221).

Pl. 216

214

208 *Two Studies of a Lion.* 1521. Silver-point. 12.2 × 17.1. Kupferstich-kabinett SMPK, Berlin.
This drawing, as well as a single study now in Vienna, were made while Dürer stayed in Ghent from 9 to 11 April 1521. The lions were kept at the Prinzenhof, the palace of the Dukes of Flanders (where Charles V was born in 1500). Dürer noted in his diary of the journey to the Netherlands: "Then I saw the lions and made a picture of one of them with the silver-point." It is possible that this was the first time that Dürer saw living lions, an event he thought noteworthy enough to record in his diary.

fancy dresses for the carnival festivities of 1521. He and his wife were invited to a banquet to be held on the morning of Shrove Tuesday by the goldsmiths of Antwerp.[325] It is striking how close Dürer's contacts with the representatives of this profession were; it is tempting to assume that they knew that he came from a family of goldsmiths and had learnt their trade.

Dürer began to make preparations for the homeward journey as early as mid-March, when he handed two carriers a small bale and a barrel for transport to Nuremberg.[326] He also remembered his Nuremberg friends and their wives and bought presents for them: braids, gloves, cloth and berets, also curios and sweetmeats such as pistachios. However, it was to be another four months before he could start on his return journey.

In the meantime, Dürer, the Bruges painter Jan Provost and the Augsburg patrician Hans Lieber went to Bruges a week after Easter. Provost, in whose house Dürer stayed, showed his guest the artistic sights of the town: the altarpiece by Rogier van der Weyden, the *Death of the Virgin* by Hugo van der Goes, the *Madonna of Canon George van der Paele* by Jan van Eyck and Michelangelo's marble statue of the *Virgin and Child* which had been in the church of St. Jacques since 1506.[327] In the evening the

painters gave a banquet in their Guild Hall for their south German colleague and later accompanied him back to Provost's house with lanterns, as the Antwerp painters had done.

The next day Dürer went on to Ghent where he was given a ceremonial welcome by the dean and members of the Painters' Guild. They showed him the main sight of the town, the *Ghent Altarpiece* by the brothers Hubert and Jan van Eyck. In his diary, Dürer especially praised the large figures of Adam and Eve and of the Virgin and God the Father in the upper part of the altarpiece.[328] While at Ghent he drew a lion in a cage he saw at the royal residence, the Pl. 208 Prinzenhof.

A few days after his return to Antwerp, Dürer fell ill with a serious fever which was accompanied by fainting fits, depression and headaches; he himself believed he had caught the illness on his journey to Zeeland.[329] He repeatedly had to consult a physician and buy medicaments during the following months of his stay in Antwerp. Today it is thought certain that this "illness of which I have never heard from any man", as Dürer wrote, must have been malaria.[330] The marshy lowlands of the province of Zeeland were a suitable breeding ground for the insects which transmit this disease.[331] Foreigners appear to have been particularly vulnerable, as the young Archduke Maximilian had also fallen ill with an infectious disease of this kind in 1480 and again in 1497, and Bishop George de Selve, one of the two ambassadors in Holbein's famous painting, died in 1541 of a fever he had caught in the Netherlands.[332] It appears that Dürer never fully recovered either. This is suggested by the description of his illness in a letter which Pirckheimer wrote to Hans Tucher five years after Dürer's death.[333]

On the other hand, Dürer seems to have recovered quickly from his acute fever, because early in May he was a guest at the wedding of Joachim Patenier whom he calls a landscape painter—the first time that this term is used in the German language. Dürer had recovered sufficiently to take up work again and seems to have painted two portraits in the space of a fortnight: "a face of a duke" of whom nothing is known (A. 161V), and the treasurer Lorenz Sterck. It is very likely that this last portrait is the magnificent *Portrait of a Man,* of Pl. 207 1521, in the Prado.

Dürer's next entry in his diary, dated 17 May, is his famous lament at Luther's arrest;[334] its authenticity has recently been questioned, but without justification.[335] Dürer could not have known that Luther's "arrest", which took place at Castle Altenstein near Eisenach on 4 May, was a

209 *Portrait of Agnes Dürer in Netherlandish Costume.* 1521. Metal-point on grey-purple primed paper. 40.7×27.1. Kupferstichkabinett SMPK, Berlin.

As Dürer notes in the inscription at the top, he drew this portrait of his wife on the occasion of their twenty-seventh wedding anniversary on 7 July 1521. After almost a year in the city on the Schelde, Agnes Dürer had become so accustomed to the foreign surroundings that she exchanged her usual dress for a Netherlandish costume. As the wife of the celebrated painter she had not simply lived a retiring life in the small suite of rooms in Planckfelt's inn, but had also been a guest at several of the festivities organized in her husband's honour. On one of these occasions she was ceremoniously escorted home late in the evening by her hosts carrying torches.

210 *Portrait of a Nun.* 1520. Charcoal. 40.4×27.4. F. Lugt Coll. Fondation Custodia, Institut Néerlandais, Paris.

This interesting charcoal drawing, which was only published a few years ago, has been interpreted—presumably correctly—as the portrait of a nun. It may be the nun whom Dürer mentions in his diary of the journey to the Netherlands, to whom he gave seven *Weisspfennige* and several of his prints.

measure which had been taken with the knowledge of Luther's sovereign, the Elector Frederick of Saxony, to protect the reformer from the ban of the Empire he had been threatened with. Dürer's description, mentioning precise locations, the number of mounted soldiers who had been present, and the role which the imperial herald Kaspar Sturm had played in the proceedings, makes it likely that Sturm himself or one of his pursuivants had spread the news in Antwerp.

Every line of Dürer's lament expresses the heart-felt piety of an exceptionally cultured man who knew that Wyclif had first attempted reform in England more than a century earlier. Dürer addresses Erasmus of Rotterdam towards the end of his lament: "Hear me, thou knight of Christ, ride out beside the Lord Jesus Christ..." But the great Humanist, to whose *Handbook of the Christian Knight* Dürer's form of address presumably referred, was not one to become either a knightly protector or a suffering martyr of the new doctrine.

Dürer's moving words show clearly that he, like many of his friends both in Nuremberg and Antwerp,[336] believed in Luther's teaching. It may, therefore, seem strange that Dürer reverently went to see the relics in the cathedral treasury in Aachen during his travels. In Düren he looked at the head of St. Anne which had been stolen from Mainz cathedral; in Cologne he made a point of going to the church of St. Ursula to visit the grave of the martyr, and in Antwerp he even went to confession. However, it must be remembered that the Reformation was only beginning and the significance of the saints, or even the relics, had not yet been questioned.

Although Dürer repeatedly had to consult a physician during the second half of May, he was able to entertain Konrad Meit at his house over Whitsun and to make four designs of a St. Christopher on grey paper for Joachim Patenier. As the date for his departure approached, he once more (on 5 June) entrusted a carrier with a large bale to be

211 *Head and Shoulders of a Twenty-Four-Year-Old Girl, with the Abbey of St. Michael at Antwerp.* 1520. Silver-point. 13.3 × 19.4. Musée Condé, Chantilly.

Of the two sketch-books which Dürer used during his journey to the Netherlands, the one in landscape format with silver-point drawings is the better known. On a number of sheets Dürer combined particularly delicately drawn portraits with landscapes or architectural backgrounds. It is difficult to know whether these were intended to be coherent compositions, or whether the landscapes were drawn beside the figures because of lack of space. The person depicted in this drawing is usually, but erroneously, called a young man; however, the patterned collar covering the shoulders was definitely part of female dress, so that the sitter must have been a young girl.

212 *The Negress Katharina.* 1521. Silver-point. 20 × 14 (enlarged). Gallerie degli Uffizi, Florence.   ▷

Dürer inscribed the drawing at the top: "Katharina, twenty years old". The girl shown was a servant in the house of the Portuguese factor João Brandão, who conducted his business from Antwerp and with whom Dürer was in close contact during his stay in the city on the Schelde. An entry in Dürer's diary specifically mentions that he drew the "moor".

taken to Nuremberg. The following day he and his wife went to Mechelen, presumably to take their leave of Margaret of Austria. Dürer took this opportunity to show the princess his portrait of her late father Maximilian, but unfortunately she did not like it.[337] However, she spent some time showing the painter her own art treasures which included Jan van Eyck's *Arnolfini Couple* and about fifty small panels from Queen Isabella of Spain's retable done by Juan de Flandes. Dürer was also shown a sketchbook of Jacopo de' Barbari who had been in Margaret's service from 1510 onwards. Dürer asked the princess to give it to him as a present, but to his disappointment she refused, saying she had already promised it to her current court painter, Barent van Orley. In Mechelen, as everywhere, Dürer had been given a banquet by the painters and sculptors. Being a man of wide interests he took the opportunity to visit the gun foundry of Hans Poppenreuther, who had originally come from Nuremberg, and made a drawing of the mortar in his sketchbook (W. 783).

In the weeks immediately preceding Dürer's departure the painter Lucas van Leyden had come to Antwerp and visited him.[338] On 2 July Dürer had already sent his luggage ahead, ordered the carriage and was ready to depart with his wife and maid, when King Christian II of Denmark summoned the artist to paint his portrait. The following day, Dürer travelled to Brussels with his wife Agnes and the maid Susanna and witnessed the reception given outside the city gates by the Emperor for his royal brother-in-law, King Christian II. He was admitted to the princes' banquet as a spectator. On 7 July Christian of Denmark gave a banquet and this time Dürer was a guest. Dürer took ten days to paint the king's portrait in oils, basing the painting on a drawing—this included all the preparatory work, such as obtaining a wooden panel and having the colours ground. Christian rewarded the artist with a princely sum, paid through his Amsterdam banker Pomponius Occo.[339]

Dürer left Brussels to start on his return journey exactly a year after his departure from Nuremberg. He travelled by way of Louvain, Aachen and Jülich to Cologne, and it is here that his diary ends.

Several aspects have to be considered in trying to take stock of Dürer's journey to the Netherlands. In spite of many difficulties, he had achieved the immediate goal of his journey, i.e. the assurance that his pension would be continued. But the prolonged stay of three people in a foreign city had cost a lot of money. He had raised half the sum through a loan of 100 florins from Alexander Imhoff, and by selling prints and occasionally charging fees for portrait drawings.[340] It is true though that he had adapted to the Antwerp life style and had lived like a wealthy citizen. He, his wife and his maid had been well dressed, and he had generously given away prints, paintings and drawings, because as the "prince among northern painters"—as the Netherlandish artists called him—he must have felt obliged to live in style and demonstrate his munificence. Not only had his colleagues shown him respect, but also scholars, diplomats and even princes, with the exception of the young emperor whom Dürer appears to have seen only from a certain distance. The Antwerp magistrate had made the artist a generous offer, similar to that made by the Signoria in Venice, if he agreed to stay in the city.[341]

The new surroundings had obviously had a stimulating effect on him as an artist. They revived his creative powers as is shown by the wealth of drawings and paintings he mentions—more than a hundred in all—of which only a fraction have survived. Not only is the amount of work completed in a single year admirable, but also the new expressive force shown in these works. It was in the Netherlands that Dürer developed his monumental portraits: the Madrid *Portrait of* Pl. 207 *a Man*, the large charcoal drawings (W. 807–10), the Pl. 210 drawings done with a metal-point, and the small silver-point Pl. 211 works. Dürer's stay in Antwerp also renewed his interest in compositions of a multitude of figures.

A negative result—not just from the point of view of later generations—was the malarial infection which was to be the cause of Dürer's premature death.

XI. The Last Years: 1521–8

The Reformation in Nuremberg · Supremacy of Painting · The Manuals

Dürer, his wife Agnes and his maid Susanna (who later married Dürer's journeyman Jörg Pencz) appear to have arrived back in Nuremberg early in August, 1521. There were still outbreaks of the plague, which delayed the establishment of the Imperial Chamber and the Imperial Regiment in Nuremberg decreed by the Estates of the Empire. But eventually princes and officials arrived in the city, as had been stipulated at the Diet of Worms. Now Nuremberg really was a kind of capital of the German Empire. However, the council had the difficult task of maintaining the distinguished status of the city by being particularly loyal to the emperor, while at the same time being unable to make concessions on the religious question, since a large number of patricians as well as other citizens were followers of Luther.[343] They therefore tried to introduce reforms gradually. During 1521, for instance, three preachers who had had a Humanist education were employed in the two parish churches and the Hospital of the Holy Spirit—Andreas Osiander, Dominikus Schleupner and Thomas Venatorius. Lazarus Spengler, who was very active in furthering the cause of church reform in Nuremberg, had been instrumental in having them appointed.

The first Diet of the new king, in 1521, could not be held in Nuremberg (as had been stipulated in the Golden Bull) because of the plague, and had to be held in Worms; it was then decided that the Assembly of the Estates should take place in Nuremberg in 1522.[344] The council wanted to be able to offer the new king and the representatives of the estates a suitably dignified venue and therefore decided to have both the interior and the exterior of the old main hall of the town hall redecorated with paintings. This was a natural suggestion since the hall's old wooden ceiling, formerly a pointed barrel vault, had just been replaced with a fashionable coffered ceiling and a round barrel vault by Hans Behaim the Elder. Dürer was commissioned to design the rest of the decorations. As early as 11 August, the council passed a resolution to have the interior decorations exe-

cuted according to Dürer's instructions.[345] Of these designs there survive a pen and wash drawing for part of the window wall (W. 921) and a sketch for the *Calumny of Apelles* (W. 922) for the opposite wall. The triumphal chariot of the Emperor Maximilian, which was to decorate the remainder of this wall, was transferred from the existing design (W. 685); the artist published this design at the same time as a woodcut made up of eight separate sheets. It is still not known whether Dürer was also responsible for the paintings of the façade which are mentioned as early as September. In 1522 Dürer was paid the considerable sum of 100 florins for his work, which may have included the cartoons necessary for the execution of the paintings as well as the actual designs.[346]

Scholars now believe that the paintings in the main hall and the three exterior walls of the town hall were executed by Hans Springinklee and Hans von Kulmbach. They used a mixed-media technique of oil and tempera[346a] which no one else except Leonardo da Vinci employed for wall paintings, and which has not proved durable either in his frescoes or in those in Nuremberg.

Drawings of 1521 show that, apart from working on the decorative scheme for the town hall, Dürer also planned a number of multi-figure compositions: a representation of the *Virgin and Child with St. Anne* (W. 885 and 539), a *Holy Family* (W. 852), scenes from the *Passion* (W. 880–2) and above all a large design for a "sacra conversatione" in Pl. 213 the Italian manner. Four sketches for its overall composition (St. 1521/81–3 and 91) reveal how the basic idea for this picture was conceived and developed. A number of individual studies (St. 1521/84–90, 92–6) indicate that prepara- Pl. 214 tions for the painting were considerably advanced when Dürer stopped work on it in 1522 (St. 1522/1–6). It has been suggested that the altarpiece panel was executed for the church of St. Peter in Riga and destroyed as early as 1524 by iconoclasts, but there is no documentary or literary evidence to support this hypothesis.[347] The only completed painting

213 *Enthroned Madonna with Ten Saints.* C. 1521. Pen. 31.5 × 44.4. Musée Bonnat, Bayonne.

of these years is the *Man of Sorrows* (A. 170K), painted in 1522 for Cardinal Albrecht of Brandenburg. In one of the studies for this picture, (W. 886) Christ's face is clearly reminiscent of Dürer's own features.

Dürer's graphic work fared scarcely any better. A large engraving of about 1523 — which would have been his only picture of a Crucifixion, except for the woodcut of 1494–5 — remained unfinished even though the contours of the figures and landscape had already been engraved on the Pl. 215 plate. Preliminary studies made in 1521 and 1523 (St. 1521/72–8, 1523/2–5) are much larger than the engraving itself. The figures are monumental and their emotions strongly expressed; it is thus all the more surprising that Dürer used two of the delicate, detailed silver-point sketches dating from his journey to the Netherlands for the background landscape. In the same year, Dürer completed one single woodcut for the *Passion* cycle, using a landscape format which he had already worked on in the Netherlands. This Pl. 216 was the *Last Supper*, remarkable for its extreme formal simplicity. As a portraitist Dürer continually developed new and unusual formal solutions regardless of whether he was Pl. 224 working with metal point or burin, whether he was painting, or drawing the features of a sitter on the wood block for the wood-cutter. Portraits in profile were among his important formal innovations in graphic work. A pure profile of a head does not, however, have a very sculptural effect, so the artist often retained the slightly foreshortened oblique position of the sitter's body and shoulders, a feature of conventional portraits. With this device of differentiating

between the position of the head and shoulders, Dürer achieved both a monumental, sculptural effect and an impression of movement. By achieving this balance between calm grandeur and lively movement Dürer had attained the ideal of classical art. He varied this basic conception according to the personality of the sitter. In his woodcut of the emperor's protonotary Ulrich Varnbüler, done in 1522, the cartouche bearing the inscription and also Varnbüler's beret Pl. 217 are decorative features that also help characterize the energetic Swiss Humanist. In comparison, the engraved portrait of the Elector, Albrecht of Brandenburg, completed in 1523 when Albrecht was only thirty-four years old, appears almost insignificant. The portrait engraving of the Humanist Philipp Melanchthon, made in 1526, shows Luther's friend Pl. 218 before a background that is partly left uncut, and partly covered with parallel hatchings, a device which helps emphasize the portrait's impression of nervous sensibility.

Dürer's ability to reveal a man's character purely through engraved lines is demonstrated particularly well in two portraits he completed in 1523 and 1524, one of the Elector Frederick the Wise of Saxony and one of Willibald Pirck- Pls. 219–20 heimer. In both cases an inscription at the bottom of the picture is surmounted by the shoulders of the sitter which are partly cut off by the frame, the two impressive heads taking up most of the restricted space of the picture plane. This makes the two men appear thick-set and heavy, a feature which reveals their character, but also reflects contemporary stylistic convention.

The portrait engraving of Erasmus of Rotterdam of 1526 Pl. 222 is quite different. Dürer began work on it after much hesitation and after repeated admonitions by the Humanist; he based the portrait on the drawing made in Brussels in the presence of Nikolaus Kratzer (cf. p. 206). It became Dürer's most lavish portrait engraving and the only one which

214 *St. Apollonia.* 1521. Chalk on green primed paper. 41.4 × 28.8. Kupferstichkabinett SMPK, Berlin. ▷

After his return from the Netherlands Dürer was intensely preoccupied with the composition of a picture showing the Madonna amid many saints. This is one of the few of Dürer's works for which we have a considerable number of drawings illustrating both how the composition evolved and how details were determined with the help of studies from nature. The drawing in Bayonne (Pl. 213) presumably shows the final version of the composition before Dürer decided to change the transverse format into an oblong one. The Berlin study of the bust-length figure has been identified as St. Apollonia by the pair of tongs with the tooth which this saint holds as her attributes in the Bayonne drawing (second from the right). The angle of her head and her lowered eyelids are largely identical with this study from nature. In spite of his sympathies for the Reformation Dürer still revered the Virgin Mary.

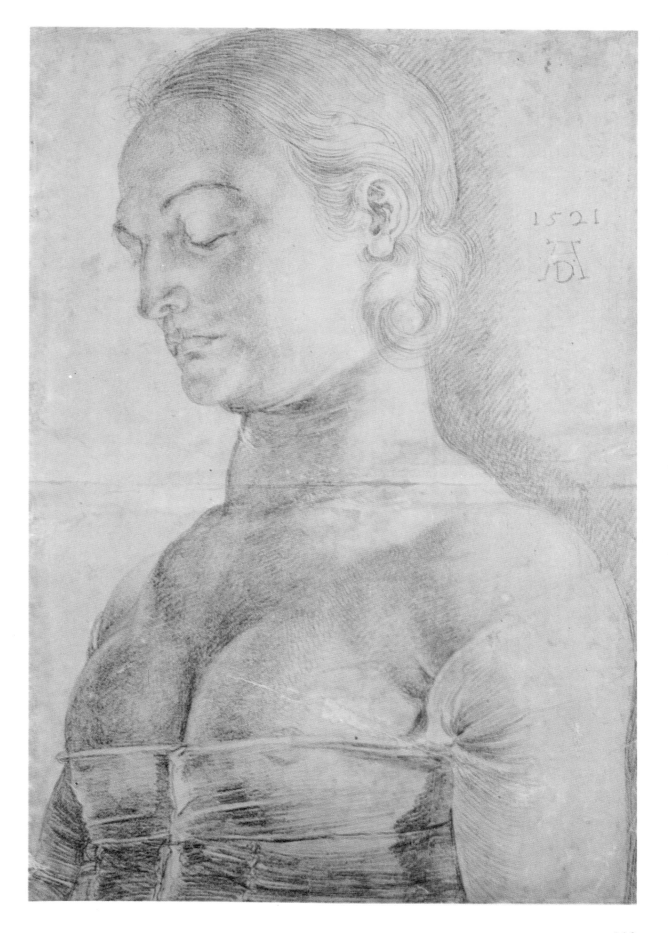

shows the sitter engaged in activity. The overall effect of the engraving and, by implication, the way Erasmus is characterized are largely determined by the clear geometric shapes of the table, the books and the large panel bearing the inscription. Dürer tried to create a portrait which reflected the greatness of the scholar, but Erasmus was none the less dissatisfied with the result.[348]

The year 1526 was once again a time of intense artistic activity for Dürer. As well as working on his theoretical

215 *Mary Magdalene Kneeling at the Foot of the Cross.* 1523. Metal-point heightened with white on green primed paper. 29.5 × 20.6. Cabinet des Dessins, Musée du Louvre, Paris.

This impressive drawing of Mary Magdalene clasping the foot of the Cross was one of a number of studies for a large engraving (32 × 22.5) of a Crucifixion, which remained unfinished. As the figures in the studies are considerably larger than those in the engraving, it has often been thought that Dürer originally planned a painting and that the engraving is only a copy of this lost work.

writings and portrait engravings, Dürer again turned to painting. During this year he painted his last picture of the *Virgin and Child,* portraits of two close friends, the patricians Hieronymus Holzschuher and Jakob Muffel (A. 178), and the strange portrait of Johann Kleberger which represents an entirely new departure in Dürer's portrait painting. Pl. 232 Pl. 221 Pl. 223

However, the most important work of this year is the double panel of the *Four Apostles.* Among Dürer's paintings, it marks a peak in both his artistic and intellectual development comparable to the *Melencolia I* among his engravings. The final versions of the more than life-size figures of the Apostles John and Peter on the left-hand panel, and Paul and Mark the Evangelist on the right-hand panel had evolved slowly; their formal antecedents go back to the two small engravings of apostles completed in 1514. Dürer then made three more engravings for this series in 1523; four large preliminary drawings for further engravings were executed in 1522 and 1523. The figure of Paul on the right-hand panel of the *Four Apostles* was based on the same study of 1523 on which Dürer had based his *St. Philip* later in the same year. Pls. 228–9 Pl. 171 Pls. 230–1 Pl. 227

At Dürer's request, the calligrapher Johann Neudörffer inscribed quotations from the apostles' writings on the lower edge of the two tall narrow panels of the *Four Apostles.* In October, 1526 the artist presented the panels to the council of his home town for commemoration.[349] In return for his gift the council rewarded him with a honorarium of 100 florins.[350] According to Neudörffer[351] Dürer had intended the four figures to represent not just preachers of the Christian faith but also the four temperaments. He therefore emphasized both individual and typical features.

Much has been written on the significance of the two panels and particularly on their inscriptions which urge the council to refuse to listen to false prophets. Dürer's message can only be understood if one takes the general religious situation in Germany into account. At the time when the artist was working on the designs for the town hall and Luther was still in the Wartburg, Luther's colleague, Andreas Bodenstein from Karlstadt, had taken over the leadership of the reform movement. In November, 1521 he had dedicated his pamphlet on the doctrine of the Last Supper, "On the Adoration and Reverence for the Miracles of the New Testament", to Dürer.[352] This pamphlet showed him to be a moderate, but less than a month later he was heading the radicals who, early in February, 1522, were to destroy the first pictures in Wittenberg. Bodenstein also supplied the theological justification for the condemnation of pictures in another of his pamphlets, published in the

216　*The Last Supper*. 1523. Woodcut. 21.3 × 30.1. Kupferstichkabinett SMPK, Berlin.

The grouping of the apostles in Dürer's last woodcut of the *Last Supper* reflects his knowledge of Leonardo da Vinci's famous wall painting in the refectory of the monastery of S. Maria delle Grazie in Milan. Dürer presumably knew one of the engravings which had been made soon after the completion of the painting. Dürer's composition differs in several important ways from earlier representations of this theme. The traitor Judas has already left the room, and Christ talks to the disciples. The table is empty except for the cup placed in the gap between Christ and the group of apostles on the left. In the foreground to the extreme right are the basket of bread and wine jug. The elements of the eucharist are emphasized so strongly by formal means, that they must be understood as a reference to communion in both kinds, as it was celebrated in Nuremberg for the first time in the same year. It is very likely that this was intended to be the first woodcut of a Passion cycle for which Dürer had already made preliminary designs in the Netherlands (Pl. 206).

same year, entitled "On the Abolition of Images".[353] Dürer, too, was against the excesses of image worship, as is made clear by his comment on a copy of Michael Ostendorfer's woodcut *The Pilgrimage to the Beautiful Virgin Mary at Regensburg*.[354] However, he could not have condoned the abolition of all religious images, since this would have meant not only losing much of the work on which his livelihood depended, but also that an essential part of his work so far would be called into question. He formulated his opinion on this issue, which must have concerned him deeply, in the introduction to his *Teaching of Measurements*, published in 1525: "Although there are people here and now who despise the art of painting very much and say it is idolatrous, any Christian man is as little drawn to superstition by a painting or a portrait as a pious man is drawn to murder just because he carries a weapon by his side. Only a truly

VLRICHVS VARNBVLER ZC. M.D.XXII.

Albertus Dürer Noric
hac imagine Ulrichum cognom
Varnbüler, Ro. Caesarei Regimini
in Imperio, à Secretis, simul
Gramaticum, ut quem amet
unice, etiam posteritati
cognitum reddere
conatur.

◁ 217 *Portrait of Ulrich Varnbüler.* 1522. Woodcut. 43 × 32.3. Kupferstichkabinett SMPK, Berlin.

Varnbüler, the protonotary of the Imperial Chamber, was friendly with Pirckheimer and Dürer, who drew the portrait of the Swiss Humanist during the Nuremberg Diet of 1522. The large beret and the head itself with its beaked nose and full lips seem to belong to a Swiss mercenaries' leader rather than to a scholar who was in contact with Erasmus of Rotterdam; but the inscription definitely reads: "Albrecht Dürer from Nuremberg wishes to make Ulrich—with the family name Varnbüler, which he loves very much—the private secretary of the Roman imperial regiment, known to later generations and tries to honour him (with this portrait)."

218 *Portrait of Philipp Melanchthon.* 1526. Engraving. 17.4 × 12.7. Kupferstichkabinett SMPK, Berlin.

Melanchthon (1497–1560), Luther's closest friend and collaborator, had come to Nuremberg in 1526 to give the council advice on the institution of a Latin (grammar) school. The scholar, who was not yet thirty years old, was a well-liked guest in Pirckheimer's house; it was here that he met Dürer whom he grew to admire, as is shown by several of his comments on the painter. A preliminary pen drawing for this engraving is in a private collection in Florence. The inscription reads: "Dürer was able to draw Philipp's features from life, but the trained hand could not capture the spirit."

219 *Portrait of Frederick the Wise of Saxony.* 1524. Engraving. 18.8 × 12.2. Kupferstichkabinett SMPK, Berlin.

The Elector Frederick III of Saxony (1463–1525), who had long been a patron of Dürer, was known to his contemporaries as "the Wise" because of his balanced policies aimed primarily at the welfare of the Empire. The inscription reads: "He was dedicated to Christ and loved the word of God with great piety, worthy to be revered by posterity. Albrecht Dürer from Nuremberg drew Frederick, Duke of Saxony, Arch-marshal and Elector of the Holy Roman Empire. He drew the picture for the man of great merit, as a living man for the living man."

senseless man could worship a painting or an image made of wood or stone. A painting which is well made and fashioned with wonderful art improves a man rather than gives him pleasure." Dürer could quote Luther as his authority for this argument, because in the same year Luther had published a pamphlet *Against the Heavenly Prophets*, in which he had opposed the foolish adoration of images yet was prepared to tolerate crucifixes and pictures of saints.[355]

At Easter, 1523 Holy Communion was administered according to both creeds for the first time at the Augustinian monastery in Nuremberg, and Dürer published his woodcut of the *Last Supper,* which testified that his sympathies lay with the Reformation.[356] However, the real break with religious traditions in general did not take place until 1524–5. During and after the third Nuremberg Diet (4 January– 18 April 1524), provosts and preachers abolished numerous rites and introduced the German language into church services without asking the council for its consent.[357] Then the peasants' uprising, which had originally been socially motivated but now turned into a religious campaign, reached Nuremberg territory and spread to the urban proletariat. As a result the council felt compelled, in the summer of 1524 as well as in May, 1525, to negotiate both with the usually well-to-do peasants and with the urban poor and to make concessions.[358] These events are reflected—albeit in a modest way—in Dürer's design for a *Monument for the Defeated Peasants* in his *Teaching of Measurements.*

But Dürer must have been more deeply affected by the appearance of Anabaptists and zealots in the city. He was directly concerned, because not only the rector of the Sebald school, Hans Denk, who was also a protégé of Pirckheimer, and the painter Hans Greiffenberger, but also his own journeyman Jörg Pencz and the young painters Sebald and Barthel Beham caused offence by their partly atheistic, partly communistic speeches. The council summoned Hans Denk and the "godless painters" to appear in court in January, 1525,[359] and, with the agreement of the clergy, expelled them from the city at the end of the month.[360] It was an even harder blow for Dürer when the wood-cutter Hieronymus Andreae was arrested for his connections with the rebellious peasants, because Andreae, known as Form-schneider, had worked with Dürer for several years.

In March of the same year a religious disputation took place before the council between representatives of the Dominicans and Franciscans on the one hand and the Lutheran preachers on the other. A clear victory for the preachers resulted in the abolition of the monasteries by the authorities; it was said that "the pope had been given leave". But the arrogant behaviour and far from evangelical conduct of the preachers, or at least Osiander, gave rise to fierce criticism.[361] Pirckheimer and Scheurl were outraged by these developments and turned to the old faith with renewed strength. These developments have led Dürer scholars to interpret his inscriptions on the *Four Apostles* as

220 *Portrait of Willibald Pirckheimer.* 1524. Engraving. 18.1 × 11.5. Kupferstichkabinett SMPK, Berlin.

This engraving was completed twenty-one years after the portrait drawing (Pl. 96). The chin and neck have become puffy and the eyes have a resigned look, but Dürer nevertheless succeeds in conveying something of the pugnacious energy and outstanding intelligence of his friend who suffered severely from gout. Part of the inscription reads: "The spirit will survive, the rest will die."

221 *Portrait of Hieronymus Holzschuher.* 1526. Oil. 48 × 36. Gemälde-galerie SMPK, Berlin.   ▷

One of the most striking features of Dürer's last years is the large number of portraits he completed. Among them the portrait of Hieronymus Holz-schuher, now in Berlin-Dahlem, is particularly famous. Holzschuher (1469–1529) was a member of an old Nuremberg patrician family. He had studied in Italy, had been a member of the council of his home town since 1499, and supported the Reformation in Nuremberg.

a critical comment on the actions of the "godless painters" and the behaviour of the new clergy.[362] But linguistically as well as thematically, the inscriptions are closely related to Luther's preface to his "testament" of September, 1522 and other reformatory writings[363], so that they must in fact be seen as a declaration of loyalty to the Reformation. It is very unlikely that the rash youthful behaviour of the painters inspired Dürer to create the panels in order to condemn the painters through the inscriptions. Such an action on Dürer's part, almost two years after the sentence which moreover

had already been partially revoked, [364] is inconceivable. Nor was the behaviour of Andreas Osiander, though it provoked strong criticism, important enough to inspire Dürer to create two monumental paintings. On the other hand the much more serious threat to the Nuremberg Reformation, of armed intervention by the emperor and the south German princes, could well have provided Dürer with the incentive to appeal to the responsible government of the city[365] to stay on the religious course it had so far adopted[366] and ignore the false prophets in the opposite camp. This is the only sensible explanation of Dürer's gift of the *Four Apostles,* which was also designed to keep the memory of himself and his art alive.

Dürer's concern was for the pure, unadulterated word of God. He expressed this concern in the inscriptions as well as symbolically; the motif of the words of the Bible recurs three times, in the shape of two books and a scroll. It is unlikely that the quotations from the Bible were meant to symbolize anything but a profession of faith in the word of God as restored by Luther, for the simple reason that no one could be sure that events which happened locally in Nuremberg would be remembered by later generations.

It could be said that Dürer's painting of the *Virgin and* Pl. 232 *Child* of 1526 and his last woodcut of a religious subject, a representation of the Virgin (B. 98), do not support this interpretation of the *Four Apostles.* Furthermore, Dürer's repeated mention of the last rites in his family chronicle (a customary piece of writing in Nuremberg patrician circles)[367], which he wrote in 1523 from notes made by his father, has been said to reflect his adherence to the old faith. But it has to be remembered that most of the traditional church ceremonies were not abolished in Nuremberg until 1524,[368] and that until then only the iconoclasts had taken a definite stand against the cult of the Virgin Mary and the worshipping of saints.[369] At that time neither the followers of Luther nor the representatives of the old doctrine could conceive that Western Christendom would be divided into two separate churches.

222 *Portrait of Erasmus of Rotterdam.* 1526. Engraving. 24.9 × 19.3. Kupferstichkabinett SMPK, Berlin.

During his stay in the Netherlands Dürer often met Erasmus of Rotterdam (1465–1536), the most important scholar of his day, and drew him twice. Erasmus wanted a portrait engraving by Dürer, but the artist hesitated and had to be repeatedly urged to start work. The formal arrangement of this engraving makes it one of the artist's most important graphic works; yet when Dürer had completed it, Erasmus was very disappointed, since he did not consider it a good likeness. The inscriptions read: "Portrait of Erasmus of Rotterdam, drawn from the living model by Albrecht Dürer" (in Latin). "His writings portray him better" (in Greek).

223 *Portrait of Johann Kleberger.* 1526. Oil. 37 × 37. Kunsthistorisches Museum, Vienna. ▷

The portrait of the Lyons merchant Johann Kleberger (1486–1546) is one of Dürer's most idiosyncratic works, since it is a painting copying a classical relief. Kleberger, who had been born in Wertheim on the Main, had quickly acquired considerable wealth in the service of the Paumgartner and Imhoff families; he had settled in Lyons where his charity had gained him the epithet "le bon alleman". He sympathized with the Reformation, but also appears to have studied the occult sciences, as the strange signs on this painting testify.

232

◁ 224 *Portrait of Ulrich Starck*. 1527. Metal-point. 41×29.6. Department of Prints and Drawings, British Museum, London.

This is Dürer's last portrait drawing and shows a particularly balanced formal arrangement. The blank rectangle in the upper right-hand corner, intended for date and signature, is consciously made part of the composition. The drawing technique is limited to restrained lines indicating shapes and textures and simple diagonal hatchings, used both in the modelling of the figure and the background. Ulrich Starck (1484–1549) was a member of the Nuremberg patriciate.

225 *Design for a Monument for the Defeated Peasants*. 1525. Woodcut illustration from *The Teaching of Measurements*. C. 26 high. Kupferstichkabinett SMPK, Berlin.

The manual, published in 1525, included instructions for the design of commemorative columns. An imaginative monument commemorating the suppression of the peasants uprising of 1525 is one of several designs illustrated. The arrangement shown here combines plinth and column proper, which are illustrated on two pages of Dürer's manual. The numbers indicate the proportions.

Therefore, all that can be said about Dürer's religious attitudes during the last years of his life is that he sympathized with Luther's doctrines, but within the framework of one common Christian faith. This did not exclude him, or Pirckheimer, from viewing certain symptoms of the new religious trend with concern. Dürer's last years were spent against a background of sectarianism and intolerant disputes over doctrine among followers of the same camp. There was also a constant fear that the religious freedom which had only just been won might be lost again, and the additional threat of the Turkish army advancing relentlessly towards the borders of the empire from the south-east.

In 1527, Dürer again turned to painting. However, of the three pictures he executed, only the *Bearded Youth* (A. 186) has survived in the original. Only copies remain of a small grisaille painting of *Christ Carrying the Cross* which was based on sketches and designs made during the journey to the Netherlands. The *memento mori* image of a *Sleeping Child* (A. 185K) has survived only in a coarsened woodcut version which gives the vaguest indication of what the original must have been like.

PL. 206
PL. 233

Looking at Dürer's output during the last seven years of his life, one sees that he was yet again capable of an artistic revival which resulted in works of great simplicity and monumentality. Compared with earlier years, however, the number of paintings and graphic works completed during this time is small. Moreover, they were done in 1521–3 and 1526–7, while Dürer seems to have produced nothing but a few engravings in the intervening years. However, these late works show that there was no general deterioration in Dürer's powers. It would be unfair to say that these works represent a last flickering of his artistic vitality; the wealth of new ideas and solutions makes such an interpretation untenable. Several causes seem to have been responsible for the fact that Dürer only completed relatively few works during his last years. The malaria he had caught in the Netherlands undoubtedly weakened his creative powers.

The sensitive artist may have been even more deeply affected by the psychological strain occasioned by the political and religious events of those years than by his physical illness. On the one hand, he himself had been "helped out of great fears" by Luther's works, as he had

233

written as early as 1520; on the other, he must have been deeply troubled by the fierce controversy over the value and meaning of works of art in the context of the faith and the iconoclasm which followed it.

But Dürer was not idle; as his personal crisis weakened his artistic activities, he threw himself with all his force into his theoretical works. The first two books of his manual on proportions had been almost ready for printing before he left for the Netherlands. After his return he decided to start the work with a general introduction on geometry. This introduction was to explain the various means of measuring used in the manual on proportions, and provide information on the essential prerequisites for all artistic creation.

Although Dürer could use the notes he had made in earlier years[370] for his new project, the completion of the text and

226 *Head of Mark the Evangelist.* 1526. Metal-point on brown primed paper. 37.3 × 26.4. Kupferstichkabinett SMPK, Berlin.

227 *Apostle.* 1523. Metal-point, heightened with white, on green primed paper. 31.8 × 21.3. Graphische Sammlung Albertina, Vienna.

Dürer used this monumental drawing of an apostle for his engraving of the apostle Philip, which was intended, together with engravings of Bartholomew and Simon, to form part of the series of small-format representations of the apostles begun as early as 1514 (cf. Pl. 171). The engraving of Philip was not immediately published. This study, however, was used again in 1525–6 as a model for the Apostle Paul on one of the two panels of the *Four Apostles*, painted in 1526.

228–9 *The Four Apostles.* 1526. Oil. 204 × 74 each. Bayerische Staatsgemäldesammlungen, Munich.   ▷

The *Four Apostles* are rightly considered Dürer's most important work. However, the title is not entirely correct, as only the Apostles John, Peter and Paul are represented on the two panels; the fourth figure is Mark the Evangelist. The inscriptions, which were added by the calligrapher Johann Neudörffer, declare Dürer's belief in the Reformation and warn the Nuremberg Council not to deviate from the doctrine proclaimed by Luther.

the preparation of the necessary geometric drawings and other illustrations must have taken quite a long time. It is true that there already were a number of previous publications on the subject in German. However, Dürer's project was much more ambitious than those of his predecessors, and since he intended his book to be used by artists and skilled artisans alike, he had to make comprehensive studies, going as far back as to classical sources. He had purchased a Latin edition of Euclid in Venice as early as 1507. It is likely that Pirckheimer and Johannes Werner, a trained mathematician and vicar of St. Johann, helped him translate the Greek and Latin terminology into German.

Dürer's work starts with an explanation of basic geometric principles, such as point and line. After discussing

230 *The Apostle Bartholomew.* 1523. Engraving. 12.2×7.6. Kupferstichkabinett SMPK, Berlin.

231 *The Apostle Philip.* 1526. Engraving. 12.2×7.6. Kupferstichkabinett SMPK, Berlin.

232 *The Madonna with the Pear.* 1526. Oil. 43×32. Gallerie degli Uffizi, Florence. ▷

Dürer's last picture of the Madonna was painted at a time when Nuremberg had already turned away from the papacy. The carefully thought-out composition, delicate colours and sensitive expressions that characterize this painting testify to Dürer's continuing veneration of the Madonna.

237

lines, including complicated curves, he progresses in the second book to planes and solids and then describes a number of special problems. The two last books begin with a discussion of solids, but mainly deal with artistic and practical questions, such as the construction of sun-dials, alphabetical letters and various types of columns. The work ends with a short treatise on perspective and instructions on the use of various drawing devices.

Pl. 234

Dürer seems to have started on his second theoretical work, a manual on the art of fortification, immediately after finishing work on the *Teaching of Measurements*. This second book, the first study to be published in German on the problems of fortification created by the development of artillery, must be regarded as another part of the comprehensive manual for painters which Dürer planned. However, his decision to write about the subject may well have been precipitated by the increasing threat of a Turkish invasion. As a result of the taking of Belgrade in 1521 by the

Pl. 235 (margin, left of first paragraph)

belligerent Sultan Suleiman, a commission was set up at the Nuremberg Diet of 1522 to consider defensive measures against the Ottoman. The architect Johannes Tschertte was present,[371] which implies that questions of fortifications were discussed. At the beginning of his book, Dürer states that he undertook this project because of the Turkish threat, and dedicates the work to Ferdinand, the brother of the Emperor Charles V, who had become King of Bohemia and Hungary early in 1526.

233 *Christ Carrying the Cross*. 1527. Oil. (Copy after a lost original by Dürer.) Accademia Carrara, Bergamo.

Apart from the *All Saints* picture completed in 1511 (Pls. 131, 132) *Christ Carrying the Cross* is Dürer's last composition incorporating a multitude of figures. The original small grisaille painting is lost, but there are three copies which give an accurate impression of what it must have looked like.

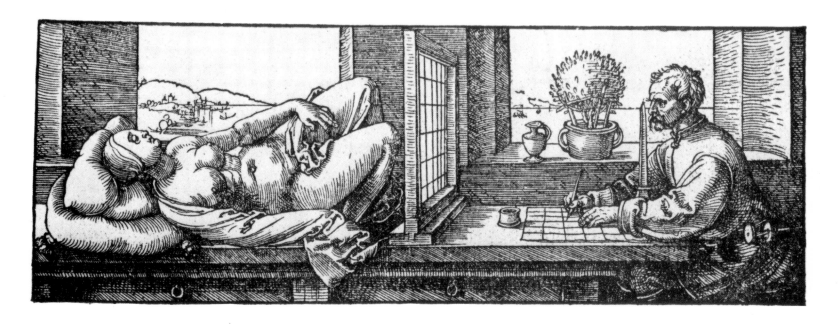

234 *Draughtsman Drawing a Recumbent Woman.* 1525. Woodcut illustration from *The Teaching of Measurements.* 7.5×21.5. Kupferstichkabinett SMPK, Berlin.

Towards the end of his manual Dürer gives instructions on how to draw a visually accurate picture with the help of various devices. This illustration shows a man drawing a woman reclining on cushions. He uses an upright grid and draws on paper which has a corresponding grid division, a device invented in Italy in the fifteenth century. The draughtsman's eye has to be directed to his subject over the top of a rod.

235 Manuscript Page of the Fair Copy for *The Teaching of Measurements.* 1524–5. Paper. 30×21.8. British Library (Sloane 5229, f. 102ʳ), London.

Only two pages (both in London) of Dürer's fair copy for *The Teaching of Measurements* survive. The page illustrated here concerns the theory of curves dealt with in the first book. Dürer describes the transformation of a curve by means of a triangular construction illustrated on the previous page. Such transformations of curves were used in architecture to construct vaults of different spans but of equal height, as Dürer demonstrates on subsequent pages.

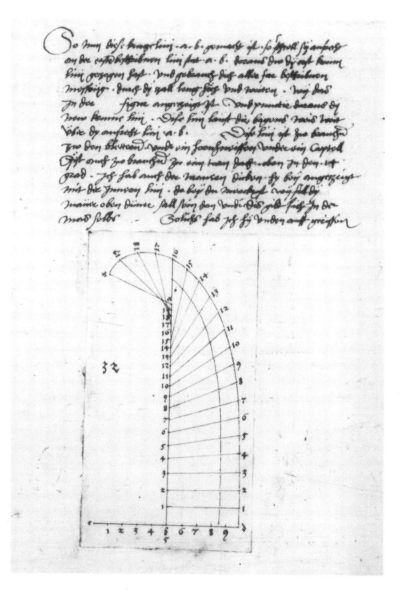

In the first part of his book, *Various Instructions for the Fortification of Towns, Castles and Large Villages,* Dürer describes three different methods of construction of round bastions which could withstand bombardment by heavy siege-artillery and at the same time allow cannons to be set Pl. 236 up for active combat with the enemy. In the next section the artist develops a plan for a fortified capital in which the residential districts are grouped symmetrically around a fortified palace. It is the site plan of an ideal town on a square grid with a network of roads running at right angles to each other; the branches of different trades and occu-

pations are distributed according to practical and social considerations in a carefully thought-out scheme. The third part deals with the construction of a circular barrage fortification between mountains and the sea. The last chapter deals with the reinforcement of mediæval fortifications.

Dürer's theory of fortification is based on the "old Italian manner", as it came to be called, which had been developed by Alberti, Filarete, Francesco di Giorgio, Leonardo da Vinci and Bramante, and of which a few examples already existed in Italy. It is not yet known, however, whose writings Dürer could have used and which modern fortifications he had seen for himself.[372]

Finally, Dürer was able to prepare for the printing of the most important part of his theoretical works so far, the treatise on human proportions. The subject had occupied him since his first meeting with Jacopo de' Barbari in Venice (cf. p. 48). Dürer had turned the Italian artists' search for

236   *Siege of a Town*. 1527. Woodcut. 22.4 × 72.7. Kupferstichkabinett SMPK, Berlin.

This woodcut was printed from two separate plates and is an interesting example of how Dürer gave visual, artistic expression to his ideas on a new kind of fortification capable of withstanding artillery fire. The town, on the extreme left, is protected by an immense bastion, such as Dürer described in his *Theory of Fortification* of 1527. A besieging army advances from the right. The square formations of the mercenary foot-soldiers can be clearly distinguished from the wedge-shaped cavalry units; there are also field- and siege-guns and accompanying carriages carrying ammunition. Last of all comes the baggage train, including herds of cattle necessary for the soldiers' provisions.

the ideal measurements of the human body into a system of human proportions devised according to different body types. By linking different physical types with the theory of Pls. 237–8 the four temperaments Dürer was the first to formulate an idea which went far beyond the theories of his age and has

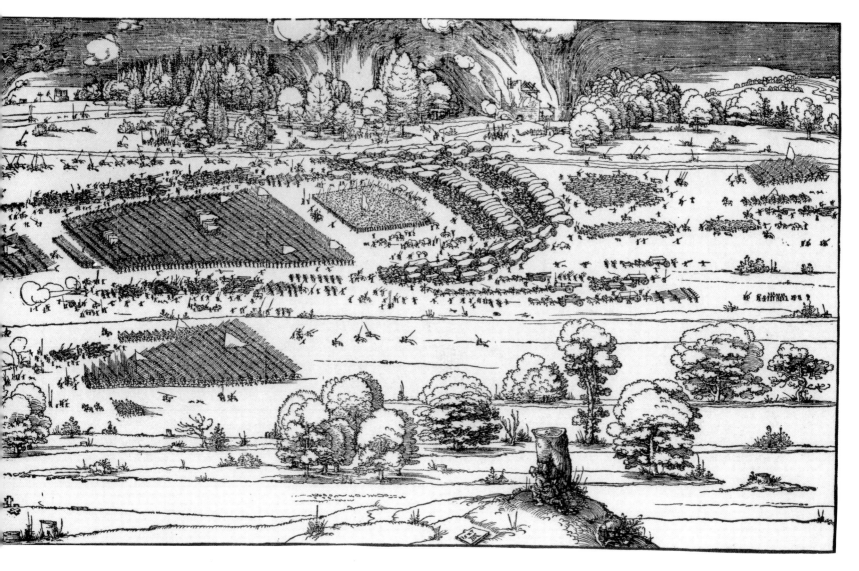

indeed only recently been taken up: the idea that the human frame and personality are linked.[373]

Dürer's most important theoretical insights into art are contained in the famous "aesthetic excursus" at the end of the third book of the *Four Books on Human Proportion*.[374] It comes immediately after a description of the "faker", a device by which the different proportional types described in the first two books can be varied by means of geometric projection. Dürer explains in the accompanying text that such variations are necessary to give individual shape to these physical types. He is thus at pains to differentiate clearly between the unique appearance of a person and the general features of the physical type to which this person belongs— this is in direct contrast to the theories of the Italian writers.[375] These comments by Dürer formulate the theoretical rule which he had already expressed in a work of art, namely the *Four Apostles*.

Dürer draws two conclusions from these findings: one is that it is necessary for an artist to be absolutely true to nature; the other, arising from the first, that he is justified in depicting ugliness[376]—provided he is talented enough to do so. These ideas are the key to some of Dürer's works, such as the *Portrait of his Mother*, and his various pictures of peasants.[377] Pl. 179 Pls. 47, 17

Dürer, in contrast to Alberti, comes to the logical conclusion that the significance of a work of art is independent of the beauty of the figures it represents. What is essential is that the work is coherent. In other words, Dürer differentiates between natural beauty which, as far as human beings are concerned, is of necessity imperfect, and the beauty to be realized in a work of art.[378]

From a starting-point based on Italian theory of art in general, and Alberti's writings in particular, Dürer arrives at conclusions, based on his own thoughts and experiences,

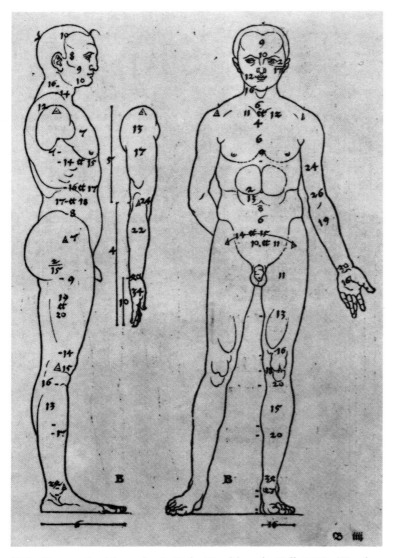

237 *Figure of a Man who is Eight Head-lengths Tall*. 1528. Woodcut illustration from *The Four Books on Human Proportion*. Kupferstich-kabinett SMPK, Berlin.

After studying the problem of the proportions of the human body for almost thirty years, in 1528 Dürer was ready to have his findings printed; but he did not live to see their publication. After repeated experiments Dürer chose the head as the ratio for the measurements of all other parts of the human body. He drew the side view of the arm separately, to avoid confusion and overlaps. The view from the back is illustrated on the next page.

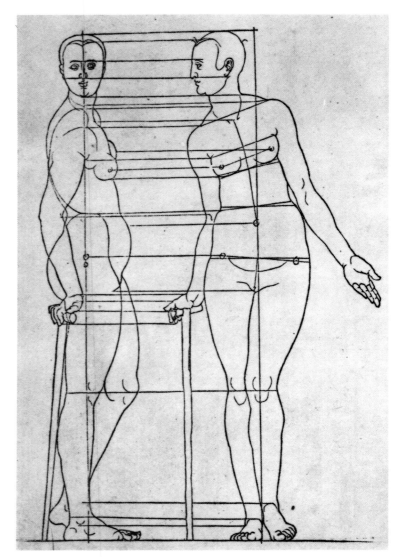

238 *Figure of a Woman shown in Motion*. 1528. Woodcut illustration from *The Four Books on Human Proportion*. Kupferstichkabinett SMPK, Berlin.

Dürer expounds his theory on how to depict the human figure in motion in the last of his *Four Books on Human Proportion*. This illustration shows two views of a female figure.

which differ markedly from those of the Italians, indeed, are in direct contrast to their ideas on art. It may be assumed that Dürer was at least partially aware of this.

There is a famous statement in the "aesthetic excursus": "For truly art is inherent in nature / he who can tear it out possesses it / if you acquire it / it will guard you against many faults in your work, and with the help of Geometry

you may demonstrate much about your work." This state-ment is occasionally even today misinterpreted as an affir-mation of naturalism in art, although it has long been estab-lished that in this context the term "art" *(kunst)* means order or regularity.[379] What Dürer means is that the artist who recognizes order inherent in nature (that is in the shaping of the human body) and can reduce it to mathemati-cal principles is spared many mistakes which might be made by a painter working merely to workshop traditions. With these words Dürer gives a theoretical justification for his

242

239 *Dream Vision*. 1525. Watercolour. 30.5×42.5. Kunsthistorisches Museum, Vienna.

As the long inscription explains, on the night of 7 to 8 June 1525, Dürer had such a vivid dream of torrential rain that he woke up horrified. It is known from other written sources that Dürer frequently suffered from nightmares, but this dream is generally thought to be particularly important. It has been linked to Dürer's malaria (cf. p. 216) as well as a fear of a new Flood, which had been prophesied by various astrologers for the year 1524.

treatise on proportions which aligns him with those who endeavoured to have painting acknowledged as a "liberal art".

Dürer's findings in his treatise on proportions are, together with Leonardo da Vinci's, the most important contributions to Renaissance art theory. Dürer was the first to have made his findings accessible to a large public through a printed publication. He did not live to see the publication of his main theoretical work on 31 October 1528. He died on Pl. 240 6 April shortly before his fifty-eighth birthday, after having corrected the proofs for the first book. Although he seems to have been unwell for some time, his death came as a surprise. He was buried in the tomb of the Frey family in the cemetery of St. John. The next day the Nuremberg painters disinterred his body to make a death mask.

XII. Dürer

The Man · His Work · His Importance

The series of self-portraits are an obvious starting-point in trying to establish what kind of man Albrecht Dürer was. These personal testimonies begin with the silver-point drawing of 1484 and end with the representation of the forty-year-old painter as one of the minor figures on the *Landauer Altarpiece*, completed in 1511. After that there were no more direct self-portraits.

Throughout the Middle Ages there had been artists' self-portraits in the form of dedication pictures, supplemented by autobiographies in the late Middle Ages and the Renaissance. Dürer's family chronicle and his fragmentary *Gedenkbuch* may be interpreted as the first beginnings of a literary autobiography, but his character and development as a man and artist are revealed more clearly in his painted and drawn self-portraits than in these biographical notes.

It would be doing the self-portraits an injustice to think of them merely as products of a narcissistic temperament. According to a comment by the Humanist Joachim Camerarius, in the introduction to his Latin translation of the *Four Books on Human Proportion*, Dürer always maintained a critical attitude towards himself and his work. This is confirmed by a statement by the artist—recorded by Melanchthon—that he had preferred colour and variety in his youth, but was now, with growing maturity, trying to capture something of the simplicity of nature in his works. His remark that while he often saw pictures of great beauty in his dreams, he was never able to create such pictures in his waking life,[380] expresses a similar attitude.

Even bearing in mind Dürer's self-critical attitude, it is still surprising to find a man at the beginning of the modern era who was preoccupied with his own person so early in life and so consistently. The Vienna silver-point self-portrait of the thirteen-year-old, which may have been preceded by earlier attempts, is an astonishing testimony of this exceptionally early self-awareness. This is further emphasized by the inscription, added after 1500.

The next self-portrait is the Erlangen pen drawing which Dürer sketched during his days as a journeyman when he

Pl. 7

Pl. 22

was about twenty-one years old. However it is interpreted, whether as a preliminary study for a painting or as an expression of psychological or physical disquiet, it remains an intense facial and psychological appraisal unknown to artists before Rembrandt. The drawing gives a strong impression that by sketching his own features the young artist was critically examining his own artistic activity.

The Paris painting of 1493 (of which there is a preliminary study, W. 27, in the Metropolitan Museum in New York) appears almost like an answer to the tormented restlessness of the Erlangen sketch. Two features characterize it as a confession of faith: the eryngo which the painter holds in his hand, a symbol of Christ's Passion, and the inscription above the self-portrait: *My sach die gat / Als es oben schtat* ("My fate is determined above"). If the twenty-two-year-old painter confesses, as he does in these two lines, that his fate lies in God's hands, this should not be interpreted as a sign of resignation but as an expression of a heart-felt trust in God. As is shown in this picture for the first time, Dürer was a deeply religious man, and this had a decisive influence on the whole of his work.

Pl. 24

Dürer's Madrid self-portrait of 1498, completed in the same year as the *Apocalypse,* is his most appealing and shows no trace of religious anguish. Instead, the painter appears self-confident, as if wanting to express his superior artistic ability in his exterior appearance. He is dressed according to the bizarre fashion of the time, but in carefully chosen colours; his hair is foppishly long and frizzed and he has a beard, which was still uncommon then; his gloved hands are casually folded. The manly adornment of the beard became the object of much ridicule among his friends even in later years, but, as in the case of the poetry competition with the town clerk Lazarus Spengler, he countered it with superior self-irony by calling himself "the hairy, bearded painter".

Pl. 76

The fashionable elegance of Dürer's Madrid self-portrait, which some observers have thought excessive, reflects the wish, often encountered in artists, to resemble the upper class of their society. Peter Paul Rubens for instance is said to have adopted a privilege of the gentry by always carrying a sword, even when painting. There is documentary evidence that Richard Wagner wore a loose silk cloak when composing. Thomas Mann's upper middle-class behaviour is similarly documented. Less well known is the dandyish behaviour of George Grosz, who is famous for the social criticism expressed in his paintings. Even better known than these painters, musicians and writers, including Dürer, are the Bohemian artists who, in contrast, express their contempt for convention in their life style and dress.

Dürer, who by origin and profession belonged to the upper level of the artisan class, had been admitted to Humanist and patrician circles. It may have been because of his wife's relation to the patrician families Rummel and Haller that he was taken up by the intellectual and social élite. In this context it is perhaps not quite so surprising that the twenty-six-year-old painter tried to emulate his friends in his outward appearance as well, particularly as he seems to have been very partial to elegant dress.

At the age of twenty-eight, Dürer painted himself dressed Pl. 1 in a dark brown patrician fur-lined cloak. This Munich self-portrait of 1500 may well be the most famous of any artist. Its fame rests less on its artistic quality, however, than on a lack of understanding of observers of the artist's Christ-like appearance, which was first noted a century ago by the Viennese scholar Moriz Thausing. Until recently Dürer's way of representing himself in this portrait was thought to be arrogant and blasphemous. Critics have felt that Dürer's vanity, which had already been a feature of the Madrid self-portrait, is here carried to excess.

However, this is a misinterpretation of the self-portrait of 1500. Rather, it should be seen as a formal expression of the important role early modern artists throughout Europe accorded themselves. The portrait refers not only to the biblical account of the Creation, according to which God created man in His own image, but also to the philosophical ideas of Plato, Augustine, Bonaventura and Nicholas of Cusa, as well as to Florentine Neoplatonic thought. The central subject of the picture is not the person Dürer, but his creative artistic talent, which was intended to represent all the artists of his time.

Dürer used a geometric system to emphasize his Christ-like appearance, showing the importance he attached to measurement in art. This is confirmed by several of his statements: "...that measure is so highly regarded by the All-Mighty that He created all beings according to number, weight and measure";[381] and: "nothing needs measure in

more or more varied ways than the art of painting";[382] or: "the measurement of the earth, water and the stars has been made intelligible through painting, and many other things have also been made known to men through the medium of painting."[383]

This puts Dürer among those artists, mostly Italian, who demanded, as did, for example, Leonardo da Vinci, that painting should no longer be classified as a mechanical art but, because of its links with mathematics, should be seen as one of the seven liberal arts, which included geometry. Against this intellectual background Dürer's Munich self-portrait becomes one of the high-points of the artists' perpetual struggle to clarify their own role. The Munich panel, more than any other work of European painting, represents the Renaissance artist, the "new Apelles" as the Humanists called Dürer.

Two further drawings belong to the first group of self-portraits: a brush drawing on green primed paper, now in the Palace Museum in Weimar (W. 267), and a pen and wash drawing (W. 482), formerly in the *Kunsthalle* in Bremen, but which has been missing since the end of World War II. This last drawing has been variously dated between 1506 and 1521. In the Weimar drawing, which appears to have been executed between 1500 and 1505 and is an almost full-length portrait, Dürer has portrayed himself in the nude, a unique occurrence in pre-twentieth century art. This drawing reveals a self-awareness which goes far beyond the consciousness of rank represented by dress and adornments. It is the exact antithesis of the self-portrait of 1500 whose typicality is clearly underlined by the contrasting intimacy of the Weimar drawing, where the body is depicted with merciless realism. These two works epitomize the range of Dürer's art, which encompasses works that are unerringly true to nature as well as those that are highly formalized.

The Bremen drawing in which Dürer also appears almost nude and which bears the inscription: "The yellow spot which I point out with my finger is the place which hurts" is less important than the Weimar nude. It gives information on a medical fact, but adds nothing to our knowledge of Dürer's character.

Dürer himself seems to have realized that the (Munich) self-portrait of 1500 could not be surpassed, since in later years he appears merely as a minor figure in some paintings: *Feast of the Rose Garlands, The Martyrdom of the Ten* Pls. 114, 12 *Thousand*, the *Heller Altarpiece* and *All Saints*. His presence Pls. 127, 13 in these pictures doubtlessly reflects his pride in his own achievement, particularly as in all four he holds a piece of paper or a panel bearing an extensive signature. At the same

240 *Dürer's Grave.* Denkmalsarchiv, Hauptamt für Hochbauwesen, Nuremberg.

Dürer was buried in the tomb of the Frey family in the cemetery of St. John in Nuremberg. The appearance of the grave today is due to the intervention of the painter and art critic Joachim von Sandrart, who had Dürer's neglected grave repaired in 1681. It was then that the large brass plate was added which bears Latin and German inscriptions written by Sandrart. The plate at the head of the grave bears the Latin inscription written by Pirckheimer.

time this device represents a clear shift in emphasis: now the artist is both creator and created.

With growing maturity Dürer, the man, is less and less apparent in his work. When he once more took up the problematical subject of an artist's existence, in the 1514 Pl. 170 engraving of *Melencolia I,* all subjective elements were eliminated. The theme is no longer the artist as *alter deus* (other god), but a combination of melancholy and divine passion *(furor divinus),* i.e. the reason behind certain men's artistic creativity. In the subsequent history of art this inspired translation of abstract idea into concrete image has never been surpassed.

Mathematics plays a vital role in the *Melencolia I,* as in other pictures. The tools lying at the feet of the symbolic figure are in some way connected with architecture or sculpture, which in turn can be traced back to geometry. The three basic biblical categories which Dürer quotes, namely measure, number and weight, are represented in this composition by an hourglass, a number square and a pair of scales.

A conception of Dürer's character, as established from his self-portraits, still lacks several essential features. His manuscripts, of which a considerable number survive, provide further clues. The description of his father's death in 1502 in the fragmentary *Gedenkbuch*[384] reveals true filial

247

love and devotion. Dürer's attachment to his mother, Barbara Dürer, is perhaps even more apparent, because the description of her last hours is supplemented by the large charcoal drawing made a few months before her death. The merciless portrayal of decay in this sixty-three-year-old woman makes her picture one of the most moving documents of human life. Moreover, the inscription in Dürer's portrait of his teacher, Michael Wolgemut, shows that Dürer was similarly attached to other people who were close to him.

Dürer's human warmth, courtesy and amiability may be deduced from his friendships with Konrad Celtis and Willibald Pirckheimer, and are affirmed by many references in letters by his contemporaries, who regarded him as a loveable man as well as a supremely gifted artist. Joachim Camerarius, for instance, stresses these features in his introduction to the *Four Books on Human Proportion*; he writes that Dürer had been a sociable man, able to entertain a whole table with his stories. He seems moreover to have been a humorous man as well; this is illustrated in the letters he wrote from Venice to his friend Pirckheimer, where he makes mocking remarks about the latter's achievements in rhetoric and mnemotechny (the art of improving the memory)[385] as well as his many love-affairs.[386]

Dürer's love of gambling, documented in many entries of the diary he kept during his journey to the Netherlands, is also part of this sociability. However, he recorded his losses and much rarer gains with a quite surprising meticulousness bordering on parsimony. This striving for financial gain is confirmed by many other records, such as contracts with agents selling his prints, his letters to Jakob Heller, the diary of his journey to the Netherlands, and his discussion of a painter's pay in the manual on painting. His attention to money matters eventually gained him financial success. At his death he left his wife 6,848 florins (approximately £60,000 by 1980 standards); this made him one of the hundred most wealthy citizens of Nuremberg.[387]

Dürer's striving for financial gain must be seen in the context of the early capitalist era to which he belonged, but the historical situation alone does not explain his greed. In a letter written in November, 1530 to Johannes Tschertte in Vienna,[388] Willibald Pirckheimer accuses Dürer's wife Agnes of being responsible for her husband's premature death, because she had urged him to earn more and more money despite his illness. It must be remembered that Pirckheimer (who was to die a month later) was in a pessimistic frame of mind and also that he did not like the wife of his dead friend. Therefore, this letter can hardly be regarded as an objective account. If one looks at the issue dispassionately, it becomes clear that both partners were interested in acquiring adequate financial backing for the social standing they had attained.

Practically nothing else is known about Dürer's relationship with his wife Agnes. Dürer's own comments about her are objective and sober. Only the inscription "my Agnes" on the Vienna drawing hints at affection. However, the state of Dürer's marriage can hardly be deduced from this. It had been arranged by their parents, as was the general practice; marriages were primarily considered as economic unions, with mutual affection a pleasant but by no means vital extra. Seen in this context, Dürer and his wife presumably had an entirely normal marriage, though there were no children.

A close examination of the artist's character is mainly interesting for what it reveals about his work. In retrospect it can be summarized as follows: Albrecht Dürer, who came from a German-Hungarian family of skilled artisans, was a man of exceptional artistic talent as well as intellectual ability. This rare and happy combination made him a great artist, who was encouraged by his parents and astonishingly sympathetic fellow citizens. His immense inventiveness is illustrated particularly clearly in his engravings and woodcuts; he favoured these media since they allowed him independence from the wishes of patrons. Prints also proved almost ideal in that they represented a constant source of income, which was important for Dürer. Through his woodcut sequences and engravings he became famous even outside Germany while he was still comparatively young; this made him more self-confident, but also encouraged him to further efforts.

Another advantage graphic works held for Dürer was that he could apply his theoretical findings much more easily to them than to paintings, which were usually commissioned. The fat peasant-like man and the corresponding woman for instance, which were the first figures Dürer constructed in his treatise on proportions, reappear in the engraving of *Peasants at the Market*, executed in 1519. The engraving bears out Dürer's words in the so-called "aesthetic excursus" at the end of the third book of the treatise on proportions, that "a knowledgeable, experienced artist can demonstrate his great power and art even in coarse peasant figures".[389]

This statement shows how far away Dürer had moved from the search for ideal human proportions characteristic of Italian theorists; none the less Dürer's examination of these problems had necessarily been based on the Italians' studies of proportion and perspective. He adopted a number of ideas of Leon Battista Alberti and Marsilio Ficino, and through his publications made them available to those who had no access to the Italian originals, which existed in manuscript form only. It is difficult to judge what effect Dürer's books had on his contemporaries, but the fact that his treatise on proportions was translated into Latin and his *Teaching of Measurements* appeared in a new, enlarged edition in 1532, implies that both works made their mark. Yet Dürer's writings do not appear to have become a widely used manual for intending artists; their demands on the reader were too high for this, as a note by Hieronymus Rodler in his book on *The Art of Measurement*, Simmern 1531, testifies.[390]

However, even if Dürer was not widely influential as a writer, he certainly was as an artist. His exceptional talent enabled him early on to create a new, coherent style based on the grandiose, formal art of painters like Mantegna as well as on the detailed realism which characterized his own style. His new, monumental works, particularly prints, became known not only to other artists but also to the public at large, familiarizing them with Renaissance forms modelled on classical art. In this way Dürer—as Panofsky has pointed out—helped subsequent generations to appreciate classical art itself.

Dürer did not merely gain inspiration from the Italians; he in turn influenced them through his engravings and woodcuts. His accomplished engraving technique had a decisive influence on Marcantonio Raimondi, for instance, and his landscapes inspired many Italian painters and draughtsmen. It is therefore no exaggeration to call Albrecht Dürer one of the central figures of European art at the beginning of the modern era; his influence extends beyond national borders and the limits of time and continues to be felt today.

Notes

1 Endres, pp. 246 f.
2 Stromer, 1978, pp. 63–7
3 Waetzoldt, p. 243
4 Gümbel, pp. 9–11
5 Schnelbögel, 1970, pp. 216 ff.
6 Cremer, p. 127
7 Hirschmann, p. 45
8 Mummenhof, p. 82
9 Baader, pp. 40 ff.
10 Knappe, 1971, pp. 247 f.
11 Rupprich, vol. 1, pp. 28–31
12 *Dürer*, 1971, no. 7
13 Solleder, 1934; Rupprich, vol. 1, p. 252
14 Rupprich, vol. 1, p. 28
15 Caesar, p. 31
16 Hase, p. 17
17 Rupprich, vol. 1, p. 225
18 Hase, p. 23
19 Hampe, 1928, pp. 197–206
20 Rücker, p. 14
21 Hofmann, p. 7; Schultheiss, p. 234
22 Rupprich, vol. 1, p. 30
23 Leder, p. 29
24 Machilek, p. 18
25 Flechsig, vol. 1, pp. 166 f.; Waetzoldt, p. 93
26 Rupprich, vol. 2, p. 92
27 Schultheiss, p. 229
28 Rupprich, vol. 1, p. 221
29 Rupprich, vol. 1, p. 52
30 Heller, vol. 2, 1, p. 74
31 Rupprich, vol. 1, p. 113
32 Rupprich, vol. 1, pp. 86, 113
33 Flechsig, vol. 1, pp. 166 f.; Rupprich, vol. 2, p. 19
34 Braunfels, 1971, p. 138
35 Heerwagen, pp. 31 f.
36 Rosental, p. 47
37 Strieder, 1974, pp. 45 ff.
38 Rupprich, vol. 1, pp. 294 f.
39 Rupprich, vol. 1, p. 31
40 Meder, 1919, pp. 20, 207–18

41 Zahn, pp. 21 ff.
42 Rücker, Pl. 49
43 Rupprich, vol. 1, p. 297
44 Rupprich, vol. 1, p. 31
45 Brand Philipp, pp. 5 ff.
46 Panofsky, 1960, pp. 165 ff.
47 Rupprich, vol. 1, p. 31
48 Rupprich, vol. 1, p. 295
49 Rupprich, vol. 1, p. 295
50 Van Mander, pp. 71, 95
51 Sandrart, p. 63
52 Rupprich, vol. 1, p. 28
53 Anzelewsky, 1954, pp. 6 f.
54 Schürer, pp. 173 ff.
55 Panofsky, 1945, pp. 23 f.
56 Anzelewsky, 1971, p. 87
57 Evers, *Dürer bei Memling*
58 Châtelet, pp. 60 f.
59 Wiesflecker, vol. 1, pp. 220–8
59a Strauss, 1974, vol. 1, Appx. I, 1
60 Panofsky, 1945, pp. 5, 23; *Dürer,* 1971, p. 74
61 Flechsig, vol. 1, p. 134
61a Anzelewsky, 1971, no. 6
62 Anzelewsky, 1954, pp. 12–27
63 Winkler, 1951, p. 70
64 Landolt, pp. 38 ff. and Hieronymus, pp. 271 ff.
65 Lefebvre, pp. 90 ff.
66 Könnecker, p. 73
67 Gaier, p. 5
68 Leitschuh, p. 164; Zarncke, p. XXIX
69 Lefebvre, pp. 77 f.
70 Köhler, p. 43
71 v. Borries, pp. 25 f.
72 Anzelewsky, 1971, p. 119
73 Wiederanders, pp. 11 f.
73a Stauber, p. 5
74 Grote 1964, pp. 30 f.
75 Anzelewsky, 1971, p. 25
76 Meder, 1923, p. 34
77 Ficino, pp. 605 f.
78 Goldschmidt, pp. 26 f., 59 ff.

79 Stauber, p. 9
80 Hase, p. 20
81 Meder, 1911–12, pp. 198 ff.
82 Rusconi, pp. 121 f.
83 Hase, p. 353
84 Braghirolli, pp. 370 f.; Wind, 1948, pp. 4 f.
85 Anzelewsky, 1971, pp. 159, 210
86 Simon, pp. 21 ff.
87 Anzelewsky, 1955, Pls. 1–5
88 Rupprich, vol. 1, p. 102
89 Hase, pp. VI–CXXIV
90 Rupprich, vol. 3, p. 488
91 Rupprich, vol. 1, p. 244
92 Lehrs, 1882, pp. 211 ff.; Boehn, pp. 9 ff.; Weiss, p. 49
93 Rupprich, vol. 1, p. 152
94 Sachs, p. 186
95 Winkler, 1957, p. 74
96 Panofsky, 1930, p. 168
97 Grote, 1954–9, p. 55
98 Burger, p. 272
99 Goldschmidt, pp. 115–45
100 Reimann, pp. 152 ff.
101 Cassirer, p. 71; Chastel, pp. 101 f.
102 Cf. the corresponding chapter in my forthcoming *Dürer-Studien*
103 Leitschuh, p. 133; Baxendall, p. 413
104 Wuttke, 1967, pp. 321 ff.
105 Rupprich, vol. 2, Pls. 40 ff.
106 Rupprich, vol. 2, pp. 12, 35
107 Rupprich, vol. 2, pp. 36, 38, 39
108 Rupprich, vol. 1, p. 72
109 Reimann, p. 164, A. 4
110 Peuckert, p. 106
111 Levebvre, p. 90
112 Brant, Varia Carmina, 1498, no. 51
113 Peuckert, pp. 195 ff.
114 Koepplin, p. 193; Adel, p. 53
115 Chastel, p. 61
116 Giehlow, 1904, p. 6
117 Ficino, pp. 296 ff.

118 Schrade, p. 25; Bainton, pp. 269 ff.; Anzelewsky, 1971, no. 10
119 Rupprich, vol. 2, pp. 106 ff.
120 Panofsky, 1945, 3rd chapter
121 Kirn, pp. 130 ff.
122 Wuttke, 1967, pp. 321 ff.
123 Panofsky, 1920, pp. 359 ff.
124 Giehlow, 1902, pp. 25 f.
125 Meder, 1932, pp. 22 ff.
126 Pauli, 1910, p. 58
127 Alberti, pp. 78–9
128 Filarete, pp. 603–5
129 Rupprich, 1930, p. 23
130 Malaguzzi Valeri, p. 464
131 Richter, vol. 2, no. 716–18
132 Pauli, 1914, pp. 105 ff.
133 Rupprich, vol. 2, p. 87
134 Hind, Pls. 613–15
135 Rupprich, 1960–1, p. 229
136 Frenzel, pp. 193 ff.
137 Rupprich, vol. 1, p. 55
138 Gombrich, p. 77; Ficino, p. 118
139 Rupprich, vol. 1, p. 162
140 Pigler, pp. 281 ff.
141 Anzelewsky, 1979, p. 527
142 Wölfflin, p. 161
143 Anzelewsky, 1971, no. 82
144 This will be discussed in detail in my forthcoming Dürer-Studien
145 Ginhart, pp. 129 ff.
146 Rupprich, vol. 1, pp. 41–60
147 Rupprich, vol. 1, pp. 43 f.
148 Rupprich, vol. 1, p. 49
149 Vasari, vol. 5, p. 406
150 Rupprich, vol. 1, p. 52
151 Grote, 1956, p. 5
152 Rupprich, vol. 1, p. 59
153 Rupprich, vol. 1, pp. 44, 46
154 Rupprich, vol. 1, p. 110
155 Rupprich, vol. 1, p. 59
156 Hofmann, pp. 4, 6
157 Rupprich, vol. 1, p. 55
158 Rupprich, vol. 1, p. 42
159 Rupprich, vol. 1, p. 45
160 Anzelewsky, 1971, pp. 64 ff.; Cat. no. 93
161 Rupprich, vol. 1, pp. 55, 57
162 Rupprich, vol. 1, p. 57
163 Rupprich, vol. 1, p. 245
164 Rupprich, vol. 1, p. 53
165 Rupprich, vol. 1, p. 36
166 Schultheiss, p. 226
167 Noack, p. 29
168 Wiesflecker, vol. 3, pp. 345 f.
169 Rupprich, vol. 1, p. 59
170 Rupprich, vol. 1, p. 294
171 Cantor, pp. 467 f.

172 Harnest, 1972, p. 198
173 Strauss, 1974, no. 1506/44–8, HP 1506/3–5
174 Stechow, p. 251; Strauss, 1976, p. 159
175 Strauss, 1972, no. 130–3
176 Anzelewsky, 1971, p. 62
177 Hirschfeld, p. 107
178 Codex Esurialensis, p. 106
179 Anzelewsky, 1971, p. 42
180 Anzelewsky, 1971, Cat. no. 98
181 Rupprich, vol. 1, p. 253
182 Simler, pp. 124 ff.; Laufner, p. 252
183 Rupprich, vol. 1, p. 49
184 Meister um Albrecht Dürer, Cat. no. 251
185 Rupprich, vol. 1, pp. 246 f.
186 Meister um Albrecht Dürer, Cat. no. 150
187 Rupprich, vol. 1, p. 49
188 Rupprich, vol. 1, pp. 226 f.
189 Hampe, 1928, p. 43; Kauffmann, 1972, pp. 13 f.
190 Grünhagen, p. 375
191 Rupprich, vol. 1, pp. 68, 256
192 Anzelewsky, 1971, p. 78
193 Rupprich, vol. 1, p. 64
194 Hirschfeld, pp. 130–9
195 Rupprich, vol. 1, p. 64
196 Kristeller, vol. 2, p. 109
197 Anzelewsky, 1971, p. 76
198 Anzelewsky, 1971, p. 45
199 Rowlands, p. 32
200 Ficino, p. 1031
201 Rupprich, vol. 1, p. 289, no. 142
202 Rupprich, vol. 1, pp. 277 ff.
203 Rupprich, vol. 1, pp. 229 ff.
204 Grote, 1964, p. 32
205 Anzelewsky, 1971, no. 117 V
206 Würtenberger, pp. 51–3
207 Panofsky, 1945, pp. 146 ff.
208 Dürer, 1971, no. 707
209 Stafsky, pp. 18 f.
210 Anzelewsky, 1971, p. 189
211 Rupprich, vol. 1, p. 255
212 Dürer, 1971, no. 698
213 Rupprich, vol. 2, pp. 373–6
214 Brion-Guerry, pp. 120 f.
215 Strauss, 1974, no. AS: 1509/1
216 Petz, p. 254
217 Rupprich, vol. 2, pp. 81 ff.
218 Rupprich, vol. 2, p. 84
219 Rupprich, vol. 2, pp. 100 f.
220 Alberti, pp. 150–3
221 Rupprich, vol. 2, p. 113
222 Alberti, pp. 88 f.
223 Rupprich, vol. 2, pp. 104, 116 ff.

224 Anzelewsky, 1979, pp. 528 ff.
225 Graf, p. 24
226 Rupprich, vol. 3, p. 296, no. 57
227 Giehlow, 1904, p. 66 A.4
228 Rupprich, vol. 2, p. 101
229 Giehlow, 1904, pp. 63 f.
230 Rupprich, vol. 2, p. 109; Panofsky, 1960, pp. 69–71
231 Waetzoldt, p. 239
232 Rupprich, vol. 2, pp. 128–41
233 Wiederanders, p. 21
233a Cremer, pp. 125 ff.
234 Rupprich, 1969, pp. 47–55
235 Fichtenau, pp. 25–34
236 Strauss, 1974, no. 1512/8, 10; vol. 5, pp. 2667–701
237 Österr. Nationalbibliothek, Vienna, Cod. 2835, 2837
238 Giehlow, 1903, p. 93
239 Of the group of the procession Hans Burgkmair designed 67 and Albrecht Altdorfer 38
240 Koepplin, p. 104, A. 267
241 Volkmann, pp. 81–95
242 Giehlow, 1904, p. 69
243 Rupprich, vol. 1, pp. 77 f.
244 Rupprich, vol. 1, p. 77, no. 24
245 Rupprich, vol. 1, p. 110
246 Rupprich, vol. 1, p. 79
247 Rupprich, vol. 1, p. 249
247a Strauss, 1974, pp. 1–112 prayer-book
248 Rupprich, vol. 1, p. 257
249 v. Tavel, pp. 64 ff.; Vetter and Brockhaus, pp. 70 ff.
250 Rupprich, vol. 1, p. 261
251 Rupprich, vol. 1, pp. 154, 157
252 Grimm, pp. 534 ff.; Weber, pp. 13–44
253 Rox, pp. 67 ff.
254 Rupprich, vol. 2, pp. 55 ff.
255 Harnest, 1971, p. 53
256 Rupprich, vol. 1, p. 297
257 Giehlow, 1904, p. 14; Panofsky and Saxl, 1923; Horst, 1953; Klibansky, Saxl and Panofsky, 1964; Schuster, 1974; Hoffmann, 1979
258 Klibansky, Saxl and Panofsky, pp. 256 ff.
259 Panofsky, 1945, vol. 2, no. 177
260 Hamann, pp. 152 ff.; Harnest, 1979, pp. 152 ff.
261 Dürer, 1971, no. 581
262 Rupprich, vol. 1, pp. 36 f.
263 Rupprich, vol. 1, p. 258
264 Rupprich, vol. 3, p. 452
265 Rupprich, vol. 1, p. 260

266 Schubert, p. 147
267 Jeremias, pp. 36 f.
268 Jeremias, p. 170
269 Rupprich, 1975, p. 77; Seebass, pp. 107 ff.
270 Lutz, pp. 22 ff.
271 Graf, pp. 65 ff.
272 Rupprich, vol. 2, p. 88
273 Rupprich, 1959
274 Lefebvre, pp. 149–51
275 Rupprich, vol. 2, p. 106, *passim*
276 Rupprich, vol. 2, p. 104, *passim*
277 Christensen, 1970, pp. 205 f.
278 Rupprich, vol. 2, Pls. 2, 3
279 Rupprich, vol. 2, Pl. 46
280 Rupprich, vol. 2, Pl. 139
281 Kauffmann, 1924, p. 99 A.4
282 Rupprich, vol. 3, pp. 19 ff.
283 Panofsky, 1960, p. 69
283a Information kindly provided by Matthias Mende, Nuremberg
284 Anzelewsky, 1971, nos 145, 146
285 Rupich, vol. 1, p. 82
286 Rupprich, vol. 1, p. 84
287 Rupprich, vol. 1, p. 263, no. 46
288 Rupprich, vol. 1, p. 263, no. 50
289 Rupprich, vol. 1, p. 254
290 Rupprich, vol. 1, p. 264
291 Rupprich, vol. 1, p. 248
292 Sampaio, p. 13
293 Schubert, p. 153
294 Kamann, p. 284
295 Veth and Muller, vol. 2, pp. 15 f.
296 Timken-Zinkann, pp. 88 ff.
297 Rupprich, vol. 1, p. 148
298 Rupprich, vol. 1, pp. 165, 175
299 Veth and Muller, vol. 2, pp. 53 ff.
299a U. Mende, pp. 24 ff.
300 Rupprich, vol. 1, p. 154
301 Veth and Muller, vol. 2, p. 30
302 Veth and Muller, vol. 2, p. 60
303 Rupprich, vol. 1, p. 155
304 Veth and Muller, vol. 2, pp. 129 f.
305 Rupprich, vol. 1, pp. 88 ff.
306 Anzelewsky, 1956, pp. 87–100
307 Rupprich, vol. 1, p. 156

308 Waetzoldt, p. 93
309 Veth and Muller, vol. 2, pp. 69–74
310 Rupprich, vol. 1, p. 159
311 Rupprich, vol. 1, p. 159
312 Rupprich, vol. 1, p. 159
313 Rupprich, vol. 1, p. 160
314 Rupprich, vol. 1, p. 159
315 Schubert, p. 216
316 Rupprich, vol. 1, p. 160
317 Wölfflin, p. 317
317a Anzelewsky, 1956, p. 104
318 Brand, pp. 59 ff.
319 Grote, 1971, pp. 120 ff.
320 Rupprich, vol. 1, p. 154
321 Sampaio, pp. 14, 231
322 Wölfflin, p. 326
323 Rupprich, vol. 1, p. 173
324 Rupprich, vol. 1, p. 158
325 Rupprich, vol. 1, p. 165
326 Rupprich, vol. 1, p. 166
327 Rupprich, vol. 1, p. 168
328 Rupprich, vol. 1, p. 168
329 Rupprich, vol. 1, pp. 168 f.
330 Timken-Zinkann, pp. 88 f.
331 Veth and Muller, vol. 2, p. 33
332 Wiesflecker, vol. 1, pp. 155, 204
333 Rupprich, vol. 1, p. 284
334 Rupprich, vol. 1, pp. 170 ff.
335 Lutz, pp. 32 ff.; Seebass, pp. 105 f.
336 Saxl, vol. 1, p. 271; Seebass, p. 111
337 Anzelewsky, 1971, nos 145, 146
338 Rupprich, vol. 1, p. 174
339 Veth and Muller, vol. 2, p. 35
340 Rupprich, vol. 1, p. 176; Veth and Muller, vol. 2, p. 159
341 Rupprich, vol. 1, p. 120
342 Schubert, p. 135
343 Hofmann, p. 6
344 Dürer, 1971, no. 239
345 Rupprich, vol. 1, p. 242, no. 16; M. Mende, vol. 1, p. 52
346 Rupprich, vol. 3, p. 450; M. Mende, vol. 1, p. 58
346a M. Mende, vol. 1, pp. 70, 81
347 Busch, pp. 32 ff.
348 Rupprich, vol. 1, p. 276, no. 101

349 Rupprich, vol. 1, p. 117
350 Rupprich, vol. 1, pp. 242, 249; Strieder, 1973, p. 151
351 Neudörffer, pp. 37, 50
352 Rupprich, vol. 1, pp. 92 f.
353 Dürer, 1971, no. 398
354 Rupprich, vol. 1, p. 210
355 Harbison, p. 372; Christensen, 1970, p. 215
356 Panofsky, 1945, pp. 221 ff.
357 Seebass, p. 117
358 *Geschichte Nürnbergs*, pp. 154–6
359 Kolde, p. 230
360 Kolde, p. 248
361 Heidrich, pp. 61 ff.
362 Heidrich, pp. 11 ff., 69 ff.
363 Zucker, 1886, pp. 38–44
364 Heidrich, p. 20
365 Anzelewsky, 1971, p. 277
366 Wiederanders, p. 112
367 Rupprich, vol. 1, pp. 28–31
368 Seebass, p. 117
369 Harbison, p. 372; Christensen, 1970, p. 216
370 Rupprich, vol. 3, p. 310
371 Rupprich, vol. 3, p. 372
372 Reitzenstein, pp. 178 ff.
373 Kretschmer, *Körperbau und Charakter;* Waetzoldt, pp. 265 ff.
374 Anzelewsky, 1977, pp. 70 ff.
375 Waetzoldt, pp. 275 f.
376 Panofsky, 1945, p. 274
377 Anzelewsky, 1977, p. 76
378 Panofsky, 1945, p. 275
379 Waetzoldt, p. 275
380 Rupprich, vol. 2, p. 115
381 Rupprich, vol. 2, p. 127
382 Rupprich, vol. 2, p. 127
383 Rupprich, vol. 2, p. 113
384 Rupprich, vol. 1, pp. 36 f.
385 Rupprich, vol. 1, p. 55
386 Rupprich, vol. 1, pp. 44, 58
387 Stromer, 1971, p. 19
388 Rupprich, vol. 1, pp. 283–7
389 Anzelewsky, 1977, pp. 75 f.
390 Spohn, p. 80

List of Abbreviations

Institutions

FU   Freie Universität Berlin
GNM   Germanisches Nationalmuseum, Nuremberg
SMPK   Staatliche Museen Preussischer Kulturbesitz

Oeuvre Catalogues

A.   Anzelewsky, Fedja, *Albrecht Dürer.*
        Das malerische Werk, Berlin 1971
B.   Bartsch, Adam, *Le peintre graveur,* vols. 1–21,
        Vienna 1803–21
K.   Kristeller, Paul, *Engravings and woodcuts of*
        Jacopo de' Barbari. Intern. Chalcogr. Ges. 1896
M.   Meder, Joseph, *Dürer Katalog. Ein Handbuch*
        über Albrecht Dürers Stiche, Radierungen,
        Holzschnitte, deren Zustände, Ausgaben und
        Wasserzeichen, Vienna 1932
St.   Strauss, Walter L., *The complete drawings of*
        Albrecht Dürer, vols. 1–6, New York 1974;
        Suppl. 1, New York 1977
W.   Winkler, Friedrich, *Die Zeichnungen Albrecht*
        Dürers, vols. 1–4, Berlin 1936–9

Periodicals

AB   The Art Bulletin
HZ   Historische Zeitschrift
JKSAK   Jahrbuch der Kunsthistorischen Sammlungen des
          allerhöchsten Kaiserhauses (Vienna)
JPKS   Jahrbuch der (königl.) preussischen
          Kunstsammlungen
MJBK   Müncher Jahrbuch der Bildenden Kunst
MVGN   Mitteilungen des Vereins für die Geschichte der
          Stadt Nürnberg
PJ   Preussische Jahrbücher
SWI   Studies of the Warburg Institute (London)
ZBK   Zeitschrift für Bildende Kunst
ZDVK   Zeitschrift des deutschen Vereins für
          Kunstwissenschaft
ZKG   Zeitschrift für Kunstgeschichte

Bibliography

Exhibition Catalogues

Meister um Albrecht Dürer, GNM, Nuremberg 1961

Albrecht Dürer 1471–1971, GNM, Nuremberg 1971

The graphic work of Albrecht Dürer. An exhibition of drawings and prints. British Museum, London 1971 (publ. by John Rowlands)

Das alte Nürnberger Rathaus. Vol. 1: *Baugeschichte und Ausstattung des grossen Saals und der Ratsstube.* Revised by Mathias Mende, Nuremberg, Stadtgeschichtliche Museen (ed.), Nuremberg 1979 (Exh. Cat. no. 15)

Books and Articles

Adel, Kurt, *Konrad Celtis*, Vienna – Graz 1956

Alberti, Leon Battista, *Kleinere kunsttheoretische Schriften.* Original text ed., transl. and comm. on by Hubert Janitschek, Vienna 1877 (Quellenschrift für Kunstgeschichte und Kunsttechnik des Mittelalters und der Renaissance, 11)

Anzelewsky, Fedja, Motiv und Exemplum im frühen Holzschnittwerk Albrecht Dürers. Thesis, Berlin FU 1954 (typescript)

– 'Albrecht Dürers grosser Kreuzigungsholzschnitt von 1494–5', in *ZKG*, 9, 1955, pp. 137–150

– 'A propos de la topographie du parc de Bruxelles et du quai de l'Escaut à Anvers de Dürer', in *Bulletin des Musées Royaux des Beaux Arts*, Brussels 1957, pp. 87–107

– *Albrecht Dürer. Das malerische Werk*, Berlin 1971

– 'Dürers "ästetischer Exkurs" in seiner Proportionslehre' in *Kaleidoskop. Eine Festschrift für Fritz Baumgart*, Berlin 1977, pp. 70–8

– 'Ein humanistischer Altar Dürers', in *Humanistische Bibliothek*, Series 1, vol. 38 (18e Coll. internat. de Tours), *L'Humanisme allemand 1480–1540*, 1979, pp. 525–36

– Dürer-Studien. Untersuchungen zu den ikonographischen und geistesgeschichtlichen Grundlagen seiner Werke zwischen den beiden Italienreisen (in preparation)

Baader, Josef, *Beiträge zur Kunstgeschichte Nürnbergs*, Nördlingen 1860

Bainton, Roland H., 'Dürer and Luther as the man of sorrows' in *AB*, 29, 1947, pp. 269–72

Baxandall, Michael, 'Rudolf Agricola and the visual arts', in *Intuition und Kunstwissenschaft. Festschrift für Hanns Swarzenski*, Berlin 1973, pp. 409–18

Boehn, Max von, *Albrecht Dürer als Buch- und Kunsthändler*, Munich 1905

Borries, Johann Eckart von, *Albrecht Dürer – Christus als Schmerzensmann*, Karlsruhe 1972 (Bildhefte der Staatl. Kunsthalle, 9)

Braghirolli, Wilelmo, 'Carteggio di Isabella d'Este Gonzaga intorno ad un quadro di Giambellino', in *Archivio veneto*, 13, 1877, pp. 370–83

Brand, Erna, 'Untersuchungen zu Albrecht Dürers Bildnis eines jungen Mannes', in *Staatliche Kunstsammlungen Dresden*, Jb., 70–1, pp. 59–83

Brand-Philip, Lotte, 'The portrait diptych of Dürer's parents', in *Simiolus*, 10, 1978–9, no. 1, pp. 5–18

Brant, Sebastian, *Varia Carmina*, Basle, Johann Bergmann 1.5.1498

– *Das Narrenschiff.* Ed. by Friedrich Zarncke, Leipzig 1854; reprinted Darmstadt 1973

Braunfels, Wolfgang, 'Die reformatorische Bewegung im Spiegel von Dürers Spätwerk', in *Albrecht Dürer. Kunst einer Zeitenwende.* Ed. by Herbert Schade, Regensburg 1971, pp. 123–43

Brion-Guerry, Liliane, *Jean Pèlerin Viator. Sa place dans l'histoire de la perspective*, Paris 1962 (Les classiques de l'humanisme. Etudes)

Burger, Heinz Otto, *Renaissance. Humanismus. Reformation. Deutsche Literatur im europäischen Kontext*, Bad Homburg v.d.H. 1969

Busch, Nikolaus, *Untersuchungen zur Lebensgeschichte Dürers*, Riga 1931 (Abhandlungen der Herder-Gesellschaft und des Herder-Instituts zu Riga, 4, 1)

Caesar, Elisabeth, 'Sebald Schreyer', in *MVGN*, 56, 1969, pp. 1–213

Cantor, Moritz, *Vorlesungen über Geschichte der Mathematik*, 2nd ed., Leipzig 1900

Cassierer, Ernst, *Individuum und Kosmos in der Philosophie der Renaissance*, Leipzig – Berlin 1927; reprinted Darmstadt 1974 (Studies of the Warburg Library, 10)

Chastel, André, *Marsile Ficin et l'art*, Geneva-Lille 1954, 2nd ed. 1975

Châtelet, Albert, 'Dürer und die nördlichen Niederlande', in *Anzeiger des GNM*, 1975, pp. 52–64

Christensen, Carl C., 'Dürer's Four Apostles and the dedication as a form of Renaissance art patronage', in *Renaissance Quarterly*, 20, 1967, pp. 325–34

– 'Iconoclasm and the preservation of ecclesiastical art in Reformation in Nurnberg', in *Archiv für Reformationsgeschichte*, 61, 1970, pp. 205–21

Codex Escurialensis. Ein Skizzenbuch aus der Werkstatt Domenico Ghirlandaios. Ed. by Hermann Egger in collaboration with Christian Hülsen and Adolf Michaelis. Text and Pl. vol., Vienna 1906 (Special issue of the Österreichisches Archäologisches Institut, Vienna 4)

Cremer, Erika, 'Dürers verwandtschaftliche Beziehungen zu Innsbruck', in *Festschrift Nikolaus Grass*, vol. 2, 1975, pp. 125–30

Dürer, Albrecht, *Schriftlicher Nachlass*, see: Rupprich, Hans

Endres, Rudolf, 'Zur Einwohnerzahl und Bevölkerungsstruktur Nürnbergs im 15. und 16. Jahrhundert', in *MVGN*, 57, 1970, pp. 242–71

Evers, Hans Gerhard, *Dürer bei Memling*, Munich 1972

Fichtenau, Heinrich, *Die Lehrbücher Maximilian I. und die Anfänge der Frakturschrift*, Hamburg 1961

Ficino, Marsilio, *Opera Omnia*, 2 vols., 4 pts., Basle 1561, Turin 1959

Filarete, Antonio Averlino, *Antonio Averlino Filarete's Tractat über die Baukunst nebst seinen Büchern von der Zeichenkunst und den Bauten der Medici*. Ed. by Wolfgang von Oettingen, Vienna 1890 (Quellenschriften für Kunstgeschichte und Kunsttechnik des Mittelalters und der Neuzeit, N.S., 3)

Flechsig, Eduard, *Albrecht Dürer. Sein Leben und seine künstlerische Entwicklung*, vols. 1–2, Berlin 1928–31

Frenzel, Gottfried, 'Veit Hirsvogel, eine Nürnberger Glasmalerwerkstatt der Dürerzeit', in *ZKG*, 23, 1960, pp. 193–210

Geier, Ulrich, *Studien zu Sebastian Brants Narrenschiff*, Tübingen 1966

Giehlow, Karl, 'Poliziano und Dürer', in *Mitteilungen der Gesellschaft für vervielfältigende Künste*. Suppl. of *Die graphischen Künste*, 25, 1902, pp. 22–6

– 'Dürers Stich, "Melancholia I" und der maximilianistische Humanistenkreis', in *Mitteilungen der Gesellschaft für vervielfältigende Künste*. Suppl. of *Die graphischen Künste*, 26, 1903, pp. 29–41; 27, 1904, pp. 6–18, 57–78

– 'Die Hieroglyphenkunde des Humanismus in der Allegorie der Renaissance besonders der Ehrenpforte Kaiser Maximilian I. Ein Versuch'. Epilogue by v. A. Weixlgärtner, in *JKSAK*, 32, 1915, pp. 1–232

– *Kaiser Maximilian I. Gebetbuch und Zeichnungen v. Albrecht Dürer und anderen Künstlern*, facs., Vienna – Munich 1907

– 'Urkundenexegese zur Ehrenpforte Maximilian I.', in *Beiträge zur Kunstgeschichte* (dedicated to Franz Wickhoff), Vienna 1903, pp. 91–110

Ginhart, Karl, 'Dürer war in Kärnten', in *Festschrift f. Gotbert Moro, Carinthia*, I, 152, 1962, facs., pp. 129–155

Goldschmidt, E.P., 'Hieronymus Münzer und seine Bibliothek', in *SWI*, 4, London 1938

Gombrich, E.H., *Symbolic Images*, London 1972

Graf, Wilhelm, *Doktor Christoph Scheurl von Nürnberg*, Berlin 1930, reprinted 1972 (*Beitr. zur Kultur-Geschichte des Mittelalters und der Renaissance*, 43)

Grimm, Hermann, 'Dürers Ritter, Tod und Teufel', in *PJ*, 36, 1875, pp. 543–9

Grote, Ludwig, *'Hier bin ich ein Herr' – Dürer in Venedig*, Munich 1956

– 'Die "Vorder-Stube" des Sebald Schreyer. Ein Beitrag zur Rezeption der Renaissance in Nürnberg', in *Anzeiger des GNM*, 1954–9, pp. 43–67

– 'Vom Handwerker zum Künstler', in *Festschrift f. Hans Liermann zum 70. Geburtstag*, Erlangen 1964, pp. 26–47

– 'Das Männerbildnis Albrecht Dürers in Boston', in *ZDVK*, 25, 1971, pp. 115–22

Grünhagen, C., *Geschichte Schlesiens*, vol. 1 (up to 1527), Gotha 1884

Gümbel, Albert, *Dürers Bildnisse des Ehepaars Thurzo*, Strasbourg 1928 (Studien zu deutschen Kunstgeschichte, 256)

Haase, Adolf, *Die Schlacht bei Nürnberg vom 19. Juni 1502*, Greifswald 1887 (thesis)

Hamann, Günther, 'Dürers Erd- und Himmelskarten', in *Albrecht Dürers Umwelt. Festschrift zum 500. Geburtstag*, Nuremberg 1971, pp. 152–177 (Nürnberger Forschungen, 15)

Hampe, Theodor, 'Dürer als Künstler und als Mensch. Festschrift zur 400jährigen Gedächtnisfeier Albrecht Dürers', in *MVGN*, 28, 1928, pp. 1–67

– 'Sebald Schreyer vornehmlich als Kirchenmeister von St. Sebald. Festschrift zur 400jährigen Gedächtnisfeier Albrecht Dürers', in *MVGN*, 28, 1928, pp. 155–207

Harbison, Craig, 'Dürer and the Reformation: The problem of re-dating of the St. Philip engraving', in *AB*, 58, 1976, pp. 368–73

Harnest, Joseph, *Das Problem der konstruierten Perspektive in der altdeutschen Malerei*, Munich 1971 (thesis T.U., private publ.)

– 'Theorie und Ausführung in der perspektivistischen Raumdarstellung Albrecht Dürers', in *Festschrift Luitpold Dussler*, 1972, pp. 189–204

– 'Zur Perspektive in Albrecht Altdorfers Alexanderschlacht', in *Anzeiger GNM*, 1977, pp. 67–77

Hase, Oskar, *Die Koberger*, Leipzig 1885

Heerwagen, Heinrich, 'Aus einem Nürnberger Bürgerhaus zu Ausgang des 15. Jahrhunderts (Inventarium Dorothea Hanns Wynnterin… 1486)', in *Mitteilungen des GNM*, 1902, pp. 30–6

Heidrich, Ernst, *Dürer und die Reformation*, Leipzig 1909

Heller, Joseph, *Das Leben und die Werke Albrecht Dürers*, vols. 2 (1–2) – 3, Bamberg 1827

Hieronymus, Frank, 'Sebastian Brants "Sebastians-Ode" illustriert von Albrecht Dürer', in *Gutenberg-Jb.*, 1977, pp. 271–308

Hind, Arthur, *Early Italian Engraving*, vols. 1–7, London – New York 1938–1948

Hirschfeld, Peter, *Mäzene. Die Rolle des Auftraggebers in der Kunst*, Munich-Berlin 1968 (Kunstwissenschaftliche Studien, 40)

Hirschmann, Gerhard, 'Albrecht Dürers Abstammung und Familienkreis', in *Albrecht Dürers Umwelt. Festschrift zum 500. Geburtstag*, Nuremberg 1971, pp. 35–55 (Nürnberger Forschungen, 15)

Hoffmann, Konrad, 'Dürers Melencolia', in *Kunst als Bedeutungsträger. Gedenkschrift f. Günter Bandmann*, 1979, pp. 251–77

Hofmann, Hanns Hubert, 'Albrecht Dürers politische und soziale Umwelt', in *Albrecht Dürers Umwelt. Festschrift zum 500. Geburtstag*, Nuremberg 1971, pp. 1–8 (Nürnberger Forschungen, 15)

Horst, Robert W., 'Dürers "Melencolia I". Ein Beitrag zum Melancholia-Problem', in *Forschungen zur Kunstgeschichte und Christlichen Archäologie*, 2, 1953, pp. 411–31

Jeremias, Alfred, *Johannes von Staupitz, Luthers Vater und Schüler. Auswahl aus seinen Schriften*, see: Staupitz, Johannes von

Kaufmann, Johann, 'Der Nürnberger Patrizier Christoph Fürer d. Ä. und seine Denkwürdigkeiten', in *Festschrift zur 400jährigen Gedächtnisfeier Albrecht Dürers*, Nuremberg 1928, pp. 209–311 (Mitteilungen des Vereins für Geschichte der Stadt Nürnberg, 28)

Kauffmann, Hans, *Albrecht Dürers rhythmische Kunst*, Leipzig 1924

– *Albrecht Dürer 'Die Vier Apostel'*. Lecture given on 18.4.1972 at the Art-historical Institute at Utrecht, Utrecht 1972

Kirn, Paul, 'Friedrich der Weise und Jacopo de' Barbari', in *JPKS*, 46, 1925, pp. 130–4

Klibansky, Raymond, Fritz Saxl and Erwin Panofsky, *Saturn and Melancholy. Studies in the history of natural philosophy, religion and art*, London 1964

Knappe, Karl-Adolf, 'Nürnberger Malerei von 1440 bis 1490', in Pfeiffer, Gerhard (ed.), *Nürnberg, Geschichte einer europäischen Stadt*, Munich 1971, pp. 242–50

Köhler, Wilhelm H., 'Die Tafeln des Dominikaner-Altars im Hessischen Landesmuseum in Darmstadt', in *Kunst in Hessen und am Mittelrhein*, vol. 10, 1970, pp. 35–44

Könneker, Barbara, 'Eyn wis man sich do heym behalt. Zur Interpretation von Sebastian Brants Narrenschiff', in *Germ.-rom. Monatsschrift*, N.S., 14, 1964, pp. 46–77

Koepplin, Dieter, *Cranachs Ehebildnis des Johannes Cuspinian von 1502. – Seine christlich-humanistische Bedeutung*, Basle 1973 (thesis)

Kolde, Theodor, 'Beiträge zur Reformationsgeschichte. Zum Prozess des Johann Denk und "der drei gottlosen Maler von Nürnberg"', in *Kirchengeschichtliche Studien. Hermann Reuter zum 70. Geburtstag*, vol. 3, Leipzig 1888, pp. 228–50

Kretschmer, Ernst, *Körperbau und Charakter. Untersuchungen zum Konstitutionsproblem und zur Lehre von den Temperamenten*, Berlin, 20th ed., 1951

Kristeller, Paul Oskar, *Humanismus und Renaissance*, vols. 1–2, Munich 1974–6

Landolt, Hanspeter, 'Der Holzschnitt zu "Sebastian Brants Gedicht an den heiligen Sebastian". Ein neuentdecktes

Basler Flugblatt', in *Basler Zeitschrift für Geschichte und Altertumskunde*, 75, 1975, pp. 38–50

Laufner, Richard, 'Ein Mensch in seiner Gegenwart. Der Wallfahrtsbericht Peter Fassbenders von Molsberg zu Koblenz zum hl. Grab in Jerusalem 1492–93', in *Festschrift für Eberhard Heimpel*, vol. 2, 1971, pp. 247–65

Leder, Klaus, 'Nürnbergs Schulwesen an der Wende vom Mittelalter zur Neuzeit', in *Albrecht Dürers Umwelt. Festschrift zum 500. Geburtstag*, Nuremberg 1971, pp. 29–34 (Nürnberger Forschungen, 15)

Lefebvre, Joël, *Les Fols et la Folie. Etude sur les genres du comique et la création littéraire en Allemagne pendant la Renaissance*, Paris 1968

Lehrs, Max, 'Die Kupferstichsammlung der Stadt Breslau', in *JPKS*, 3, 1882, pp. 210–23

Leitschuh, Franz Friedrich, *Studien und Quellen zur deutschen Kunstgeschichte des 15. und 16. Jahrhunderts*, Freiburg (Switzerland), 1912

Leonardo da Vinci, *The Literary Works* (ed. Jean-Paul Richter), vols. 1–2, 2nd ed., 1939

Lutz, Heinrich, 'Albrecht Dürer in der Geschichte der Reformation', in *HZ*, 206, 1968, pp. 22–44

Machilek, Franz, 'Klosterhumanismus in Nürnberg um 1500', in *MVGN*, 64, 1977, pp. 10–45

Malaguzzi, Valeri Francesco, *La corte di Lodovico il Moro*, Milan 1913

Mander, Carel van, *Das Leben der niederländischen und deutschen Maler*. Text according to the edition of 1617. Transl. and com. by Hanns Floerke, vols. 1–2, Leipzig 1906

Meder, Josef, 'Zur ersten Reise nach Venedig (1494–95)', in *JKSAK*, 30, 1911–12, pp. 183–227 (Neue Beiträge zur Dürer-Forschung, vol. 2)

– *Die Handzeichnung. – Ihre Technik und Entwicklung*, Vienna 1919

– *Die grüne Passion Albrecht Dürers*, Munich 1923, (Monographien zur deutschen Kunst, 4)

– *Dürer-Katalog, Ein Handbuch über Albrecht Dürers Stiche, Radierungen, Holzschnitte…*, Vienna 1932

Mende, Ursula, 'Dürers Zeichnungen livländischer Frauentrachten und seine sogenannte Türkin', in Kunstgeschichtliche Aufsätze von seinen Schülern und Freunden…, Heinz Ladendorf gew., Cologne 1969 (typescript)

Mummenhof, E., *Der Handwerker in der deutschen Vergangenheit*, Leipzig 1901

Neudörffer, Johann, *Nachrichten von Künstlern und Kunstsachen*, 1546, Nuremberg 1828

Noack, Friedrich, *Das Deutschtum in Rom seit dem Ausgang des Mittelalters*, vols. 1–2, Aalen 1974 (reprinted)

Panofsky, Erwin, 'Dürers Darstellung des Apollo und ihr Verhältnis zu Barbari', in *JPKS*, 41, 1920, pp. 259–377

– *Hercules am Scheidewege und andere antike Bildstoffe in der neueren Kunst*, Leipzig – Berlin 1930, pp. 166–73 (Studies of the Warburg Library, 18)

– *Albrecht Dürer*, vols. 1–2, 1st ed., Princeton 1943; 3rd ed., Princeton 1948

– *Idea. Ein Beitrag zur Begriffsgeschichte der älteren Kunsttheorie*, 2nd ed., Berlin 1960 (Studies of the Warburg Library)

– and Fritz Saxl, *Dürers 'Melencolia I'. Eine quellen- und typengeschichtliche Untersuchung*, Leipzig – Berlin 1923, (Studies of the Warburg Library, 2)

Pauli, Gustav, 'Drei neue Dürerzeichnungen', in *JPKS*, 31, 1910, pp. 57–8

– 'Dürers früheste Proportionsstudie eines Pferdes', in *ZBK*, N.S., 25, 1914, pp. 105–8

Petz, Hans, 'Urkundliche Nachrichten über den literarischen Nachlass Regiomontans und B. Walthers (1478–1522)', in *MVGN*, 7, 1888, pp. 237–62

Peuckert, Will-Erich, *Die grosse Wende. Das apokalyptische Saeculum und Luther*, Darmstadt 1966

Pfeiffer, Gerhard, (ed.), *Nürnberg – Geschichte einer europäischen Stadt*. In collaboration with several scholars, Munich 1971

Pigler, Andreas, 'Sokrates in der Kunst der Neuzeit', in *Die Antike*, 14, 1938, pp. 281–94

Reimann, Arnold, *Die älteren Pirckheimer*, Leipzig 1944

Reitzenstein, Alexander, 'ETLICHE VNDERRICHT ZU BEFESTIGUNG DER STETT, SCHLOSZ UND FLECKEN', in *Albrecht Dürers Umwelt. Festschrift zum 500. Geburtstag*, Nuremberg 1971, pp. 178–92

Richter, Jean-Paul, *The Literary Works*, see: Leonardo da Vinci

Rosenthal, Erwin, 'Dürers Buchmalereien für Pirckheimers Bibliothek', in *JPKS*, 49, 1928 (fasc.), pp. 1–54; Suppl., 51, 1930, pp. 175–8

Rox, Henry, 'On Dürer's Knight, Death and Devil', in *AB*, 30, 1948, pp. 67–70

Rücker, Elisabeth, *Die Schedelsche Weltchronik – das grösste Buchunternehmen der Dürerzeit*, Munich 1973

Rupprich, Hans, *Willibald Pirckheimer und die erste Reise Dürers nach Italien*, Vienna 1930

– (ed.) *Dürer – Schriftlicher Nachlass*, vols. 1–3, Berlin 1956–69

– 'Willibald Pirckheimer – Beiträge zu seiner Wesen-erfassung', in *Schweizer Beiträge zur Allgemeinen Geschichte*, 15, 1957, pp. 64–110

– *Dürers Stellung zu den agnoëtischen und kunstfeindlichen Strömungen seiner Zeit.* Contains an unknown letter by Dürer. Munich 1959 (Sitzungsberichte der Bayerischen Akademie der Wiss., Phil.-Hist. Kl., 1959, fasc. 1)

– 'Das literarische Werk Kaiser Maximilians I.', in *Ausstellungs-Katalog Maximilian I.*, Innsbruck 1969

Rusconi, Antonio, 'Per l'identificazione degli acquarelli tridentini di Alberto Durero', in *Die graphischen Künste*, N.S., 1, 1936, pp. 121–37

Sachs, Carl L., 'Nürnbergs reichsstädtische Arbeiterschaft während der Amtszeit des Baumeisters Michel Beheim VII. (1503–11)', in *Mitteilungen des GNM*, 1914–15, pp. 141–209

Sampaio Themudo Barata, Maria do Rosario, *Rui Fernandes de Almada – Diplomata portugues do século XVI*, Lisbon 1971

Sandrart, Joachim von, *Academie der Bau-, Bild- und Mahlerey-Künste von 1675.* Ed. and com. by Arthur Rudolf Petzer, Munich 1925

Saxl, Fritz, *Jacopo Bellini and Mantegna as antiquarians*, London 1957 (Lectures 1, pp. 151–60)

Schnelbögl, Fritz, 'Leben und Werk des Nürnberger Kartographen Erhard Etzlaub (gest. 1532)', in *MVGN*, 57, 1970, pp. 216–31

Schrade, Hubert, 'Die religiösen Grundlagen von Dürers Schriften zur Kunst', in *Zeitschrift für Deutsche Bildung*, 10, 1934, pp. 22–9

Schubert, Hans von, *Lazarus Spengler und die Reformation in Nürnberg*, Leipzig 1934 (Quellen und Forschungen zur Reformationsgeschichte, 17)

Schultheiss, Werner, 'Albrecht Dürers Beziehungen zum Recht', in *Albrecht Dürers Umwelt. Festschrift zum 500. Geburtstag*, Nuremberg 1971, pp. 220–54 (Nürnberger Forschungen, 15)

Schürer, Oskar, 'Wohin ging Dürers "ledige Wanderfahrt"?' in *ZKG*, 6, 1937, pp. 171–99

Schuster, Peter-Klaus, 'Melancholia I. Studien zu Dürers Melancholie-Kupferstich und seinem Humanismus', in *Das Münster*, 27, 1974, pp. 409–11

Seebass, Gottfried, 'Dürers Stellung in der reformatorischen Bewegung', in *Albrecht Dürers Umwelt. Festschrift zum 500. Geburtstag*, Nuremberg 1971, pp. 101–31 (Nürnberger Forschungen, 15)

Simler, Josias, *De Alpibus commentarium. Die Alpen*, Munich 1931

Simon, Erika, 'Dürer und Mantegna', in *Anzeiger des GNM*, 1971–2, pp. 21–40

Solleder, Fridolin, 'Probleme um Dürers väterliche Herkunft', in *Der Heimgarten. Wochenschrift der 'Bayerischen Staatszeitung'*, vol. 12, 14.4.1934

Spohn, Georg R., 'Der Simmerner Meister HH und der Autor der "Kunst des Messens" (Simmern 1531, Duke John II. von Pfalz-Simmern?)', in *ZDVK*, 27, 1972, pp. 72–94

Stafsky, Heinz, 'Die Vischer-Werkstatt und ihre Probleme', in *ZKG*, 21, 1958, pp. 1–26

Stauber, Richard, *Die Schedelsche Bibliothek*, Freiburg i.Br. 1908

Staupitz, Johannes von, *Johannes von Staupitz, Luthers Vater und Schüler. Sein Leben, sein Verhältnis zu Luther und eine Auswahl aus seinen Schriften.* Transl. and ed. by Alfred Jeremias, Berlin 1926

Stechow, Wolfgang, 'Dürers Bologneser Lehrer', in *Kunstchronik*, 57, 1922, pp. 251–2

Strauss, Walter L., *The human figure by Albrecht Dürer. The complete Dresden Sketchbook* (ed. by), New York 1972

– *The Book of Hours of the Emperor Maximilian the First decorated by Albrecht Dürer…* (ed. and comm. by), New York 1974

– *The complete drawings of Albrecht Dürer*, vols. 1–6, New York 1974

– 'Wolfgang Stechow, Praeceptor artis extraordinarius', in *Print Review*, 5, 1976, pp. 154–9

Strieder, Peter, 'Die Bedeutung des Porträts bei Albrecht Dürer', in *Albrecht Dürer. Kunst einer Zeitwende*, ed. H. Schade, Regensburg 1971, pp. 34–100; or in *La Gloire de Dürer*, Paris 1974, pp. 45–56

– 'Albrecht Dürers "Vier Apostel" im Nürnberger Rathaus', in *Festschrift Klaus Lankheit*, Cologne 1973, pp. 151–7

Stromer, Wolfgang von, 'Nürnbergs wirtschaftliche Lage im Zeitalter der Fugger', in *Albrecht Dürers Umwelt. Festschrift zum 500. Geburtstag*, Nuremberg 1971, pp. 9–19 (Nürnberger Forschungen, 15)

– 'Der kaiserliche Kaufmann. Wirtschaftspolitik unter Karl IV.', in *Kaiser Karl IV. Staatsmann und Mäzen*, ed. Ferdinand Seibt, Munich 1978, pp. 63–73

Tavel, Hans Christoph von, 'Die Randzeichnungen Albrecht Dürers zum Gebetbuch Kaiser Maximilians', in *MJBK*, 3.F. 16, 1965, pp. 55–120 (Berne 1962, thesis)

Timken-Zinkann, R.F., *Ein Mensch namens Dürer. Des Künstlers Leben, Ideen, Umwelt*, Berlin 1972

Vasari, Giorgio, *Le vite de' piu eccellenti pittori, scultori ed architettori*, ed. Gaetano Milanesi, Florence 1880

Veth, Jan and Samuel Müller, *Albrecht Dürers niederländische Reise*, vols. 1–2, Berlin – Utrecht 1918

Vetter, Ewald M. and Chr. Brockhaus, 'Das Verhältnis von Text und Bild in Dürers Randzeichnungen zum Gebetbuch Kaiser Maximilians', in *Anzeiger des GNM*, 1971–2, pp. 70–122

Volkmann, Ludwig, *Bilderschriften der Renaissance. Hieroglyphik und Emblematik in ihren Beziehungen und Fortwirkungen*, Leipzig 1923

Waetzold, Wilhelm, *Dürer und seine Zeit*, Vienna 1935

Weber, Paul, *Beiträge zu Dürers Weltanschauung*, Strasbourg 1900 (Studien zur deutschen Kunstgeschichte, 23)

Weiss, Karl Theodor, *Handbuch der Wasserzeichenkunde*, Leipzig 1962

Wiederanders, Gerlinde, *Albrecht Dürers theologische Anschauungen*, Berlin (DDR) 1975

Wiesflecker, Hermann, *Kaiser Maximilian I. – Das Reich, Österreich und Europa an der Wende zur Neuzeit*, vols. 1–3, Munich 1971–7

Wind, Edgar, *Bellini's Feast of the Gods. A study in Venetian humanism*. Cambridge, Mass. 1948

Winkler, Friedrich, *Dürer und die Illustration zum Narrenschiff*, Berlin 1951

– *Albrecht Dürer – Leben und Werk*, Berlin 1957

Wölfflin, Heinrich, *Die Kunst Albrecht Dürers*, 6th ed., Munich 1943

Würtenberger, Thomas, *Albrecht Dürer. Künstler, Recht und Gerechtigkeiten*, Frankfurt a. M. 1971

Wuttke, Dieter, 'Unbekannte Celtis-Epigramme zum Lobe Dürers', in *ZKG*, 30, 1967, pp. 321–5

Zahn, Peter, 'Neue Funde zur Entstehung der Schedelschen Weltchronik 1493', in *Stadt Nürnberg, Renaissance-Vorträge 2/3*, Nuremberg 1973, pp. 2–41

Zarncke, Friedrich, (ed.), see S. Brant, *Das Narrenschiff*

Zucker, Marcus, *Dürers Stellung zur Reformation*, Erlangen 1886

262

Dürer's Works

Index

Photo Credits

Author and publisher wish to thank all those who kindly provided photographs for reproduction.

Accademia Carrara, Bergamo Pl. 233
Ashmolean Museum, Oxford Pl. 31
Atkins Museum, Nelson Gallery of Art, Kansas City, Pl. 98
Bayerische Staatsgemäldesammlungen, Munich (Photo Joachim Blauel) Pls. 1, 67, 68, 69, 77, 228, 229
Biblioteca Ambrosiana, Milan Pls. 59 (Intercontinentale Organizzazione, Padua), 166, 167
Bibliothèque Nationale, Paris Pls. 58, 95
British Museum, London Pl. 55, 57, 74, 83, 111, 112, 152, 159 160, 183, 199, 224
Clichés des Musées Nationaux, Paris Pls. 13, 24, 39, 127, 197, 213, 215
Courtauld Institute, London Pls. 49, 50, 190
Fitzwilliam Museum, Cambridge Pls. 32, 33
Fondation Custodia, Institut néerlandais, Paris Pl. 210
Galleria degli Uffizi, Florence (Photo studio Mario Quattrone), Pls. 12, 108, 232; (Gabinetto Fotografico) Pls. 107, 180, 206, 212
Germanisches Nationalmuseum, Nuremberg Pls. 5, 11, 118, 135, 158, 182
Graphische Sammlung Albertina, Vienna (Lichtbildwerkstätte Alpenland) Pls. 7, 27, 36, 38, 40, 73, 94, 104, 116, 128, 134, 151, 156, 161, 163, 164, 185, 196, 203, 204, 227; (Verlag Anton Schroll) Pls. 100, 102
Historisches Museum, Frankfurt-on-Main Pl. 129
Hochbauamt, Nuremberg Pls. 137, 240
Kestner Museum, Hannover Pl. 99
Kunstantiquariat Kistner, Nuremberg Pl. 75
Kunsthalle, Hamburg (Photo Ralph Kleinhempel) Pls. 23, 37
Kunsthistorisches Museum, Vienna (Photo Meyer) Pls. 113, 120, 121, 125, 126, 131, 132, 133, 187, 223, 239
Metropolitan Museum of Art, New York (Benjamin Altman Collection) Pl. 184
Musée Bonnat, Bayonne (Photo Etienne) Pls. 25, 154

Musée Condé, Chantilly (Photo Giraudon, Paris) Pls. 130, 198, 200, 211
Museo del Arte Antiga, Lisbon (Est. Mario Novaes) Pl. 205
Museo del Prado, Madrid (Photo Dominguez Ramos) Pls. 76, 123, 124, 207
Museum Boymans-van Beuningen, Rotterdam Pl. 41
Museum der Schönen Künste, Leipzig (Photo Gerhard Reinhold) Pl. 62
Narodni Galerie, Prague (Fotografoval Vladimir Fyman) Pls. 114, 115
National Gallery of Art, Washington D.C. (Samuel H. Kress Collection) Pls. 70, 71, 181
Öffentliche Kunstsammlung, Basle Pls. 16, 19, 97, 150
Photo Stickelmann, Bremen Pls. 2, 42
Photo Studio Comm. Vaghi, Parma Pl. 30
Pierpont Morgan Library, New York Pls. 88, 153
Rijksmuseum, Amsterdam Pls. 10, 149
Schäfer, Dr. G., Schweinfurt Pl. 65
Staatliche Kunsthalle, Karlsruhe Pl. 21
Staatliche Kunstsammlungen, Dresden, Pls. 66, 202
Staatliche Kunstsammlungen, Kassel Pl. 64
Staatliche Museen Preussischer Kulturbesitz, Berlin (Photo Jörg P. Anders) Pls. 3, 4, 17, 18, 20, 26, 72, 84, 117, 122, 162, 176, 194, 214, 221, 225, 235, 237, 238; (Photo Walter Steinkopf) 6, 8, 9, 14, 15, 28, 29, 34, 35, 43, 44, 45, 46, 47, 48, 51, 52, 53, 54, 56, 60, 61, 63, 78, 79, 80, 81, 82, 85, 86, 87, 89, 90, 91, 92, 93, 96, 101, 103, 109, 110, 138, 139, 140, 141, 142, 143, 144, 145, 146, 147, 148, 155, 165, 168, 169, 170, 171, 172, 173, 174, 175, 177, 178, 179, 188, 189, 191, 193, 201, 208, 209, 216, 217, 218, 219, 220, 222, 226, 230, 231, 234, 236
Staatsbibliothek, Bamberg (Lichtbildstelle Alfons Steber) Pl. 186
Städelsches Kunstinstitut, Frankfurt-on-Main Pl. 195
Thyssen-Bornemisza Collection, Lugano-Castagnola Pl. 119
Universitätsbibliothek, Erlangen Pl. 22
Wallraf-Richartz Museum, Cologne Pls. 105, 106
Wessenberg Galerie, Constance (Photo Jeannine Le Brun) Pl. 157